ART
IN THE ALPHABET

ART IN THE ALPHABET

A History of the Evolution of Hand Lettering

LEWIS F. DAY

Dover Publications, Inc.,
Mineola, New York

Bibliographical Note

This Dover edition, first published in 2016, is an unabridged republication of the work originally published by B.T. Batsford, London, and by Charles Scribner's Sons, New York, in 1910 under the title *Alphabets Old and New*.

Library of Congress Cataloging-in-Publication Data

Names: Day, Lewis F. (Lewis Foreman), 1845–1910, author.
Title: Art in the alphabet : a history of the evolution of hand lettering / Lewis F. Day.
Other titles: Alphabets old and new
Description: Mineola, New York : Dover Publications, Inc., 2016. | "Art in the Alphabet, A History of the Evolution of Hand Lettering, first published by Dover Publications, Inc., in 2016, is an unabridged republication of a work originally entitled Alphabets Old and New, first published by B.T. Batsford, London, and by Charles Scribner's Sons, New York, in 1910."
Identifiers: LCCN 2016013353| ISBN 9780486454610 | ISBN 0486454614
Subjects: LCSH: Alphabets. | Lettering.

Classification: LCC NK3600 .D22 2016 | DDC 745.6/1—dc23
LC record available at http://lccn.loc.gov/2016013353

Manufactured in the United States by RR Donnelley
45461401 2016
www.doverpublications.com

PREFACE TO THE THIRD EDITION.

A BOOK of alphabets like this, for the use of artists and others who have occasion either to work in the manner of some given period or to design lettering of their own, needs scarcely any introductory essay.

I have attempted, however, in "Art in the Alphabet," to give, as simply as possible, that amount of information about the Alphabet and its evolution without which it is not safe for the designer to depart from too familiar forms.

Fuller particulars of the various alphabets than it was possible to give in this connected and condensed account of the alphabet will be found in the Descriptive List of Illustrations.

My own ideas on lettering design, enunciated by the way, are the more frankly expressed because it must be understood that they are only personal opinions which the reader will take for what they are worth.

In the alphabets themselves the spirit of the old lettering is faithfully kept, though I have not scrupled to supply missing letters. Scholars will of course object to this; but the book is not for them; it is for working artists, who will be glad, I know, to have twenty-six letters to the alphabet.

A feature in the book is the quantity of illustrations showing the difference it makes in the character of the lettering, whether it is in wood or stone, in stuff or leather, in mosaic or stained glass; whether, for example in metal, it is cut in, grounded out, beaten up, onlaid or engraved; or whether the writing tool chances to be a chisel or a gouge, a needle or a brush, a stylus or a pen—and even what sort of pen it is.

All this is much more fully illustrated than it was in earlier editions; and, in particular, the penmanship of the 17th century for which I have been able to draw upon a unique collection of the famous "Writing Books" in the possession of the publisher.

"Alphabets Old and New"* concerns itself only with letters and the corresponding numerals. The decorative use of Lettering in Ornament is the subject of a separate volume.

LEWIS F. DAY.

15, TAVITON STREET,
March 1, 1910.

* Original title of this volume.

NOTE.

Thanks are due to Mr. George Clulow for the use of his valuable collection of old Writing Books, etc.; to Messrs. Matthew Bell & Co., W. J. Pearce, J. Walter West, C. Griffin & Co., Ltd., J. Vinycomb, Herr von Larisch, Brindley & Weatherley, Frau Bassermann Nachfolger, Munich, Martin Gerlach, Ferd. Schenk, and others, who have kindly permitted the reproduction here of alphabets drawn or copyrighted by them; and to the artists who have designed alphabets especially for this book.

TABLE OF CONTENTS.

DESCRIPTIVE LIST OF ILLUSTRATIONS.

32. BLACK LETTER painted in cobalt upon glazed earthenware—In the Victoria and Albert Museum. Chiefly Hispano-moresque dishes of the 15th and 16th centuries. There is a fantastic flourishing about the lines which tells of the brush. (Compare 33.)

33. BLACK LETTER painted in cobalt upon Italian Majolica drug pots—In the Victoria and Albert Museum. The flourishes and foliations tell of the brush. 16th century. (Compare 32.)

34. LOMBARDIC INSCRIPTION cut in brass—The background characteristically cross-hatched. Nordhausen. 1395. (Compare 77 and 78.)

35. ROMAN CAPITALS painted on wood—From the drawer fronts in a chemist's shop, now in the Germanic Museum at Nuremberg. The use of the brush is partly responsible for the shape of the letters. 1727. (Compare 36, 38, 39.)

36. ROMAN CAPITALS painted on Italian Majolica—In the Victoria and Albert Museum. Distinctly brushwork. 1518. (Compare 35, 38, 39.)

37. GILT LETTERS picked out with a point, perhaps the end of a brush—Spanish estofado. From a frame in the Victoria and Albert Museum. The ground has been gilded, the gold leaf covered with a coat of black paint, out of which the letters have been scraped whilst the pigment was in condition.

38. ROMAN LETTERS painted on wood—Italian. 15th century.

39. ROMAN LETTERS painted on glazed earthenware—In the Victoria and Albert Museum. English. 18th century. (Compare with similar brushwork, 36.)

40. LOMBARDIC LETTERS, painted, and showing the influence of the brush. German.

41. ROMAN LETTERS, executed in copper rivets on a leather belt. In the Museum at Salzburg.

42. GOTHIC CAPITALS, cut in brass. From the tomb of Mary of Burgundy, wife of the Emperor Maximilian. Notre Dame, Bruges, 1495–1502.

43. INSCRIPTION—The letters, cut out in silver and rivetted on to silver. Early Gothic.

44. RAISED LETTERS—Carved in stone, from Bishop West's Chapel in Ely Cathedral. Ca. 1534. (Compare 115.)

45. LOMBARDIC LETTERS—From a stained glass window. From a drawing by C. Winston. Early Gothic.

46. LOMBARDIC LETTERS, executed in cut leather. From an early Gothic book binding in the Hamburg Museum.

47. CAPITAL LETTERS, in stone, grounded out. St. Margaret's, King's Lynn, 1622.

48. INSCRIPTION, painted on glass. From a drawing by C. Winston.

49. ALPHABET — From the inscription on a drinking cup, engraved on silver. Engraved lines shown in black.

50. EMBROIDERED LETTERS—Worked in gold over parchment upon velvet. From the leading strings of James I.

51. GREEK INSCRIPTION, incised in marble upon an antique bust of Aristophanes in the Uffizi at Florence.

52. CROWNED LOMBARDIC LETTERS — From a stained glass window in Winchester Cathedral. From a drawing by C. Winston. The fine lines are picked out of the solid paint with a pointed stick.

53. LETTERS cut out of glazed tiles and embedded in cement. From an inscription in the Cathedral at Cordova.

54. GREEK—From an Athenian stele. Marble. Cut in with a chisel. Characteristically right-lined. Certain strokes fall short of the full length. The two sides of the stroke not always parallel, but inclining occasionally to wedge-shape. The top stroke of T is not stopped by cross-cut, but runs out. 394 B.C.

55. GREEK INITIALS—From a book printed at Basel. Wood engraving. The serif fully developed. 16th century.

56. ROMAN LETTERS cut in marble—From inscriptions in the Forum at Rome. Characteristically chisel work.

57. ROMAN—From fragments in the British Museum. Cut in stone. In E, F, L, P, R, T strokes run out. Note variety in rendering the same letter. 2nd and 3rd centuries.

58. ENGLISH, IRISH, OR ANGLO-SAXON—From illuminated MSS. Curves inclined to take a spiral direction. Considerable freedom of penmanship. Various forms of the same letter. Note long tails and unequal length of letters. 6th century.

59. FROM A CODEX in Latin—Written between ruled marginal lines. Considerable variety in the form of the same letter. Note the square C and G, and the deep waist of the B and R, which compare with alphabet 1. 7th or 8th century.

60. GALICIAN CAPITALS—MSS. 8th century. (Compare B and R with alphabets 1 and 59.)

61. IRISH—From the Book of Kells. Illuminated. Note square form of certain letters—the curious D-shaped O and the general thickening of the upright strokes at the starting point. Various forms of same letter. 8th century.

62 and 63. ANGLO-SAXON—Various MSS. Forms sometimes rigidly square, sometimes fantastically flowing. Strokes developing occasionally into spirals, or into interlacing, which ends perhaps in a grotesque head. 8th and 9th centuries.

64. SAXON AND ANGLO-SAXON MSS.—The outline penned and filled in with various tints. The scribe has not made up his mind as to any logical use of thick and thin strokes. Note square C and S, and looser T and U. 7th, 8th, and 9th centuries.

65. MS. LETTERS—More nearly resembling the orthodox Roman character, with exception of D, E, G, P, U, in which Gothic characteristics begin to appear, and perhaps a hint of future minuscule forms. 10th century.

66. FRENCH MS.—Initials in colours. More Gothic than Roman, flourishing into tails of foliation. 12th century.

67. FRENCH—From the doors of the Cathedral at Le Puy. Wood, simply grounded out. Several varieties of letter. The curved lines characteristically cusped. Probably 12 century. (Compare with 19.)

lacings. But the knotting occupies approximately the natural thickness of the letter; and, though the outline is thus broken, the form of the letter is sufficiently preserved. This splitting of the letter, as it were, into ribbons in its thickest parts was not uncommon in 16th-century initials. It is obvious that any form of letter might be elaborated after this fashion. 1523.

110. ITALIAN GOTHIC CAPITALS—After Ludovico Curione. Penwork. 16th century. (Compare with German, 105.)

111. SPANISH GOTHIC CAPITALS—From the Writing Book by Juan Yciar. The forms of the K and Y are unusual. First half of the 16th century.

112. ROMAN LETTERS cut in marble—Florentine. 15th century.

113. ROMAN ALPHABET—Engraved by Heinrich Aldegrever. 1530.

114. ELIZABETHAN LETTERING—From an inscription incised in wood at North Walsham, Norfolk. (Compare 115—133.)

115. QUASI-ELIZABETHAN ALPHABET—Freely drawn from woodcut initials in various printed books of the period; but there is practically no form for which there is not authority in the old engraved letters. (Compare 44.)

116. ITALIAN GOTHIC MINUSCULE—From the original Writing Book by Palatino. Straight-lined with elaborately flourishing extremities. It suggests the engraver. 1546.

117. ITALIAN MINUSCULE—From the original Writing Book by Vespasiano. These letters are exceedingly well shaped. Observe the second variety of the letter *r*. 1556.

118. TYPICALLY ITALIAN RENAISSANCE—"Roman" capitals, by Serlio. 16th century. (Compare with Roman, 56.)

119. GERMAN CAPITALS—By Daniel Hopfer. Renaissance or "Roman" in character, but not without traces of lingering Gothic influence. 1549.

120. ITALIAN INITIALS—From the original Writing Book by G. F. Cresci. This is a fanciful and rather elegant elaboration of forms common in Gothic writing. The familiar outline is, as it were, ornamentally fretted. 1570. (Compare with 20.)

121. ITALIAN GOTHIC CAPITALS—From the original Writing Book by G. F. Cresci. Apparently to some extent influenced by the Roman character. 1570.

122. ITALIAN MINUSCULE – From the original Writing Book by G. F. Cresci. Roman in character. 1570.

123. ITALIAN GOTHIC CAPITALS—After Cresci, etc. Penmanship. 1570.

124. BLACK LETTER MINUSCULE—From a rubbing of a memorial inscription. Flemish. 1579.

125. FLEMISH MINUSCULE—From a memorial tablet at S. Jacques, Bruges. Cut in stone. There is a suggestion of turning over and interlacing the strokes of the letters, which was very usual in engraving of the period, whether on brass or stone. 16th century.

126. ROMAN CAPITALS—From the lace-book of Giovanni Ostaus, adapted to working on a square mesh. Characteristic of the method of execution, and not of any period. 1591. (Compare 200.)

127. GERMAN—From inscriptions at Bingen and other towns. Cut in stone, showing some licence on the part of the mason. 1576, 1598, 1618.

128. GERMAN MINUSCULE Roman letters—From Bamberg, engraved on brass, the background cut away. Observe the spur on the edge of the long strokes, designed to accentuate the parallelism of the line of lettering. 1613.

129. GERMAN MINUSCULE—From a monument at Würzburg Cathedral. Incised in slate. 1617.

130 and 131. MAJUSCULE AND MINUSCULE alphabets, from a rare Writing Book of the 17th century.

132. ITALICS—The sloping form came, of course, from the use of the pen, but it was largely adopted by the masons of the 17th and 18th centuries, who copied even the most elaborate flourishes of the writing-master. 17th century. (Compare 134 *et seq.*)

133. From inscriptions rather rudely carved upon a beam of elm now in the Victoria and Albert Museum. The incised line on the face of the letters occurs only in parts. Letters G, J, K, Q, X, Z were missing. English, dated 1638. (Compare 114 and 115.)

134. PEN-WRITTEN CAPITALS—From "The Pen's Transcendency," a Writing Book by E. Cocker, 1660. Cocker was so emphatically *the* English writing-master of his day as to have given rise to the phrase, "According to Cocker." (Compare this and the following with the stone cut letters, 142, 143, inspired by them.)

135. PEN-WRITTEN MINUSCULES—From "The Pen's Transcendency," by E. Cocker. 1660.

136. PEN-WRITTEN MINUSCULES—By Lesgret, a writing-master of Paris. 1736.

137. ALPHABETS AND INSCRIPTION—From "Magnum in Parvo," a Writing Book by E. Cocker.

138. ALPHABETS AND INSCRIPTION—From the "Guide to Penmanship," by E. Cocker. 1673.

139. PEN-WRITTEN CAPITALS—From a "Guide to Penmanship," by E. Cocker. 1673.

140. MINUSCULES by Maingueneau. Paris. Early 18th century.

141. PEN-WRITTEN CAPITALS, by Lesgret. Paris. 1736.

142. ENGLISH ITALIC WRITING—From inscriptions on monuments in Westminster Abbey. Stone-cutting in imitation of penwork, not characteristic of the chisel. 1665.

143. ENGLISH ROMAN LETTERING—From engraved stone slabs at Chippenham and elsewhere. 1697.

144. MINUSCULES—From a Writing Book by Shelley. English. 1705.

145. MINUSCULES—From a Writing Book by C. Snell. English. 1715.

146. MINUSCULES—From a Writing Book by M. S. Andrade. Portuguese. 1721.

147. PEN-WRITTEN ALPHABETS by M. S. Andrade. Portuguese. 1721.

148. GERMAN CAPITALS—From the Germanisches Museum, Nuremberg. Painted on the wooden drug-drawers of an old apothecary's shop. Brushwork. Observe the bulging of the curved strokes. (Compare with 149 and 19.)

149. GERMAN CAPITALS—By J. H. Tiemroth, of Arnstadt. Pen-work. From the titles of a series of water-colour paintings of botanical specimens. Observe the swelling of the curved strokes and compare with 148 and 19. Here and there a letter shows an inclination to fall into Italics. 1738–48.

150. GERMAN LETTERING—From inscriptions at Osnabrück. Halting between majuscule and minuscule forms. Incised in stone. 1742–56.

151. FRENCH—A more reticent example of the period of Louis XV., by E. Guichard, in which it would, perhaps, be more accurate to say that the shape of the letter is broken up into ornament. 18th century.

152. FRENCH—Of the period of Louis XV., by Laurent. This is a case in which Rococo scrollwork and flowers are compelled to take the form of lettering, more or less—in this case the form of current writing. 18th century.

153. MODERN MINUSCULE—From an inscription etched on lithographic stone by John Tischberger, who was a writing-master at Nuremberg, 1765–70. The touch is neither that of the pen, nor of the brush, nor of the chisel.

154. GERMAN—From a monument at Würzburg. Incised in slate. Occasional capital letters are mixed up with the minuscule. 1784.

155. ENGLISH—Roman capitals and numerals, by William Caslon. Printed type, "old face." 18th century.

156. ENGLISH—Roman lower case, and italic upper and lower case, by W. Caslon. Printed type, "old face," 18th century.

157. ENGLISH COURTHAND—From Andrew Wright's "Court-hand Restored," a book designed to assist the student in deciphering old deeds, etc. This book was published in 1815; but the character is at least as early as the 14th century, and may have been in use a century or more before that.

158. HEBREW ALPHABET.

159. HEBREW ALPHABET—Ornamental version. From Silvestre's "Paleographie." Almost identical with a 16th-century alphabet by Palatino.

160. MODERN GOTHIC CAPITALS, executed with a quill—The forms designed for execution with two strokes of the pen. Walter Crane.

161. MODERN MAJUSCULE AND MINUSCULE, directly written with the simplest stroke of a quill pen. Walter Crane.

162. MODERN GERMAN GOTHIC CAPITALS (Facturschrift)—Penwork. Otto Hupp. In the later German character penmanship ran wild. The lettering is often quite inextricable from the tangle of flourishes in which it is involved. Herr Hupp has avoided the utmost extravagance of the national style. To anyone acquainted with the German character, it is clear enough which of his sweeping strokes mean business, and which are merely subsidiary penmanship. The happy mean is, of course, to make ornament against which the letter tells plainly enough. That is attempted also in 221.

163. MODERN GERMAN GOTHIC CAPITALS—Otto Hupp. From "Alphabete und Ornamente."

164. MODERN PEN-DRAWN ALPHABET—By Otto Hupp, from Rudolf von Larisch's "Beispiele Kunstlerischer Schriften."

165. MODERN VARIATION OF MINUSCULE GOTHIC—Intentionally rather fantastic, but not intentionally departing so far from familiar forms as to be difficult to read. L. F. D.

166. PEN-WRITTEN CAPITALS. L. F. D.

185. MODERN ITALIC CAPITALS—By Walter West. Much of the delicacy of Mr. West's beautiful penmanship is unfortunately lost in the process reproduction.

186. MODERN MINUSCULE ALPHABET—By Selwyn Image. An example of his ordinary penmanship, given as an example of a modern handwriting which may fairly be described as caligraphy.

187. MODERN CAPITALS adapted for engraving. L. F. D.

188. MODERN CAPITALS adapted for execution with single strokes of the pen. L. F. D.

189. MODERN FRENCH TYPE—Designed by Grasset, and used in France for book-work. An English version is in use for advertisements, etc.

190. MODERN VERSION OF EARLY GOTHIC CAPITALS—Adapted for engraving on metal. L. F. D.

191. MODERN CAPITALS—Twisted, blunt brushwork. Could easily be worked in "couched" cord. L. F. D. (Compare 198.)

192. MODERN VARIATION UPON ROMAN CAPITALS—Blunt brushwork. L. F. D. (Compare 201.)

193. MODERN VERSION OF EARLY SPANISH LETTERS—Adapted for cutting with a single plough of the graver. L. F. D.

194. MODERN CAPITALS, shaped with deliberate view to direct and easy expression with the chisel, the cuneiform character of the Assyrian inscriptions being taken as a suggestion that a wedge-shaped incision was about the easiest thing to cut in stone. (See p. 28.) Alfred Carpenter and L. F. D.

195. MODERN CAPITALS, designed for wood-carving, the ornament typical of the Elizabethan, Jacobean, and Henri II. periods being taken as evidence of the ease with which strap-like forms may be cut with a gouge. L. F. D.

196. MODERN ALPHABET—Designed for engraving on silver. The black stands for the surface of the plate. It is as if this were a rubbing from the engraving. L. F. D.

206. MODERN GERMAN MINUSCULE—Fancifully treated. After Franz Stuck, compiled from various designs by him, in "Karten und Vignetten," etc.

207. MODERN ROMAN, MAJUSCULE AND MINUSCULE, sans serif. These thin letters, all of one thickness, are sometimes described as "skeleton."

208. MODERN ROMAN, MAJUSCULE AND MINUSCULE, of French type, elegantly shaped and spurred. Drawn by J. Vinycomb.

209. MODERN ROMAN CAPITALS—A version of the French type (208). L. F. D.

210. MODERN ROMAN CAPITALS, not quite of the usual character and proportion. (Compare 118.) L. F. D.

211. MODERN ROMAN CAPITALS AND NUMERALS — Suggestive rather of the chisel than of the pen. J. Cromar Watt, architect.

212. MODERN ROMAN CAPITALS AND LOWER CASE—Rather further removed from orthodoxy than the last. J. W. Weekes.

213. MODERN "BLOCK" CAPITALS—Based chiefly on Roman. W. J. Pearce. From "Painting and Decorating." C. Griffin & Co., Ltd.

214. MODERN ROMAN "BLOCK," or sans serif, majuscule and minuscule, miscalled "Egyptian." J. W. Weekes.

215. MODERN CAPITALS—Inspired by Gothic. W. J. Pearce.

216. MODERN GERMAN version of Roman capitals. Otto Hupp. From "Alphabete und Ornamente." Frau Bassermann Nachfolger, Munich.

217. MODERN GOTHIC CAPITALS—Meant to be fanciful, but not to do any great violence to accepted form. An alphabet in which there is the least approach to design is always in danger of being considered illegible. Legibility is for the most part the paramount consideration; but there are cases, however rare, in which it is permitted even to hide the meaning so long as it is there, for those whom it may concern.

AMPERZANDS.

NOTE.—Other examples of amperzands occur in illustrations 134, 136, 137, 138, 141, 142, 155, 167, 171, 176, 178, 189, 208, 212, 218, 222.

NUMERALS.

ART IN THE ALPHABET.

THERE are two conditions on which the artist may be permitted to tamper with the alphabet: whatever he does ought, in the first place, to make reading run smoother, and, in the second, to make writing satisfactory to the eye. Neither of these desirable ends should, however, be sought at the expense of the other.

The way to make reading easier is to mark whatever is characteristic in the letter; to develop what is peculiar to it; to curtail, or it may be to lop off, anything which tends to make us confound it with another; to emphasize, in short, the individuality of each individual letter, and make it unmistakable. At the same time, there is no reason why reading should not be made pleasant as well as easy. Beauty, that is to say, is worth bearing in mind. It must not, of course, interfere with use; but there is not the least reason why it should. Beauty does not imply elaboration or ornament. On the contrary, simplicity and character, and the dignity which comes of them, are demanded in the interests alike of practicality and of art.

It is impossible judiciously to modify the letters of the alphabet as it is, or as at any given time it was, without thoroughly understanding how it came to be so. The form and feature of lettering are explained only by its descent.

All writing is a sort of shorthand. It is inevitable that the signs used to represent sounds should be reduced to their simplest expression. They become in the end mere signs, as unlike the thing which may have suggested them in the first instance as a man's signature, which is yet honoured by his banker, is unlike his name: enough if writing convey what we are meant to understand: the business of a letter is to symbolize a definite sound.

We arrive, then, by a process of what has been termed "degradation" of such natural forms as were first employed in picture-writing (call it rather adaptation), at an alphabet of seemingly arbitrary signs, the alphabet as we know it after a couple of thousand years and more. So well do we know it that we seldom think to ask ourselves what the letters mean, or how they came to be.

The explanation of these forms lies in their evolution.

Our alphabet is that of the Romans. We speak of it to this day as Roman, to distinguish it from Gothic or black letter. The Romans had it from the Greeks, or, if not immediately from them, from the same sources whence they drew theirs.

Certainly the Greek, Etruscan, and old Roman

alphabets were all very much alike. They resembled one another in the number of letters they contained, in the sound-value of those letters, and in the form they took. There were sixteen letters common to Greeks and Etruscans: ΑΒΓΔΕΙΚΛΜ ΝΟΠΡΣΤΥ; and this number sufficed always for

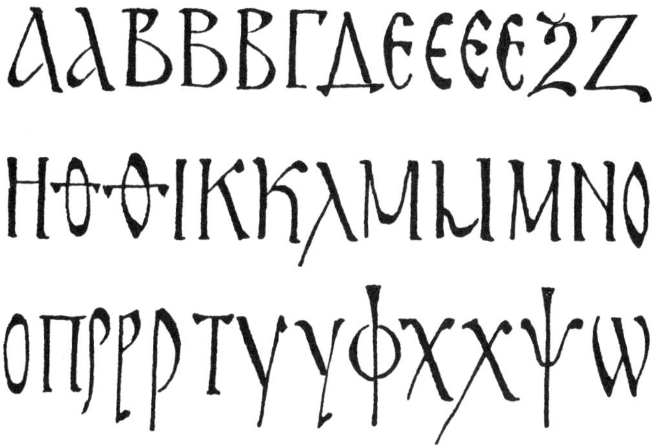

I. GREEK MS. 9TH CENTURY.

the Etruscans, the race dying out before ever it had need of more. The Greeks had no longer (as the Egyptians had) any signs to represent syllables, that is to say combinations of vowels and consonants. They added to the alphabet, which they borrowed, with modifications, from the Phœnicians, extra letters to express words of their own. The Greek ΥΦΧΨΩ do not occur in

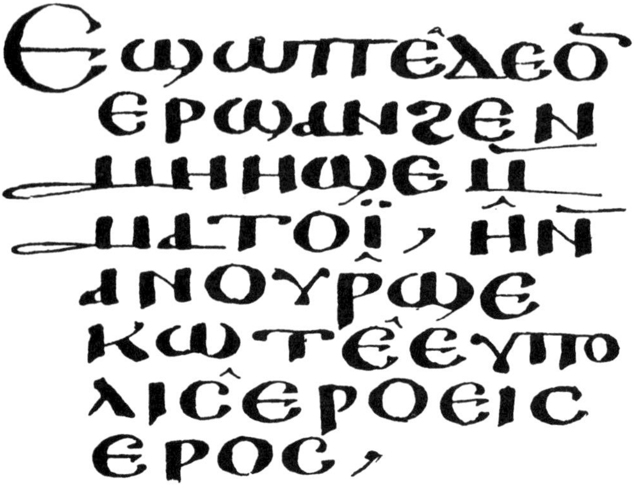

2. COPTIC MS. 5TH TO 10TH CENTURY.

the Phœnician alphabet. The Phœnicians had probably adopted from the Egyptians signs to express foreign sounds new to their own language, without knowing or caring anything about the pictorial origin of such signs. There was thus no reason why they should not modify what they regarded as arbitrary expressions of sound-values, and every reason why they should reduce them to the very simplest and most conveniently written shape—which they did ; and so it comes about that we to-day are in all probability directly indebted to ancient Egypt for at least a portion of our alphabet, far removed as it may be from the hieroglyphics of the Pharaohs That, however, is by the way, and, besides, a long way off. For present purposes we need not go further back than to ancient Greece.

The Romans dropped all compound consonants, using at first the two consonants which most nearly expressed the sound equivalent to that of the Greek double letter; for example, PH in place of Φ. But they proceeded also to devise single letters for sounds which until then had been expressed by two; F, for example, instead of PH.

A Greek alphabet of the year 394 B.C. is given in illustration 54, and a 16th-century version in 55.

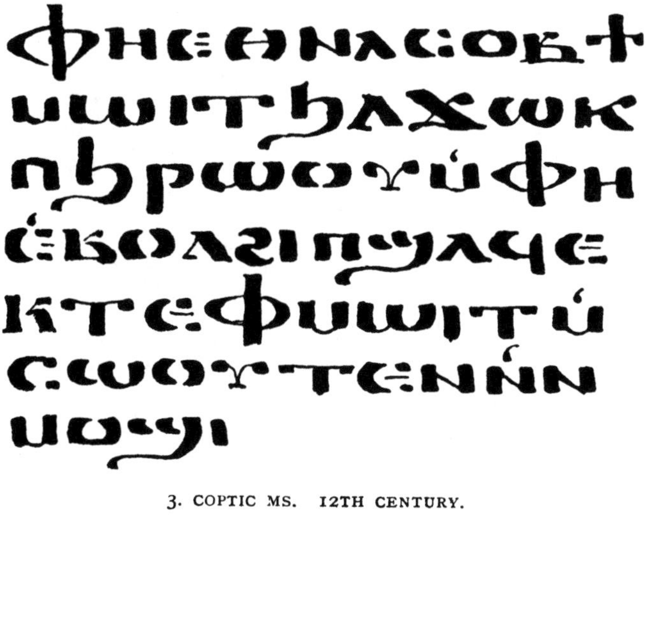

3. COPTIC MS. 12TH CENTURY.

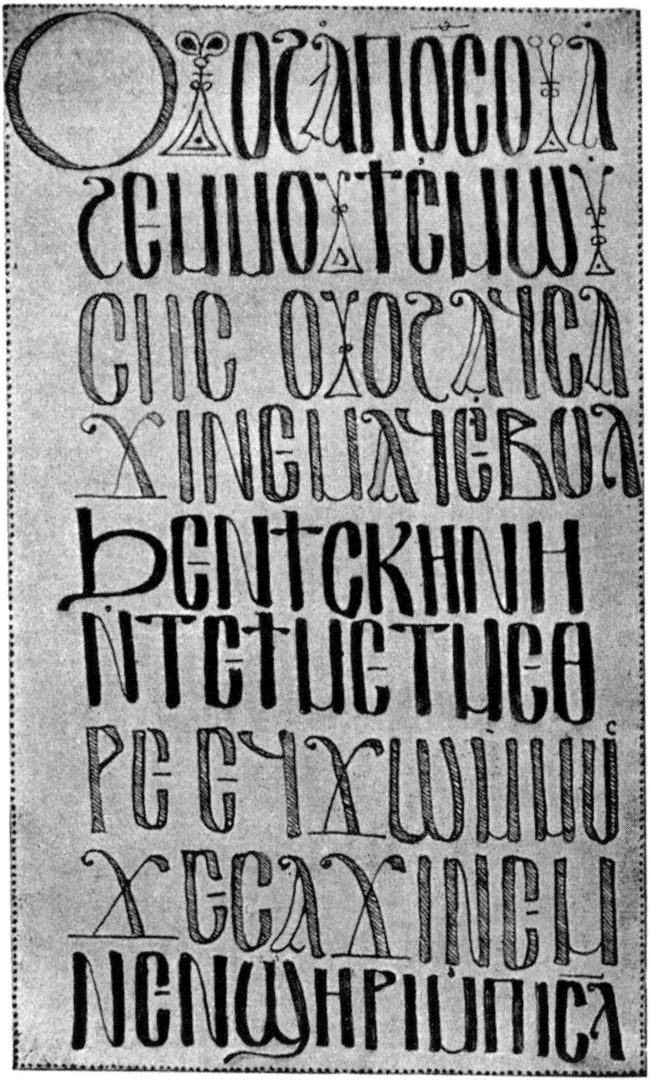

4. COPTIC MS. 14TH CENTURY.

The more cursive form employed by the 9th-century scribe is shown in the manuscript letters (1) on page 3, whilst the more careful and elaborate writing proper to gold letters is illustrated by a page of 11th-century work (5) from a MS. in the Laurentian Library at Florence.

It is interesting to compare with these the Coptic writing (2, 3, 4), which is obviously only a variant upon the Greek; for the Christianized Egyptians, when they accepted Christianity, adopted the Greek alphabet, just as the Turks took the Arabic character at the time they accepted the Koran; and when, in the 6th century, the new faith was firmly established at Alexandria, Coptic writing supplanted the old Egyptian. So it happens that the Coptic alphabet is Greek, except for seven extra signs, taken from the ancient demotic alphabet, to express Egyptian sounds for which the Greeks had no equivalent.

The early Roman or Latin alphabet differed very little from the Greek. The latest comers in it were G H K Q X Y Z.

In its adaptation to the Latin language, Greek gamma or G becomes C. G is, in fact, almost equivalent to *hard* C. To the not too subtle ear the two sounds are like enough to pass one for the other, just as *soft* C may be made to do duty for S. When G came to be used as a separate letter, distinct from C, then C in its turn was used for K, though K did not go quite out of use.

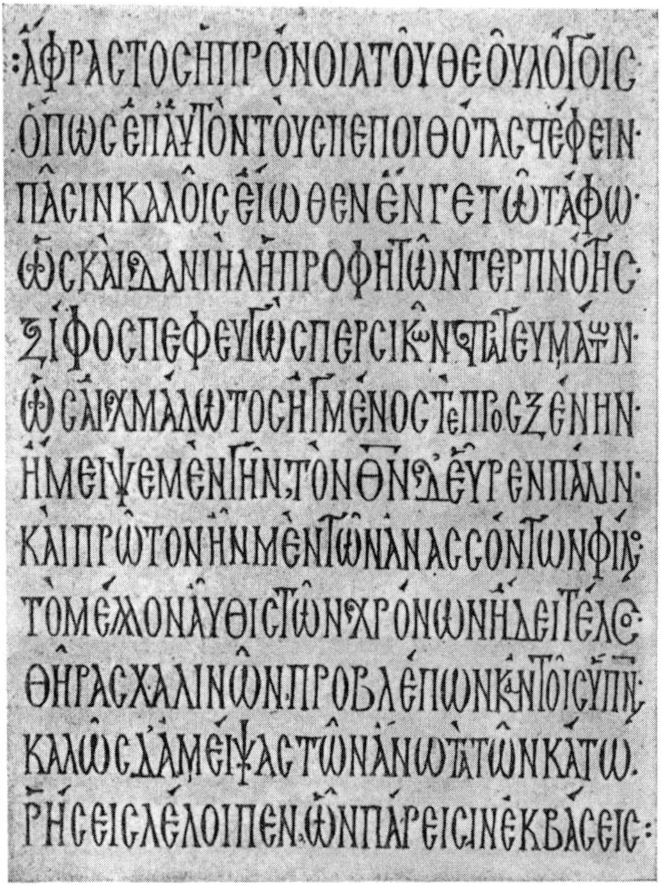
ΑΦΡΑΣΤΟΣΗΠΡΟΝΟΙΑΤΟΥΘΕΟΥΛΟΓΟΙΣ
ΟΠΩΣΕΠΑΥΤΟΝΤΟΥΣΠΕΠΟΙΘΟΤΑΣΤΡΕΦΕΙΝ
ΠΑΣΙΝΚΑΛΟΙΣΕΙΩΘΕΝΕΝΓΕΤΩΤΑΦΩ
ΩΣΚΑΙΔΑΝΙΗΛΗΠΡΟΦΗΤΩΝΤΕΡΠΝΟΤΗΣ
ΞΙΦΟΣΠΕΦΕΥΓΩΣΠΕΡΣΙΚΩΝΣΤΡΑΤΕΥΜΑΤΩΝ
ΩΣΑΙΧΜΑΛΩΤΟΣΗΓΜΕΝΟΣΤΕΠΡΟΣΞΕΝΗΝ
ΗΜΕΙΨΕΜΕΝΓΗΝ,ΤΟΝΘΝΔΕΕΥΡΕΝΠΑΛΙΝ
ΚΑΙΠΡΩΤΟΝΗΝΜΕΝΤΩΝΑΝΑΣΣΟΝΤΩΝΦΙΛΟΣ
ΤΟΜΕΣΟΝΑΥΘΙΣΤΩΝΧΡΟΝΩΝΗΔΕΙΤΕΛΟΣ
ΘΗΡΑΣΧΑΛΙΝΩΝ.ΠΡΟΒΛΕΠΩΝΚΑΝΤΟΙΣΥΠΝΟΙΣ
ΚΑΛΩΣΔΑΜΕΙΨΑΣΤΩΝΑΝΩΤΑΤΩΝΚΑΤΩ
ΡΗΣΕΙΣΛΕΛΟΙΠΕΝ.ΩΝΠΑΡΕΙΣΙΝΕΚΒΑΣΕΙΣ

5. GREEK MS. IITH CENTURY.

The letter J did not exist either in the Greek or in the ancient Roman alphabet. It is equivalent to II. Place one I over the other and you get a long $\frac{\text{I}}{\text{I}}$. Eventually the initial developed a tail, and became J. Towards the 15th century the initial I was pretty generally written J.

The Greek Υ (*upsilon*) becomes the Roman Y. The letters U and V were long considered as interchangeable; one or other of them might be used, or both at once in the same word in the same sense. It was not until the 10th century that the custom arose of using V before a vowel, and elsewhere using U.

Though Ω (*omega*) stood for long O, the Latin letter, which was derived in form from it, bore the value of W. And, as may be seen in the 9th-century alphabet on page 3, omega was sometimes *written* precisely like a W.

The alphabet, as we know it, owes something also to Scandinavia. The Runic writing, as the script of the Scandinavian and other Northern European priesthood was called, dates back to legendary days. It was the invention, they say, of Odin himself. If so, Odin, to judge by internal evidence, must have derived it from some earlier Greek or Roman source. What we know is, that it was in use from the time of the first intercourse between Scandinavians and Romans. The Christian Church forbade its use, and with the triumph

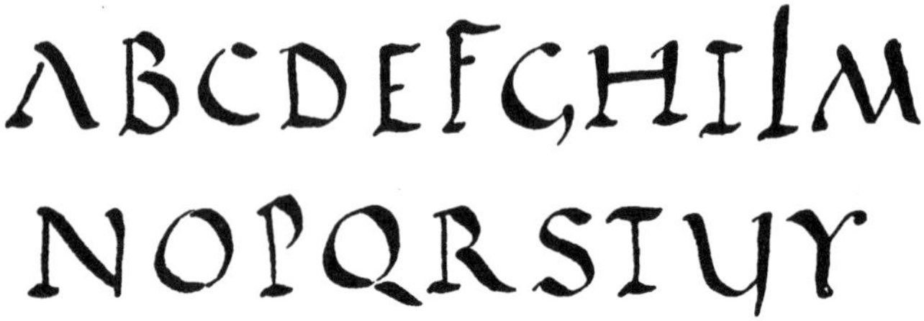

6. ROMAN MS. 4TH CENTURY.

of Christianity it passed out of currency; but it lived long enough to affect in some degree our Anglo-Saxon writing.

It will be well now to mark the more decided steps in the progress of the alphabet. The type we use takes, as every one knows, two forms—a larger and a smaller, a major and a minor, or, as printers put it, "capitals" and "lower case," or the small letters which, being most continually in request, it is convenient to keep near at hand, in the lower part of the case, from which the compositor, so to speak, feeds himself. Our written character takes the form of a "running" hand, and is known by that name, or by the more high-sounding title of "cursive."

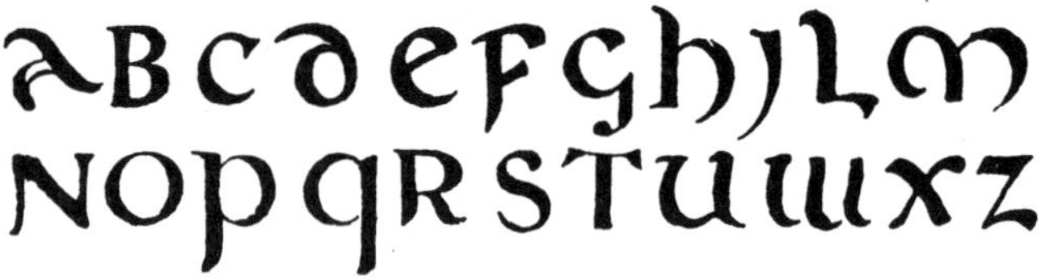

7. MS. 7TH CENTURY.

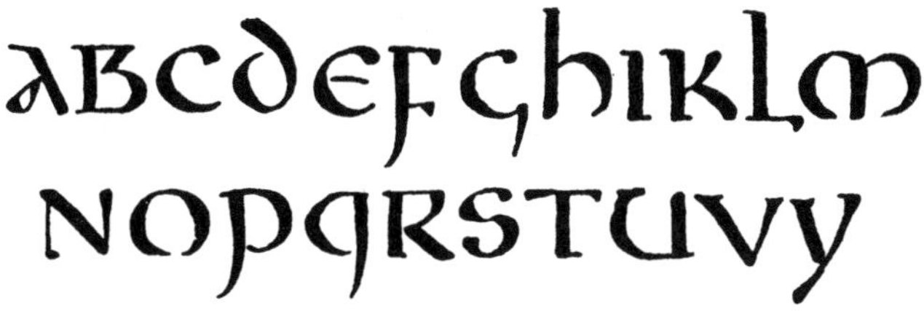

8. ROMAN UNCIALS. 8TH CENTURY.

Now, the printer's "lower case," or "minuscule," as it is also called, is practically the book form of running hand, except that the letters are quite separate, not conjoined as they are in what pretends to be only the hand of the ready writer, and does not claim to be beautiful at all.

The earlier form, whether of Greek or Roman letter, was the capital, the square shape, with relatively few curved lines, which could conveniently be cut in stone or engraved on metal. This is, in fact, the *monumental* style—adapted to, and, what is more, inspired by, the chisel or the

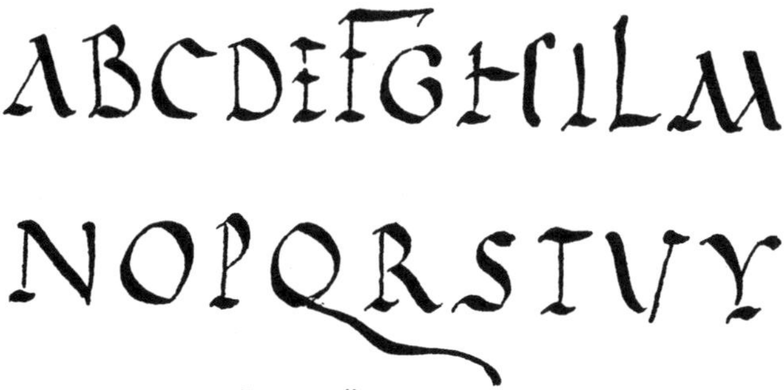

9. ROMAN "RUSTIC" WRITING. 5TH CENTURY.

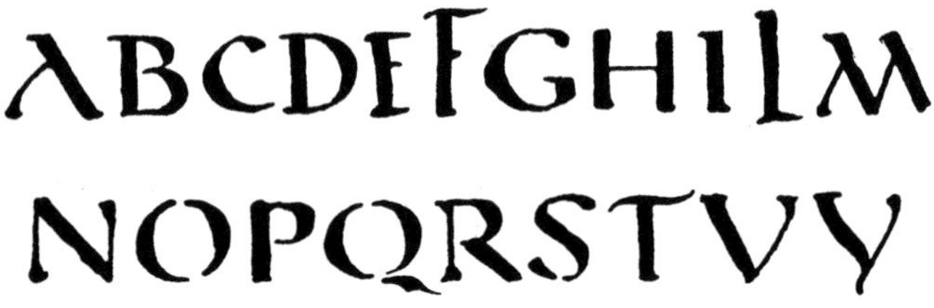

10. ROMAN MS. CAPITALS. 6TH CENTURY.

graver. You have only to look at it (54, 56, 57) to see how precisely fit it is for its purpose. There is no mistake about it, it is incision.

Manuscript writers adopted for book writing a different character, or rather they adapted the square capital letter to more ready execution with the pen, and so evolved a rounder kind of letter which is known by the name of *uncial*—not that it was invariably inch-long, as the term is supposed to imply.

The uncial form of writing is intermediate, you will see (8), between the monumental writing and the "current" hand of the ready writer. It is, if not the step between the two, a compromise between them—no matter which; what it concerns us to know is that calligraphy took that direction, which goes to explain many a later form of letter widely differing from the original square type. The relationship between these uncial letters and the cursive Greek (1) is obvious.

The uncial character does not so much affect the modern printer; but it is the form of letter from

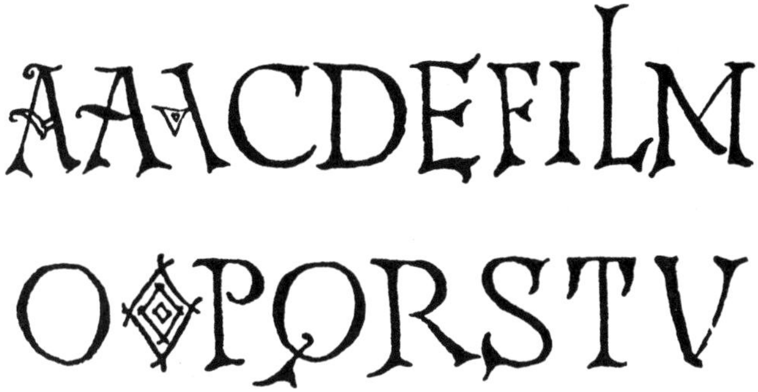

II. MS. CAPITALS. 6TH CENTURY.

which the artist who prefers his own handiwork to that of the printing press has perhaps most to learn.

A squarer form of capital employed by the Romans in manuscripts of the 5th and two following centuries, is known by the name of "rustic"; not that there was anything rustic about these capitals in our sense of the word; but the Latin word was used in the sense of free and easy, *sans gêne*. The character of the writing is not so formal as was supposed to befit the town. It is a kind of country cousin; it stands, let us say, for the Roman capital in a loose coat and a soft hat. The characteristic points about it (9) are that the vertical strokes are all very thin, and the cross-strokes broad. These cross-strokes take the form of a kind of tick, tapering at the ends; and similar ticks are used to emphasize the finishing of the thin strokes. That all of this is pen-work is self-evident. But, as before said, the more usual form of penmanship at that time was the uncial letter.

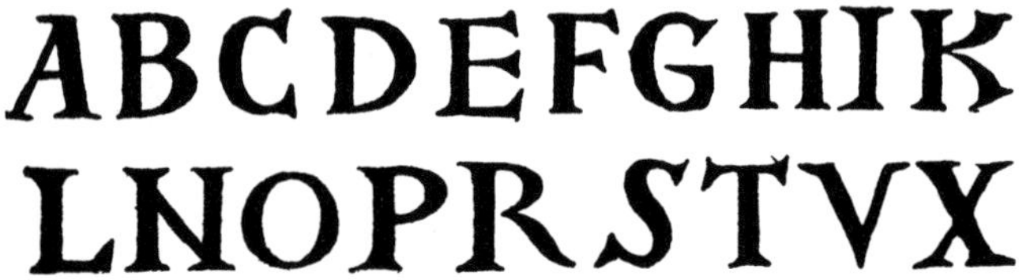

12. BYZANTINE CAPITALS. 7TH CENTURY.

Even when the Roman manuscript writers used, as they sometimes did, the square capital form, they did not confine themselves (11) to the severely simple shapes which came naturally to the lapidaries. The unequal strength of the lines, the thickening of the strokes at the ends, and the spurred or forked shapes they take, all speak of the pen; not the steel pen, of course, nor yet the more supple quill, but the reed pen—rather blunter than a quill, but pliant enough, and not given to spluttering. Moreover, it did not tempt the writer to indulge in unduly thin upstrokes.

Capitals, Greek and Roman alike, represent, roughly speaking, the first accepted shapes, engraver's or carver's work. Uncials stand for MS. writing, scribe's work, growing by degrees rounder and more current. The smaller minuscule was evolved out of the running hand of the mercantile, as distinguished from the literary, scribe. It was not used by the ancient Romans, and it was not until towards the 8th century that running hand was thus reduced to order. The greater part of what is called cursive writing scarcely concerns

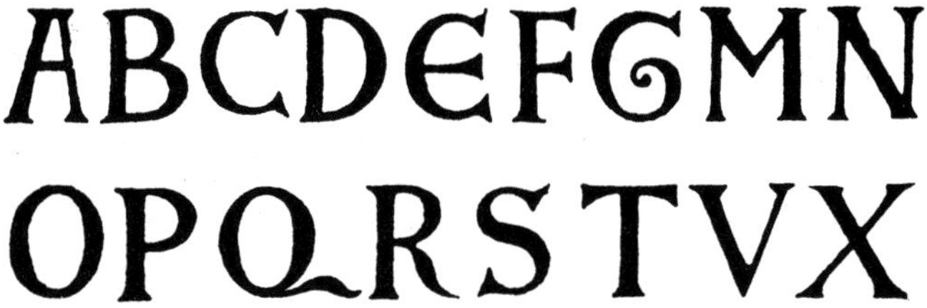

13. INSCRIPTION CUT IN STONE. A.D. 1085.

the calligrapher; it might equally be called discursive, so apt is it to run wild, in which case it tells less of the progress of writing than of the caprice or carelessness of the individual writer.

That was not the case with the various ceremonial versions of running hand employed by the writers of Papal Bulls and Royal Charters. Such "diplomatic" hands, as they are styled (because diplomas were written in them), and the so-called "Chancery" hands, are highly elaborate, and in a sense ornamental, but they are so unlike our writing as to be, practically speaking, illegible. They are very suggestive for all that. A specimen of English Court hand is given in Alphabet 157.

With the decline of the Roman empire came naturally the demoralization of the Roman character, capital or uncial; and just in proportion as Rome ceased to be the one centre of the world, and other nations rose into importance, so their writing began to show signs of nationality. At the loss of some refinement, we get thenceforth variety of character. By the beginning of the 8th century distinctly national styles of lettering were evolved.

To subdivide these styles so minutely as the learned do, is rather to bewilder the poor student by their multitude. The important European races were the Latins, the Franks, the Teutons, and Anglo-Saxons, and the Visigoths; and from them we get respectively the Lombard, the Frankish,

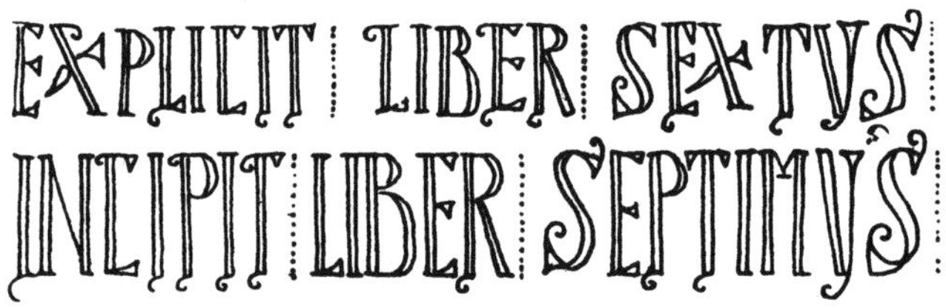

14. FRANCO-GALLIC MSS. HEADLINES. 7TH CENTURY.

the Teutonic and Anglo-Saxon, and the Visigothic types of writing, all of which eventually merge themselves in what we call Gothic, in which, nevertheless, we still find traits of nationality, English, French, Italian, German, Spanish, as the case may be.

First as to the Lombardic character, which prevailed in Italy from the 8th to the 11th century. It was not, as its name might be taken to imply, the invention of the Lombards. They were just long-bearded conquerors, and invented nothing. The character was not even confined to Northern

Italy; only it happened first to be developed there, and so all later Latin writing (after the Empire) came to be called "Lombardic."

It has already been explained how uncial writing was transitional between square "caps" and rounder pen-forms. The Lombardic shows a further stage of transition. The penman had not quite made up his mind between straight lines and curved; he hesitated between the square-lined M and N and the rounded forms (19, 20, 68). Eventually he decided in favour of the bulging shapes, which in their later development we distinguish by the name of Lombardic capitals (74).

There is a broken-backed version of the Lombard minuscule, "*Lombard brisée*" the French call it, which, though not intrinsically beautiful, is interesting as foreshadowing the later form of Gothic "lower case" which we call "black letter."

Our own "lower case" we get more or less directly from Charlemagne. He found, perhaps his friend the Pope told him, that writing had degenerated by the time he came to the throne (A.D. 800) to a state unworthy of a mighty emperor. Accordingly he ordained its reformation. He went so far as to compel bishops and other important personages who could not write decently to employ scribes who could. In this way he revived the small Roman character, which we eventually adopted for our printed type.

The scribes of Charlemagne (and for some time

after him) did not yet manage to fashion very satisfactory capitals. They still mixed up letters all of one thickness with others in which thick and thin strokes, or diminishing strokes, were used in a most illogical and awkward way (64)—indicative, of course, of a period of change. But they did arrive at a satisfactory and very characteristic rendering

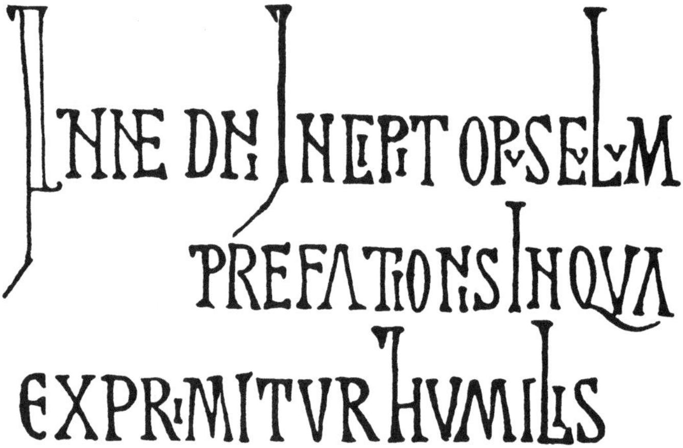

15. VISIGOTHIC MS. 10TH CENTURY.

of minuscule lettering. A conspicuous feature in it was the elongation of the longer limb of the l p g q f d—*tails*, that is to say, came into fashion, and long ones, as much as four or five times the length of the body of the letter. The letter s took also the long form, ſ. The letter t, on the other hand, does not rise much above the line, sometimes not at all.

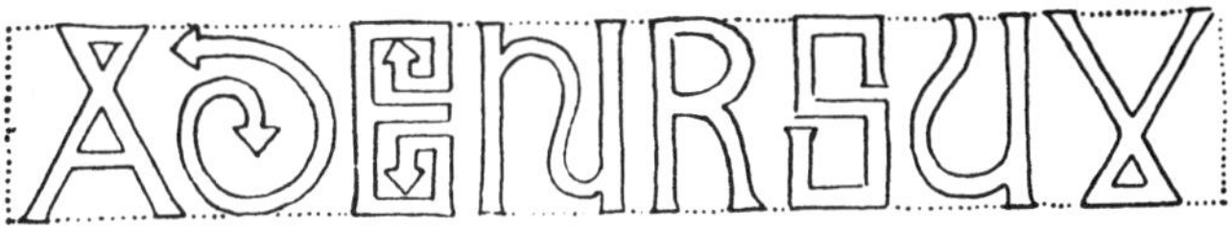

16. SAXON ILLUMINATION (CAROLINE). 9TH CENTURY.

That elongation of up-and-down strokes is characteristic of Frankish and Visigothic lettering generally. It occurs even in the case of capitals, as in the headlines of the 10th-century MS. on p. 18. There the I, the H, and the L rise high above the heads of their fellows, whilst, on the other hand, the V-shaped U in the word OPVSCVLVM is reduced to more than modest proportions.

There appears to be in Visigothic lettering, of which that is a good example, usually a trace of Moorish influence, betraying itself in the liberties taken with the *proportion* of the characters; the Moors had by that time overrun Spain.

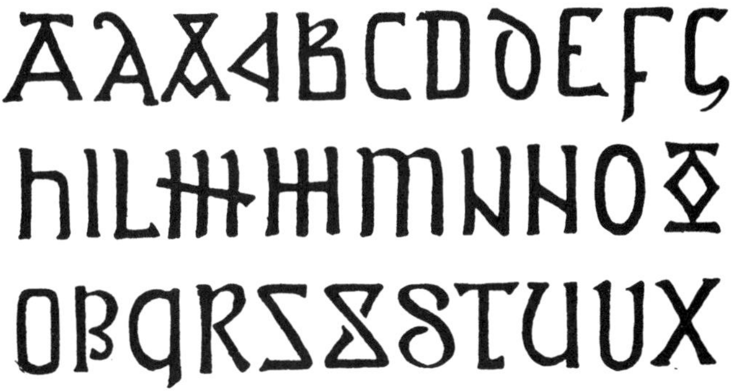

17. ANGLO-SAXON.

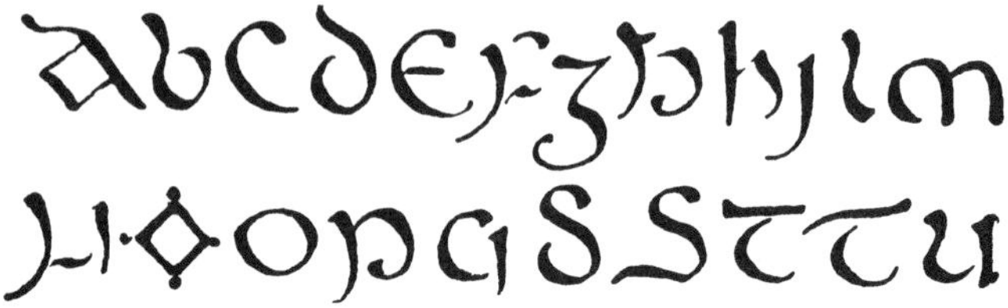

18. ANGLO-SAXON MS. 9TH CENTURY.

There is something very whimsical about the character of Anglo-Saxon capitals; at times mechanically square in form, at others exceptionally flowing and even frisky (16, 17, 62, 63). Anglo-Saxon lettering was affected by lingering traces of an obsolete alphabet derived perhaps at some remote period from the Gauls, which, to judge by internal evidence, must have been something like the Greek. In the minuscule character (18) there is a curious twist in the long stroke of the b and l.

By the 13th century the Gothic style had formed itself. In the next hundred years or more it was perfected. At the end of the 15th century it was

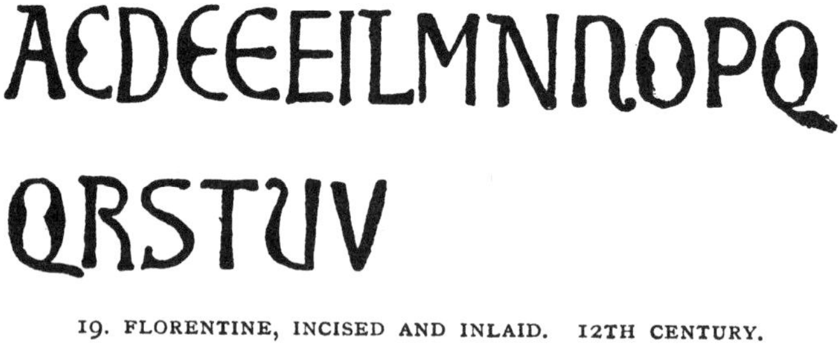

19. FLORENTINE, INCISED AND INLAID. 12TH CENTURY.

still flourishing—flourishing was the word literally —in the 16th letters were sometimes nearly all flourish: it takes an expert to read them.

The Gothic variations upon the Roman capital form are characteristic: the thick strokes are not even-sided, but expanded at the two ends or narrowed towards the centre; the curved strokes do not swell so gradually as before, but bulge

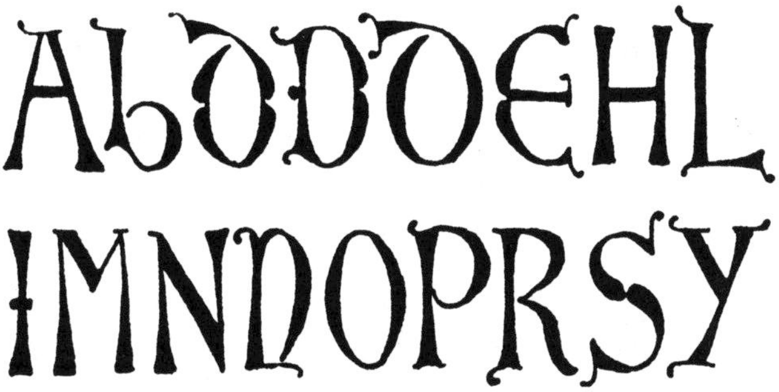

20. ITALIAN MS. EARLY 13TH CENTURY.

more or less suddenly; the tails of sundry letters break insubordinate from the ranks; and the extremities are often foliated or otherwise ornamented (66, 69, 71). Markedly characteristic of Gothic of the 13th and 14th centuries are also the "closed" letters, of which examples occur in Alphabets 76, 77, 78, 80, etc.

What are called Lombardic capitals were used, not only as initials, but for inscriptions throughout. In fact, it was not until the 15th century that inscriptions were commonly written in minuscule letters. In many cases these Lombard capitals were not written with a pen, but with a brush, from which results something of their character. The brush lines were fatter than pen strokes.

Gothic characteristics, however, only gradually

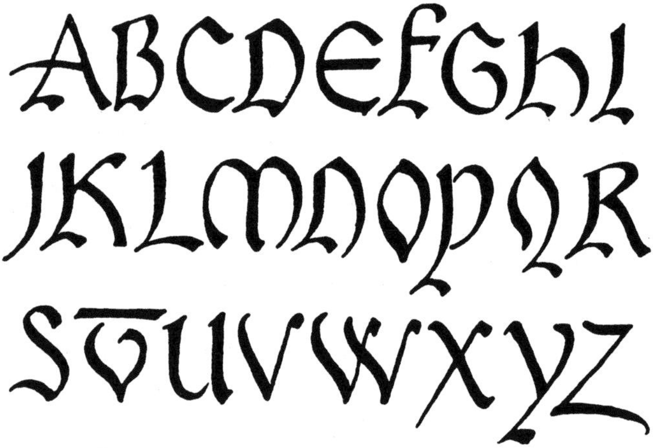

21. FREE RENDERING OF LOMBARD MSS. ABOUT 1250.

asserted themselves, and individual scribes clung tenaciously to the older forms. The alphabet opposite, for example, though of the 15th century, only mildly represents the period to which by date it belongs.

Gothic letters lend themselves to more variety in design than Roman, not being so perfect in themselves. To some, perhaps, they are more interesting on that very account: perfection palls upon us. Anyway, the Gothic forms are often very beautiful. The Roman letter is classic, and therefore fixed—or, should it rather be said, it is fixed, and therefore classic?

With regard to the Gothic minuscule character (23, 24, 25), the even perpendicularity of the broad, straight strokes gives at a glance the character distinguished as "black letter," because it is rela-

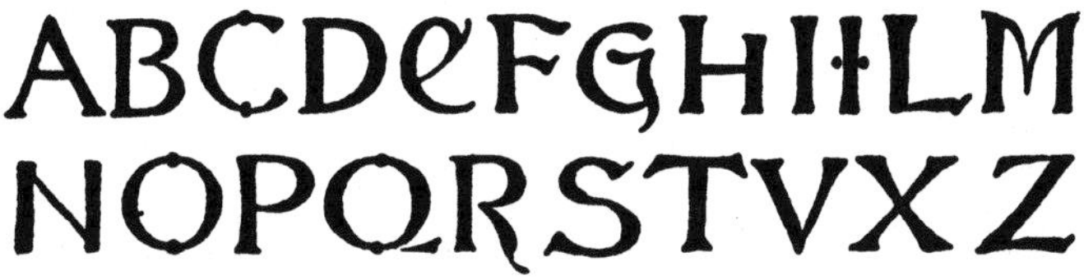

22. CAPITALS. 15TH CENTURY.

tively much heavier than the Roman minuscule. You have only to compare the two to see that the "black letter" *is* blacker.

The Germans marked this form of lettering for their own, and persevered in its use long after the rest of the world, in pursuance of the fashion of classicism prevailing in the 16th century, had abandoned it for the Roman style of lettering.

The mediæval German version of black letter was stronger than that of other countries, the French more fanciful, the Italian more refined, more perfect, but perhaps never so Gothic.

The old "black letter" varied, as will be seen,

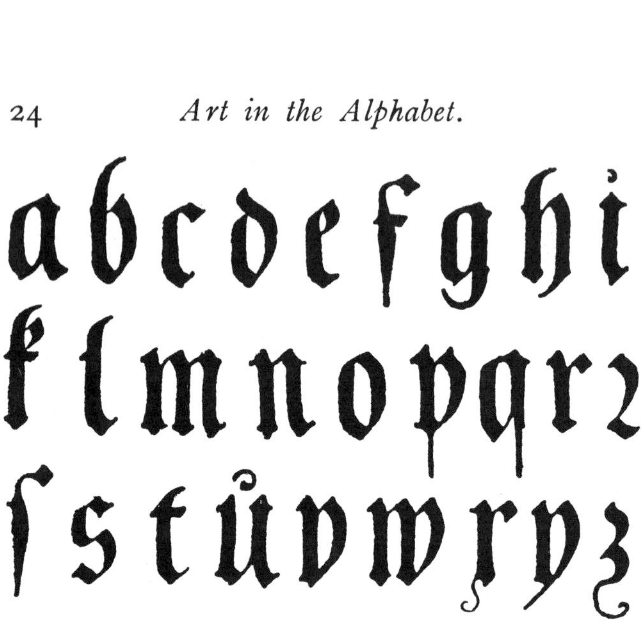

23. GERMAN GOTHIC MINUSCULE.

very much in character. The rounder form (23) is freer, easier to write, more cursive. The more regular and straight-backed letter (24, 25) went rather out of fashion for a while; but it was revived by the printers, who saw in it what they could best imitate.

The type we use nowadays has shaped itself in a more or less accidental way. In the first place, it was a copy of manuscript forms. That was inevitable. Possibly printers were anxious to palm off their printed books as manuscripts. But, apart from any such intent on their part, their text was bound to follow the written page, or no one would have been able to read it. And as, at the time of

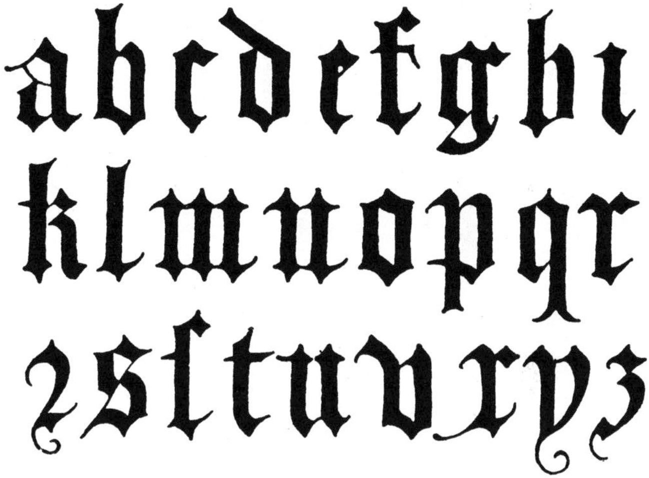

24. GERMAN GOTHIC MINUSCULE.

the introduction of printing, two styles of writing were in use for manuscripts, there arose naturally two styles of printed type—" Roman " and " black letter." In printing, as in manuscript, however, black letter gave way to the Roman character, but not all at once; there was a period of transition during which some very interesting and characteristic types were used. We in our day have arrived, by a process of copying the copies of copies of copies, from which all the virtue of vitality and freshness has died out, at a 20th century type (look at the newspapers), which compares most unfavourably with the early printing. The modern form of letter is in a measure fixed for us by

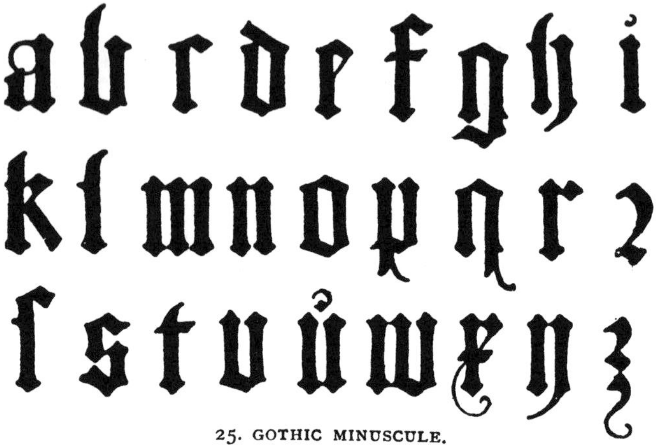

25. GOTHIC MINUSCULE.

circumstances; we cannot conveniently depart far from it; but something may be done. There is no need to revive mediæval lettering, no occasion to invent new lettering all out of our own heads, if that were possible; any new departure of ours must be very much on old lines; but at least we might found ourselves upon the best that has been done, and go straight to that for inspiration.

Type, as before said, was based on manuscript forms. These manuscript forms had been shaped with a view always to easy writing. What was difficult to pen dropped out of use, and lettering became what the scribe made it. The considerations, however, which guided the writer no longer concern the printer. It is time, perhaps, he took stock of the alphabet—looked over it with a view to its perfection, since one shape is about as easy to *print* as another. The changes which have taken place in our printed type during the last three hundred years or so may very likely have been on the whole in the direction of easy reading, but they have not been in the direction of beauty; and it is quite likely that it may be worth while restoring some obsolete forms of letter now that we have not to write them. There is inconvenience in departing in any appreciable degree from the accepted form of letter; but we have arrived to-day at a period when everyone is so familiar with the printed page that, prejudiced as we may be against any modification of it, there is no danger of our finding any real difficulty in reading an improved type. Lettering is none the more legible because it is ugly: beauty is compatible with the very sternest use.

The earliest writing was most probably scratched with a point upon whatever came handiest to the scribe—skins, palm leaves, or the bark of trees, and especially upon clay, a material which had only to be burnt to become more lasting than stone.

If, in scratching upon firm clay, the writer begins his stroke with a dig and then drags out the tool, it results in a wedge-shaped scratch. That seems to be the way the cuneiform character came about; but the lettering upon the early Babylonian "bricks," as they are called, is so precisely defined that it must have been done with a sharp graver-like point. These "wedge-shaped" or "arrow-headed" characters came to be copied, as we know, in stone, in which again they were about the simplest thing to cut. Three, or at most four, direct cuts give the Ninevite character, as we know it in the famous bas-reliefs. It is descended from clay forms, but its own mother was the stone out of which it was cut. The chisel was its father. Even in inscriptions as late as the 18th century or thereabouts, the stone-cutter lapses, as may be seen opposite, into more or less wedge-shaped incisions; the chisel tempted him, and he yielded to its persuasion.

From the cuneiform character to simple Greek (54) or Roman (56) capitals, as square as well could be, is not far; and the clear-cut inscriptions on classic monuments are still typically chisel work. Very early Greek inscriptions are, however, not much more than scratched in the granite or whatever it may be. The small Greek character on the famed Rosetta stone is *mere* scratching.

Writing done with a stylus on tablets of wax was naturally blunt. Penwork at first was also much blunter than modern writing—owing partly, no doubt, to the use of the reed pen, partly to the texture of papyrus, and partly to the consistency of the ink. The strokes of early lettering in Egyptian, Greek, and Latin manuscripts alike, are rather thick, and rounded at the angles, not sharply turned.

It was a reed pen with which the Arabs wrote,

holding it more or less horizontally so as to retain the ink, and sloping the paper or papyrus at a convenient angle; and it was in writing the Roman letters with a reed pen that the mediæval scribes gave it its Gothic character. It was not until the quill (which held the ink better) came into use that the Italians developed their minuscule letter with its thick and thin strokes.

A glance is sometimes enough to tell whether an early Egyptian manuscript was written with a pen

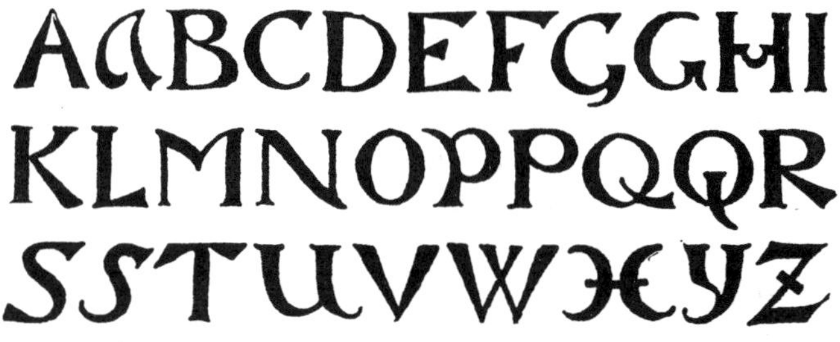

26. FROM INSCRIPTIONS CUT IN STONE. ABOUT 1700.

or with a brush. The Arab penmen, who took great pride in their art, wrote with a wonderfully elastic pen, and got out of the reed forms which remind one at times of brushwork; but the *neskhi* character is as obviously the pen form of writing as the squarer *cufic* is the monumental. So also we find among the Chinese and Japanese one form of lettering which is characteristically brushwork, and another almost rectangular, which last is clearly the monumental manner.

Even in late Gothic lettering we find a minuscule which is of the pen (23), and another (24, 25) which is monumental, adapted, that is to say, to precise and characteristic rendering with the graver upon sheets of brass. It is curious that out of this severe form of writing the florid ribbon character (108) should have been evolved. But when once the engraver began to consider the broad strokes of his letters as bands or straps, which, by a cut of the graver, could be made to turn over at the ends, as indicated in Alphabet 125, it was inevitable that a taste for the florid should lead him to something of the kind. The wielder of the brush was in all times induced by his implement to make flourishes (32, 33), in which the carver had much less temptation to indulge. The sloping or "italic" letter (27) is, on the face of it, the product of the pen.

We find, then, that the implement employed, stylus, reed-pen, brush, or whatever it may have been, goes far to account for the character of ancient lettering. So soon as the writer ceased to be satisfied with mere scratching or blunt indentation, and took to the use of the chisel, he felt the need of a square cross-cut to end the stroke of his letter. If that was broad, there was no occasion for the cut to go beyond the width of the stroke itself. If it was narrow, the easier thing to do was to anticipate the danger of overshooting the mark, and frankly extend the end cut. This method of finishing off the broad line by a projecting cross-line is technically called truncation, though literally that only means cutting off. Slight but appreciable difference in character results from the angle at which the strokes are truncated or cut off.

In working with a pen, this difficulty of ending the stroke occurs only in the case of very bold lettering. In small writing the strokes naturally

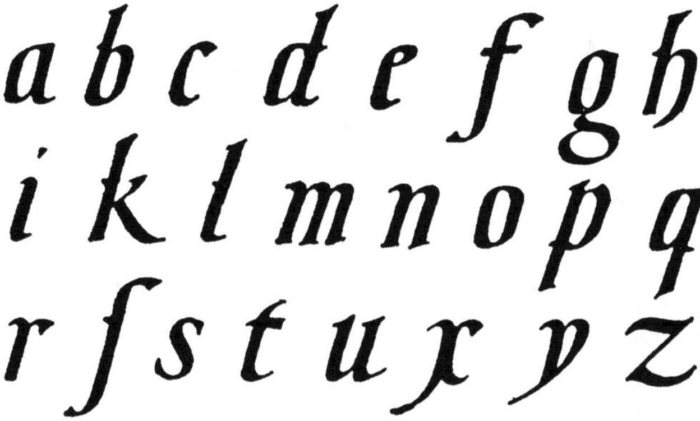

27. ROMAN ITALICS.

take pen-shape. They start square and gradually diminish, or *vice versâ*, or they thicken in the middle, according to the angle at which the pen is held, and to the pressure, which it is difficult to keep quite equal from end to end of the stroke.

It should be observed that the pressure is not naturally in the middle of the stroke, but at one end; the penman does not naturally get the symmetrical Roman O, but the Gothic O (117).

That is the pen-born shape. The even-sided O was, if not easier to cut in stone, at least as easy; there was nothing to prevent symmetry, which was accordingly the rule in sculpture. It is rather futile to aim at that kind of thing with a pen; much better let the pen have its way; and its way is otherwise (176, 179). We get so much more out of our tools by going with them, that it is rather stupid to strive against them.

In very bold writing, even with a pen, the necessity for truncating the thick strokes occurs. You cannot easily, with one stroke of the pen, make a thick line which begins and ends square. It wants trimming; and the easiest way to trim it is by means of a fine cross-stroke extending beyond its width. This cross-stroke **T** helps to preserve and to accentuate the regularity of the *line* of lettering, for which a writer worth the name naturally has a care. The broad stroke being rather loaded with ink, the fine cross-stroke is inclined, in crossing it, to drag a little of the ink with it, rounding one angle of it. The obvious way of rectifying that is to round the opposite angle also—and so we have the familiar finish T, which is equivalent to the "spur" of the chiseller mentioned just now (208).

The angle at which the cross-line joins the stroke may be softened until it disappears, and the stroke appears to be curved on either side—"dilates," to use another accepted term, at the

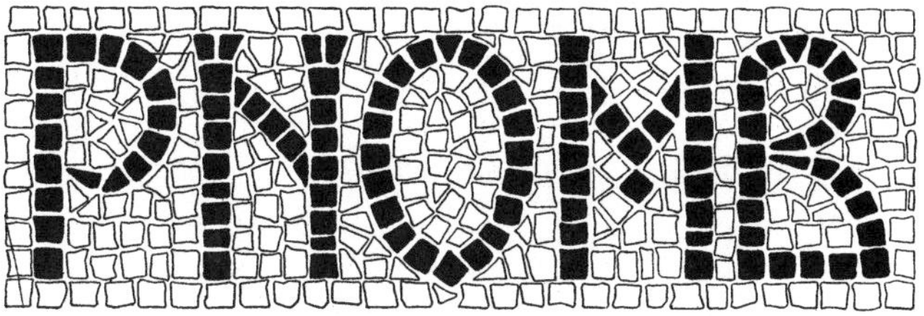

28. ROMAN MOSAIC. LOUVRE, PARIS.

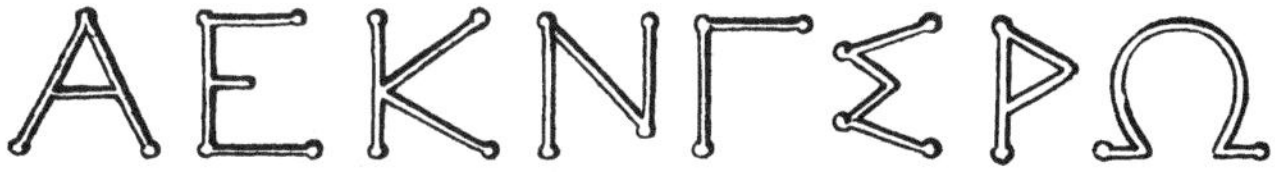

29. ENGRAVED BRONZE TABLETS. NAPLES MUSEUM.

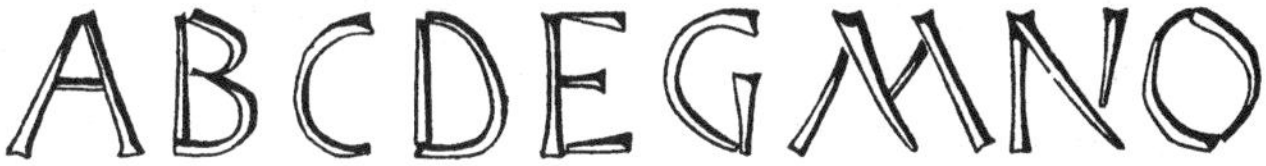

30. ENGRAVED BRONZE TABLETS. NAPLES MUSEUM.

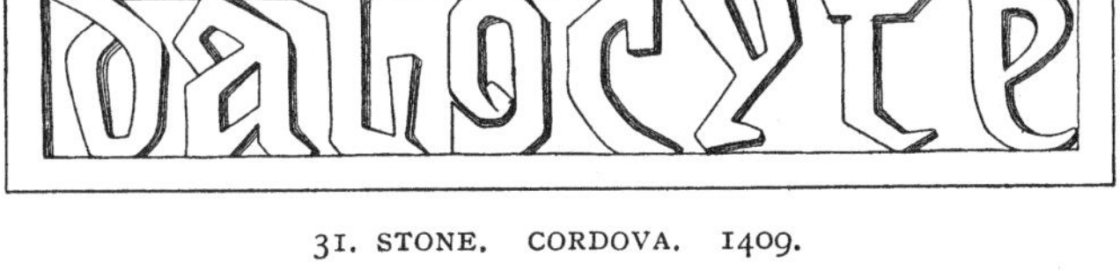

31. STONE. CORDOVA. 1409.

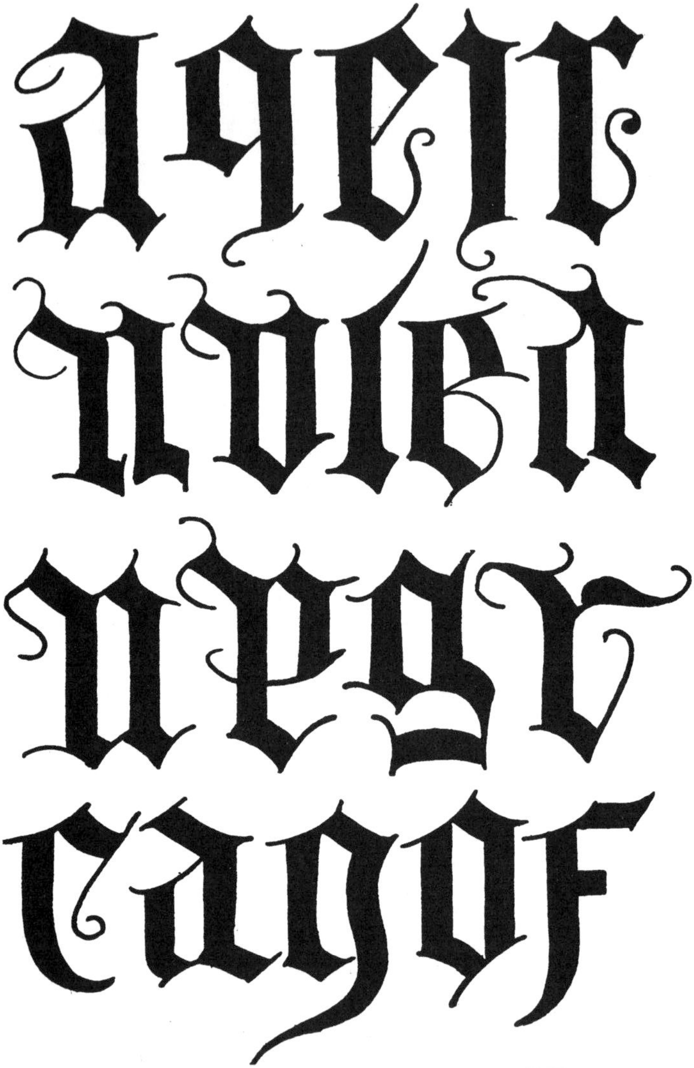

32. PAINTED ON HISPANO-MORESQUE POTTERY.
15TH AND 16TH CENTURIES.

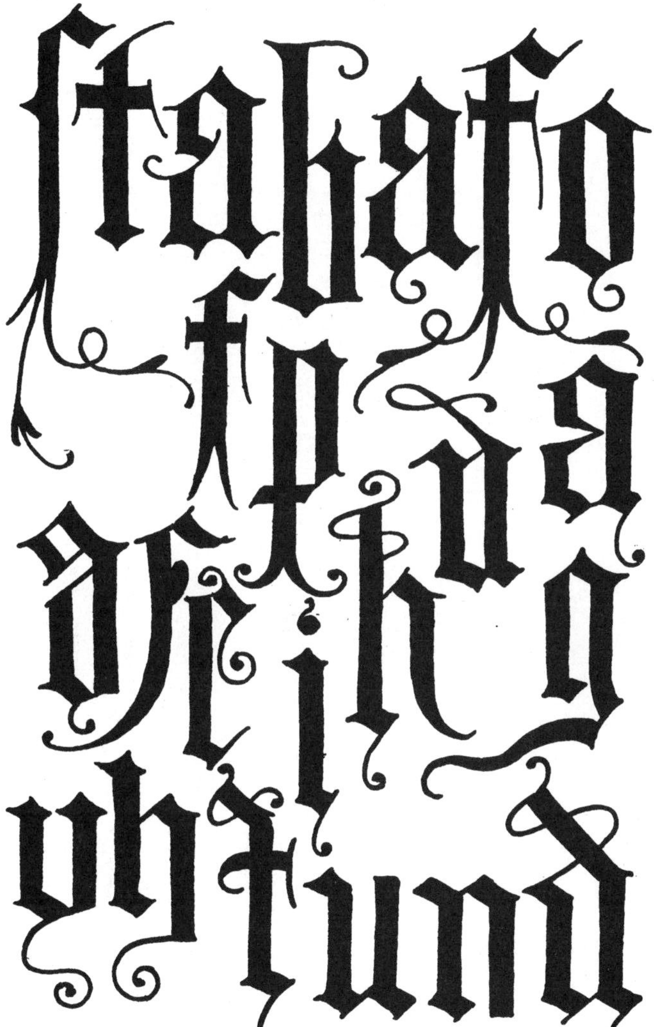

33. PAINTED ON ITALIAN MAJOLICA. 16TH CENTURY.

ends. Historically, we arrive at that in Lombardic and other writing as early as the 8th century (60).

Anticipating this dilation, the penman eventually made strokes in which the elementary straight line altogether disappears (68). Further elaborating, he arrived at the rather sudden swelling of the curved back of the letter, familiar in work of the 13th century and later (73, 87). With the forking of the terminations, and the breaking of the outline in various ways (20), we arrive at fantastic variation to which there is no conceivable end (34, 84, 88, 91, 120). Few instances, therefore, of the elaborate ornamentation of the lettering are here given (109, 120, 151, 152). Enough to give alphabets in which the ornamental design is in the construction of the letters themselves.

With the use of thick and thin strokes comes a difficulty. Which shall be thick, and which thin? The scribes were a long while making up their minds on that point, and they contrived some very awkward combinations (64). The solution we have at last come to is probably the best that could be found. We need scarcely bother ourselves about trying to improve upon modern practice in that respect; it has been a case of the survival of the fittest.

Out of the use of thick and thin strokes arises the necessity for graduated strokes, there being no other way of treating the *curved* lines intermediate between the two. Then, if the thick strokes are

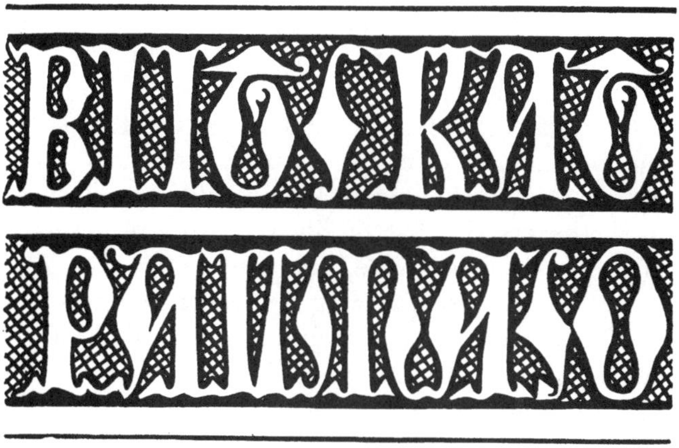

34. ENGRAVED ON BRASS. 1395.

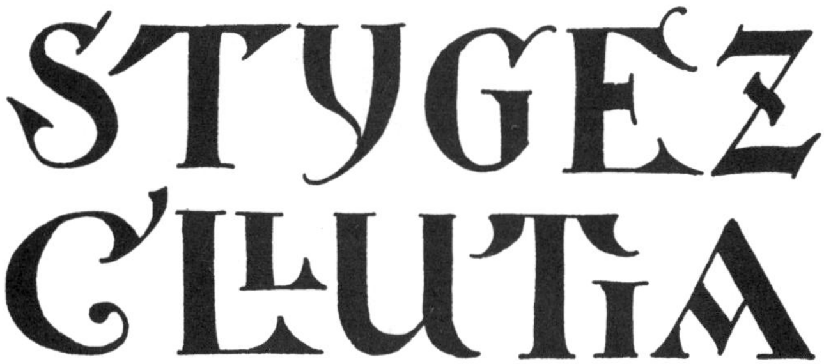

35. PAINTED ON WOOD. 1727.

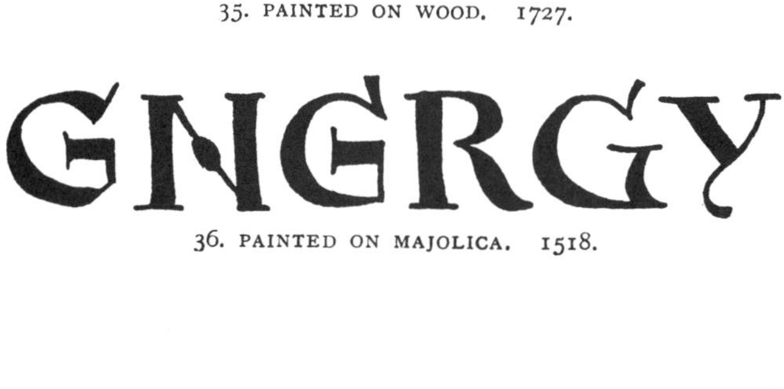

36. PAINTED ON MAJOLICA. 1518.

truncated, the thin lines appear to want corresponding accentuation at the ends; and so the "serif" runs all through the alphabet (118, 119, etc.).

The further influence of the writing tool upon the form of the letter is shown on pages 32, 33, 37, etc., and in Alphabets to which reference is made in the descriptive list of illustrations. A number of these Alphabets have been deliberately designed with a view to execution in a specific material.

With regard, now, to Numerals. Until the 15th century, the letters M, D, C, L, X, V, and I were in general use to express numbers.

The Arabic numerals, as they are called, found their way into Europe some time during the 12th century, but did not come into general use before the 15th, nor indced much before the introduction of printing, which diffused the knowledge of them. Their adoption in England was more tardy than on the continent, the beginning of the 17th century being given as the date of their universal acceptance here. The numerals, as we know them, or even as they were written in the 15th century, do not bear any marked resemblance to the genuine Arabic; numbers 1 and 9, and the all-important cypher, 0, are the only Eastern figures which seem to claim direct oriental ancestry.

The figures of the 15th century are not always at first sight very easily legible; the 7, for example (227), presents anything but a familiar appearance, but upon examination that inverted V proves to be

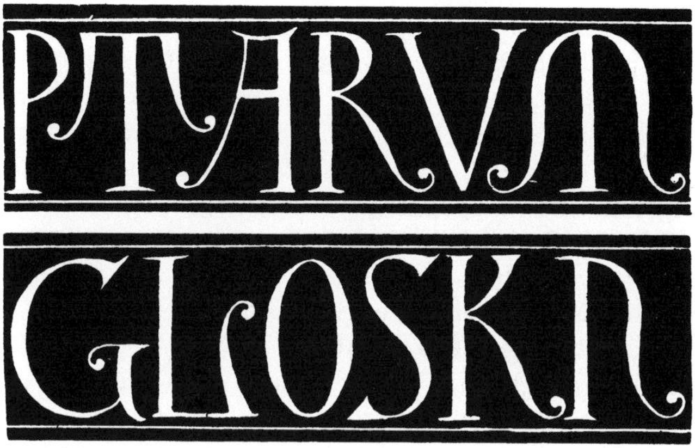

37. GOLD LETTERS PICKED OUT OF BLACK PAINT. SPANISH.

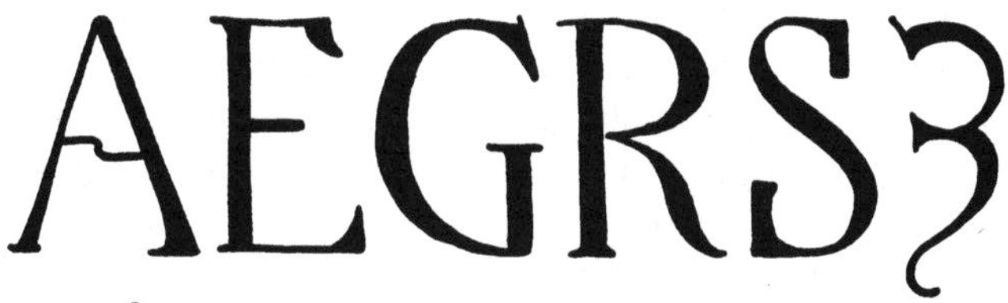

38. PAINTED ON WOOD. ITALIAN. 15TH CENTURY.

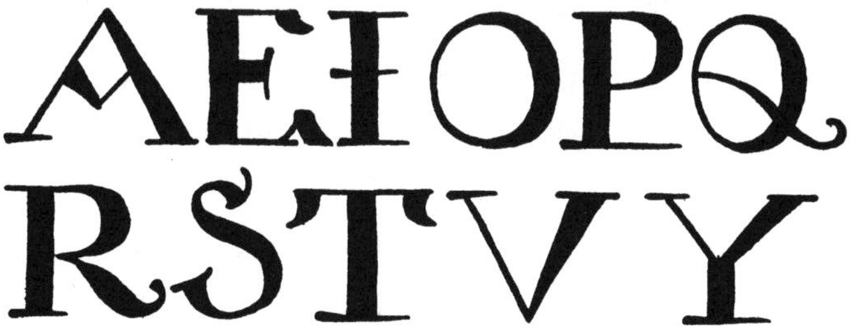

39. PAINTED ON GLAZED EARTHENWARE. ENGLISH. 18TH CENTURY.

really an equal-limbed 7 placed (as it would naturally fall) so as to rest upon its two ends: it is not the figure that is changed, but its position. Much more puzzling is the early form of 4 (227, 228, 229), a loop with crossed ends upon which it stands. The popular explanation of the figure as "half an eight," is anything but convincing; and it appears to have no Eastern prototype. There is a 17th-century version of it, however, in the Franciskaner Kirche, at Rothenburg (242), which, had it been of earlier date, might have been accepted as a satisfactory explanation. There the loop has a square end, and the figure rests, not upon its two loose ends, but partly on its point. Imagine this figure standing upright, one point facing the left, and it is seen to be a 4 of quite ordinary shape. This may not be the genesis of the form; but, if not, it is ingeniously imagined by the 17th-century mason.

Writers have from the first made use of contractions, the ready writer in order to save time and trouble, the caligrapher, sculptor, and artist generally, in order to perfect the appearance of his handiwork, and, in many cases, to make it fit the space with which he has to deal. The ends of art are not satisfied by merely compressing the letters, or reducing them to a scale which will enable the writer to bring them all into a given line (208). We, in our disregard of all but what we call practicality, have abandoned the practice of contraction, except in the case of diphthongs, and

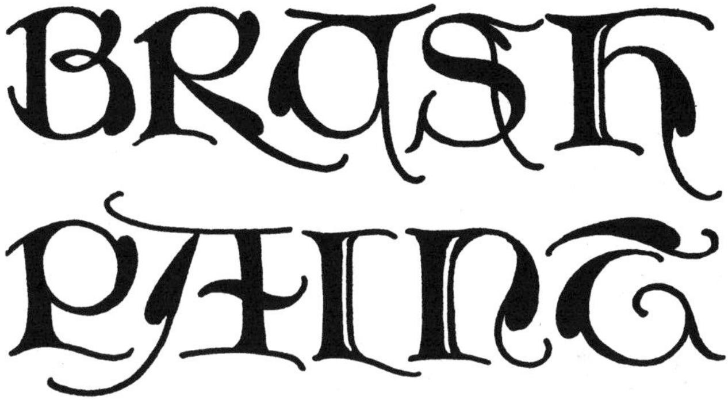

40. PAINTED, GERMAN GOTHIC, INITIALS.

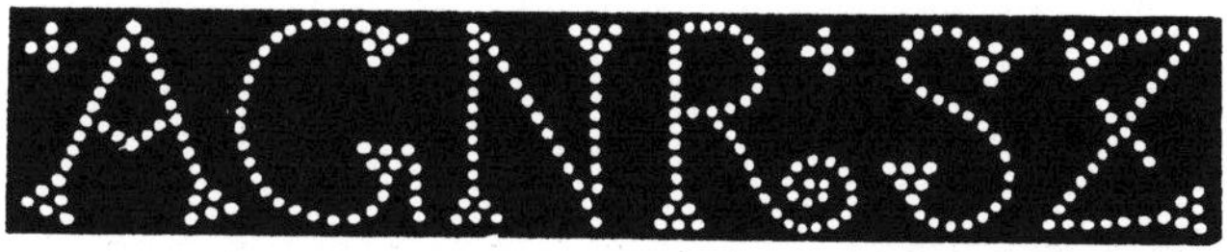

41. COPPER RIVETS ON LEATHER. SALZBURG MUSEUM.

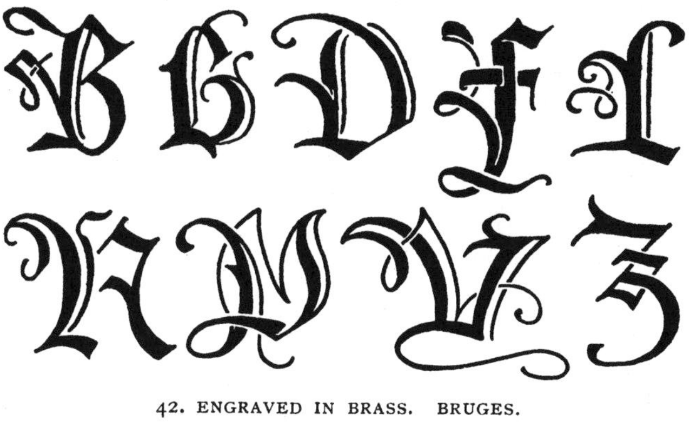

42. ENGRAVED IN BRASS. BRUGES.

in the exceptional instance of the word "et." The "amperzand," as the printer calls it (225, 226), still lingers in his founts of type, and is used even more habitually by the ordinary penman of to-day.

To what does all this investigation of the alphabet lead? It is of no use trying to evolve brand-new alphabets out of our inner consciousness. No one would understand us, and we want to be read. Originality is what we all desire; but it is scarcely the thing to seek consciously, least of all in lettering; it comes of its own accord if ever it comes. We are original or we are not.

While the alphabet is alive there will be changes in it, but they must inevitably be gradual; we can only creep on to new forms. Practically, what we have to do is to take an alphabet and modify it according to our wants or inclinations, without, as a rule, interfering much with its legibility. A man may, if he knows what he is about, make it more legible, as well as in other ways bettering it. But to do that intelligently, he should know something of the descent of the lettering on which he founds himself. That is why it has been thought worth while to discuss the subject at such length here.

An important consideration in the design of an alphabet—if design be not too pretentious a word to use in speaking of what can scarcely be much more than a variation upon orthodox forms—is that the letters should be systematically treated.

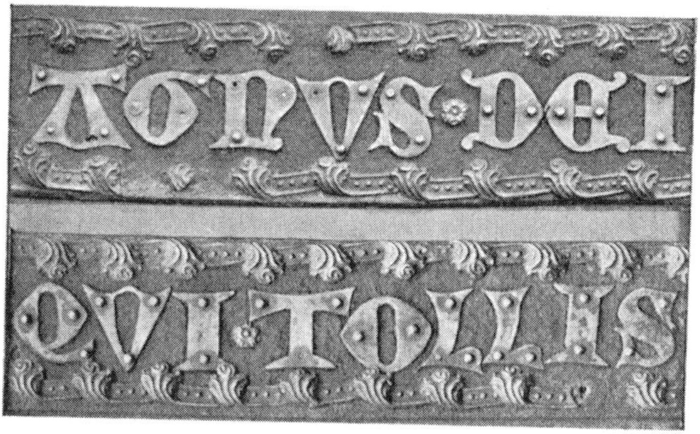

43. APPLIED LETTERS. SILVER.

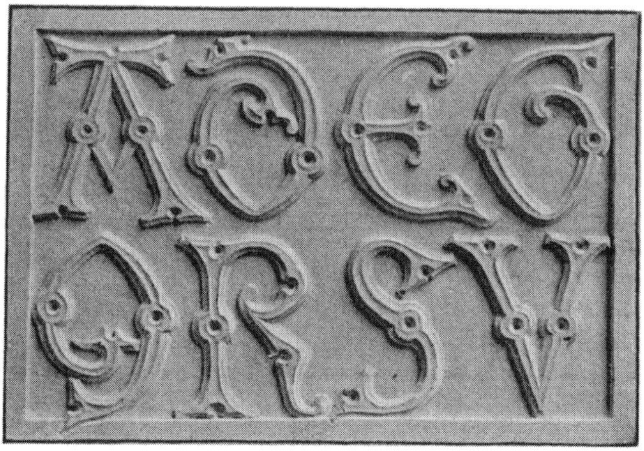

44. CARVED IN STONE. FROM BISHOP WEST'S CHAPEL, ELY CATHEDRAL. CA. 1534.

They are more likely to be all of one family if we derive them from one source. But there is no reason why we should not cross the breed in lettering, if thereby we can improve the stock. An alphabet, however, should not *look* hybrid. The artist is free to do what he can; but the test of success is that his creation should look as if it must be so, and could not have been otherwise.

Why, it is asked, should any one trouble himself about hand-drawn lettering, when he has ready to his use type, which is so much truer and more perfect? Truer, perhaps, it may be, in the sense of being more mathematically exact, but it is not necessarily so truly uniform in effect; for the unyielding letters of the type-founder come together as best they may, and if they come awkwardly he can't help it. The writer can, and indeed he should.

There is no denying that many an artist who ventures to introduce lettering into his design, does it ill, does it so carelessly, or is so easily satisfied with very indifferent penmanship, that of the two evils hard and fast letterpress would have been the lesser. None the less true is it that an artist who has been at the pains to learn to write, can, if he aim at what pen or brush will do, and refrain from entering into foolish and ineffectual rivalry with the printing press, do what that cannot do, and do better.

Looking at an early printed book, you are

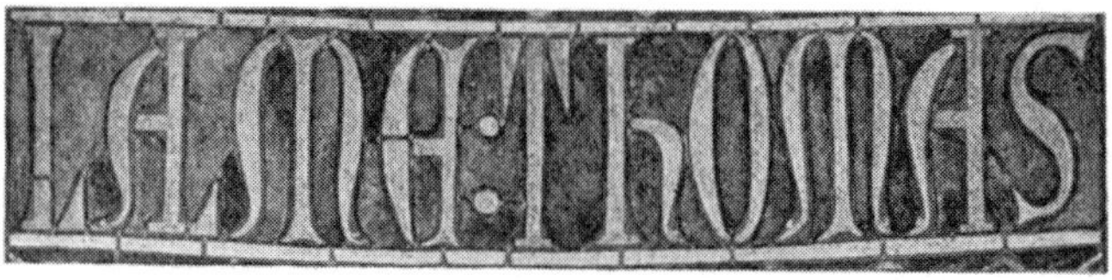

45. LEAD GLAZING. AFTER WINSTON.

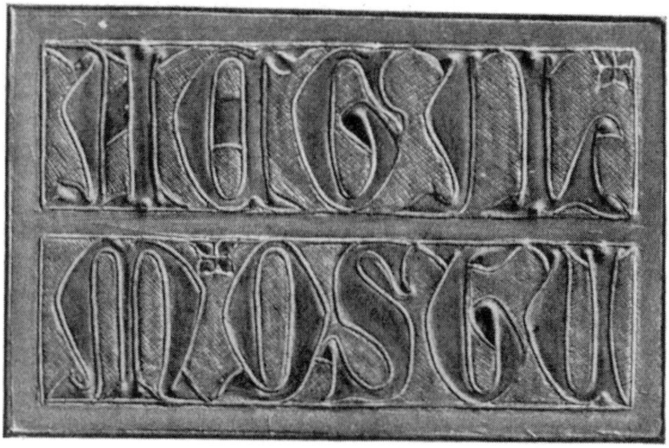

46. CUT LEATHER FROM A BOOK BINDING. HAMBURG MUSEUM.

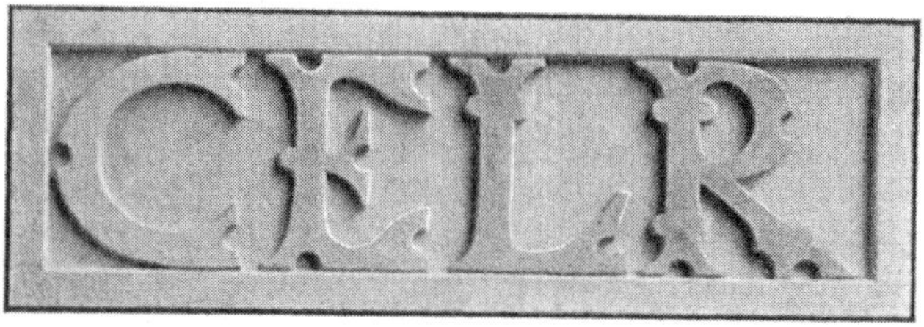

47. CARVED IN STONE. ST. MARGARET'S CHURCH, KING'S LYNN. 1622.

astonished, each time afresh, at the beauty of the page. But if you go from that straight to a fine manuscript, you realize that, after all, printing, even such printing as was done by the great printers, is a makeshift. It is a makeshift we have to put up with, and we may as well make the best of it ; merely petulant complaint is childish ; but when occasion does occur, let us have the real thing, and don't let us be persuaded by readers so greedy of print as to have lost all appetite for beautiful writing, that there is no flavour or artistic savour in it. It is not good manuscript, but their spoilt palate, which is at fault.

Having perfected machinery, we are doing our best to make ourselves into machines. Until that happens—which God forbid !—man's hand is still the best, in art at all events ; and were it not the best, it would still have the charm of character, that individual quality for which a public brought up exclusively on printed type has no relish. Print, with its mechanical smoothness, and precision, has gone far to distort the modern ideal of lettering, just as photography, with its literalness, has degraded the ideal of art. There are people who resent as a sort of impertinence anything in lettering which the printing press cannot do. They are ready to take offence at whatever is unfamiliar. Really the impertinence is in a makeshift thing like type usurping any kind of authority in a matter quite beyond its scope.

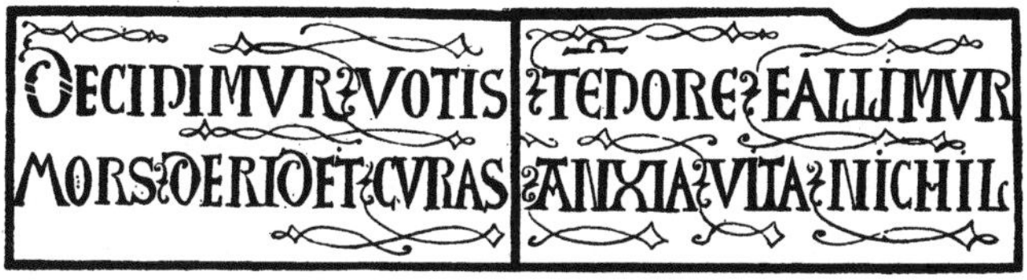

48. PAINTED ON GLASS. AFTER WINSTON.

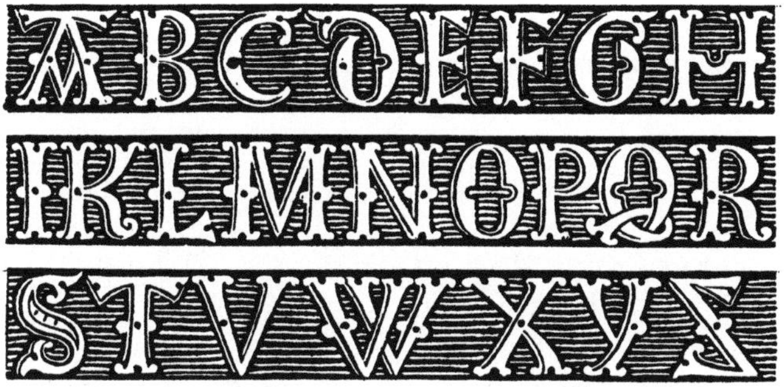

49. ENGRAVED ON SILVER. FROM A CUP.

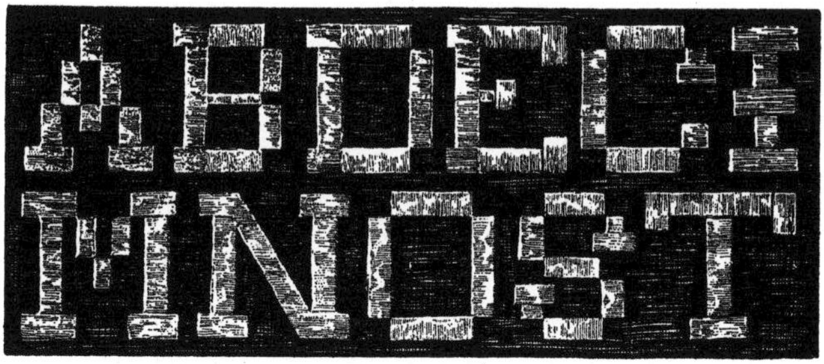

50. EMBROIDERED IN GOLD THREAD. JAMES IST.

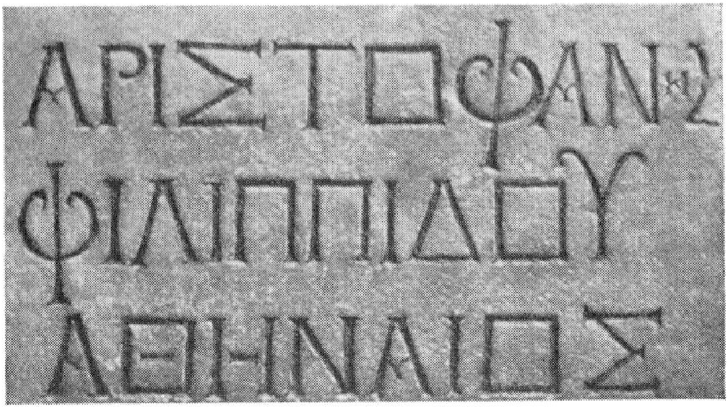

51. CUT IN MARBLE. ON AN ANTIQUE BUST OF ARISTOPHANES IN THE UFFIZI, FLORENCE.

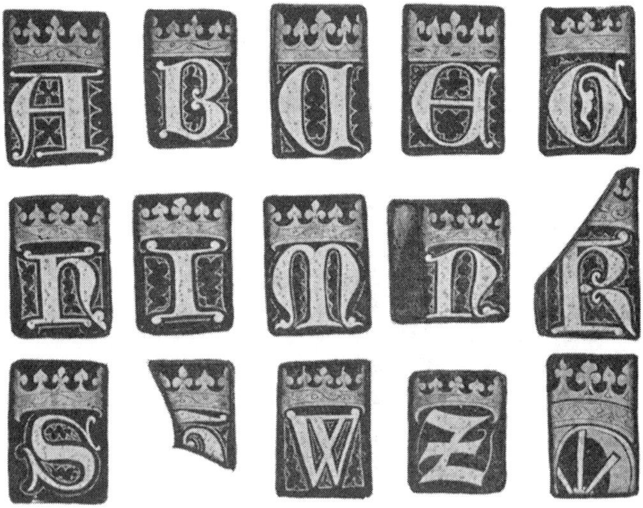

52. STAINED AND PAINTED GLASS. FROM WINCHESTER CATHEDRAL. AFTER WINSTON.

The great difference between old lettering and new is that in days before type-founding the scribe was free to play variations on the well-known alphabetical air, whereas our print is monotonous as the tune of a barrel organ.

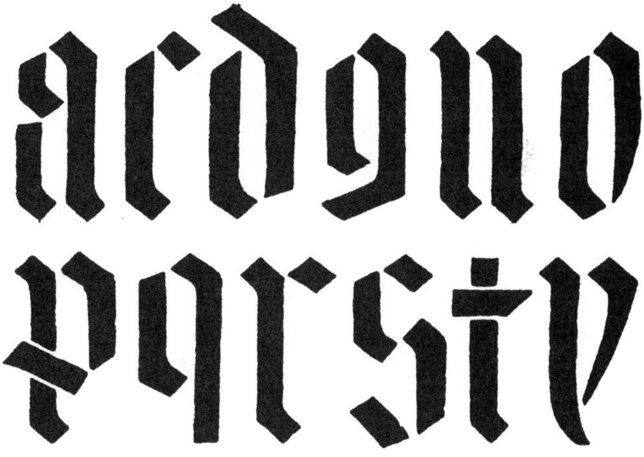

53. CUT OUT OF GLAZED TILES EMBEDDED IN CEMENT. CORDOVA.

Pedants are never happy until everything is fixed. But nothing is fixed until it is dead. Life is in movement. Philosophy has long since given up the search for perpetual motion, but that is the secret of it—life; and that is the evidence and sign of life—motion. English will be a dead language when there is no longer any possibility of change in the way it is written.

OLD ALPHABETS

ARRANGED IN ORDER OF THEIR DATE. MANY OF THEM DIRECTLY DUE TO THE USE OF CHISEL, PEN, BRUSH, &c.

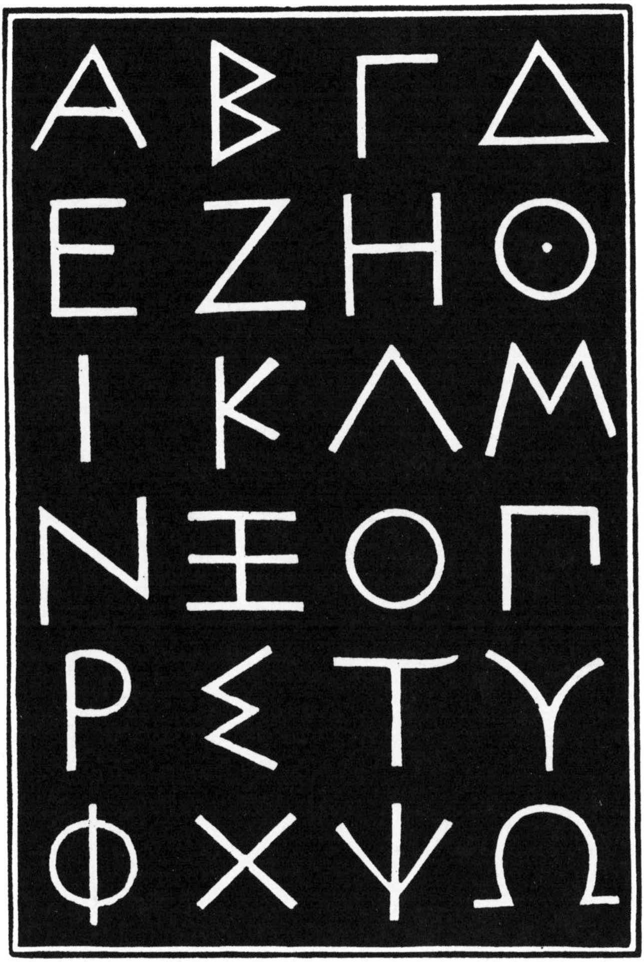

54. GREEK. FROM A STELE AT ATHENS. B.C. 394.

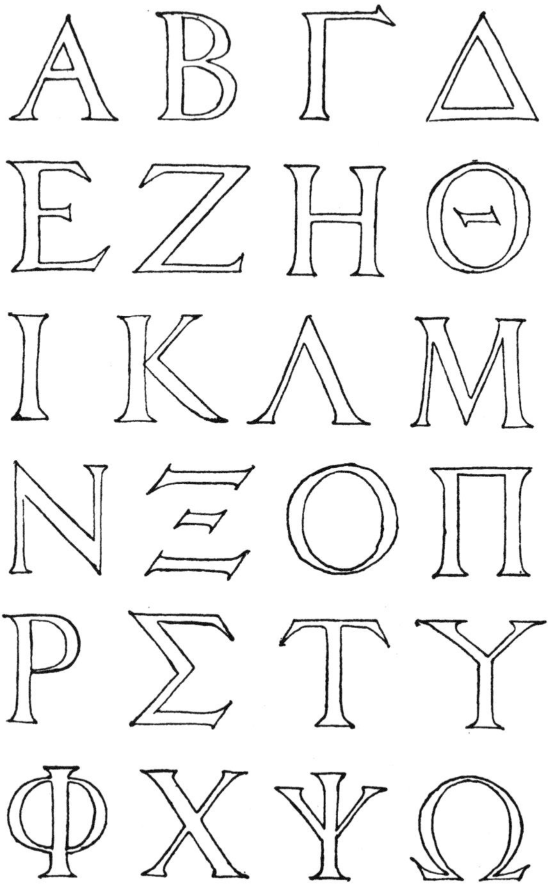

55. GREEK INITIALS, PRINTED AT BASEL. 16TH CENTURY.

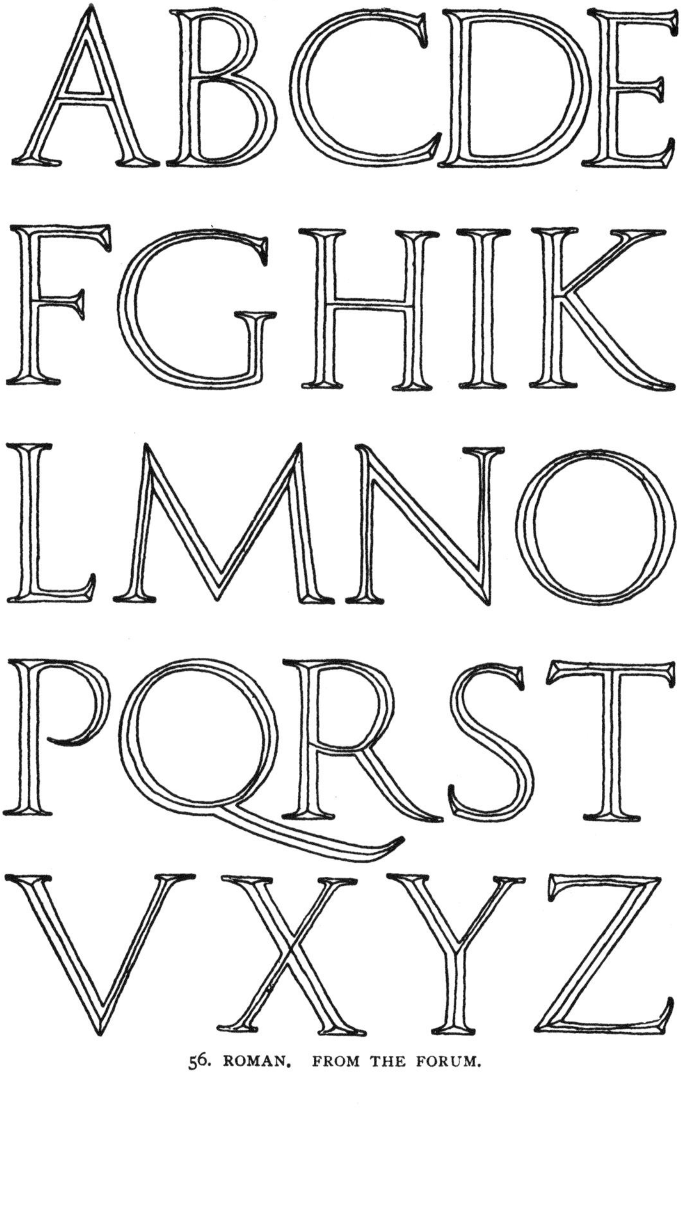

56. ROMAN. FROM THE FORUM.

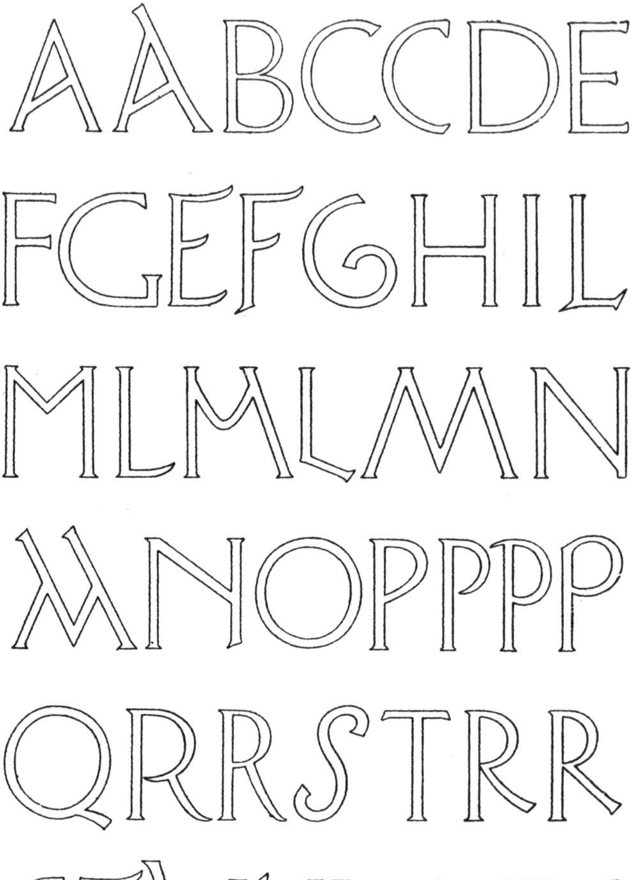

57. ROMAN. FROM SCULPTURES IN THE BRITISH MUSEUM. A.D. 150 TO 300.

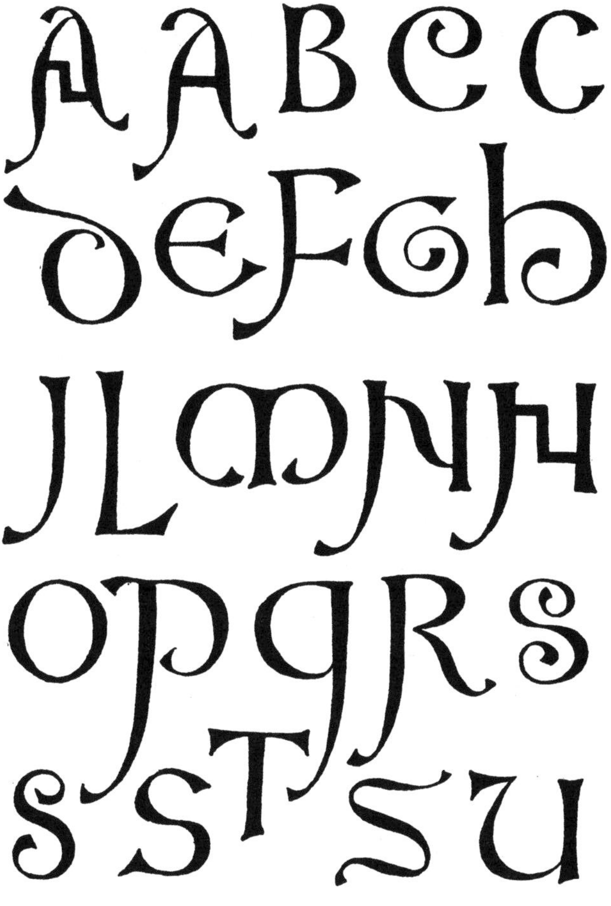

58. ANGLO-SAXON? 6TH CENTURY.

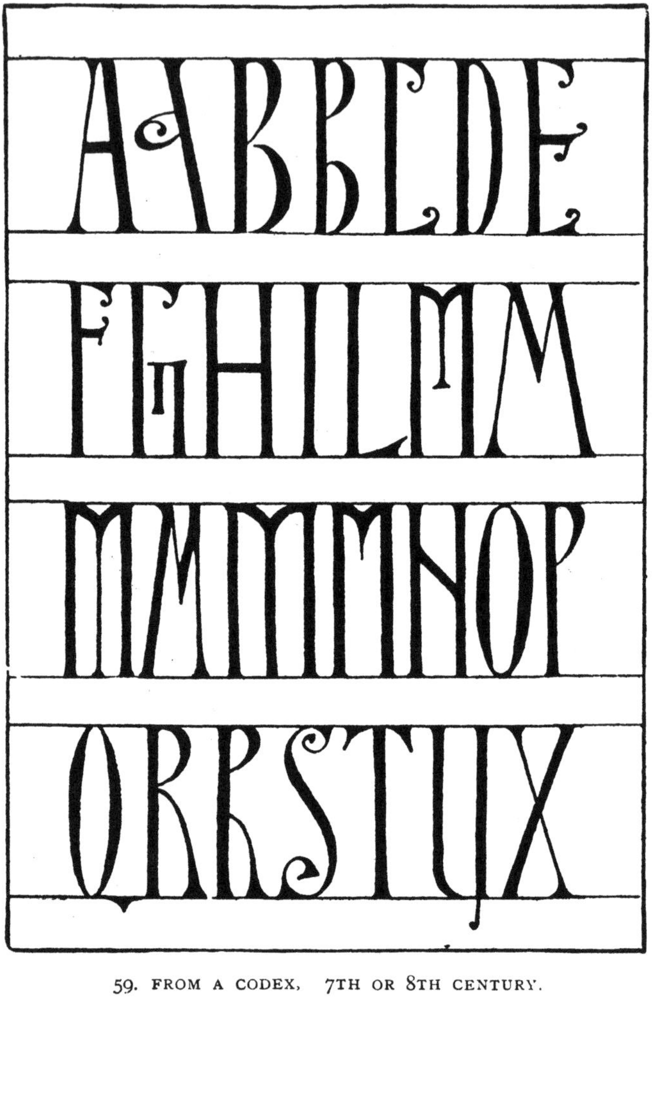

59. FROM A CODEX, 7TH OR 8TH CENTURY.

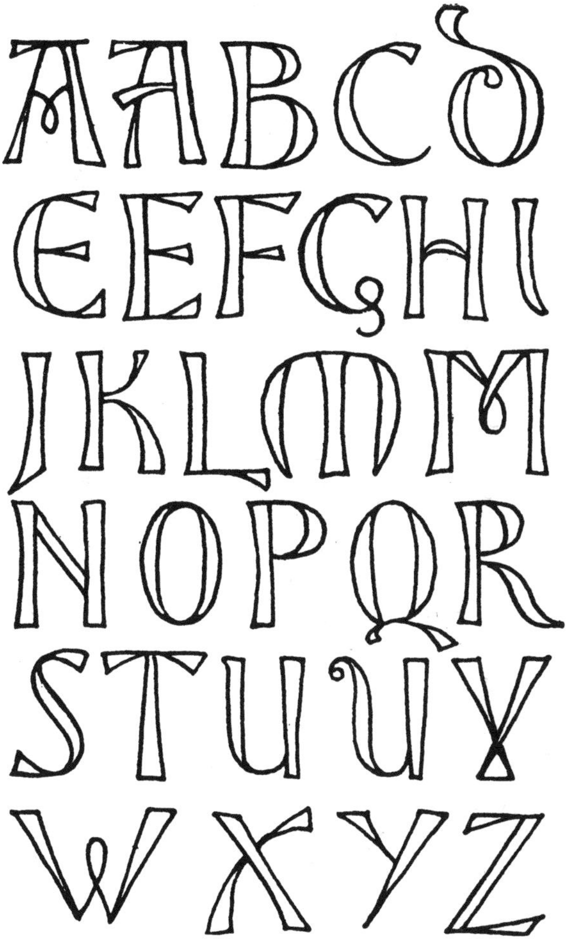

60. GALICIAN MS. 8TH CENTURY.

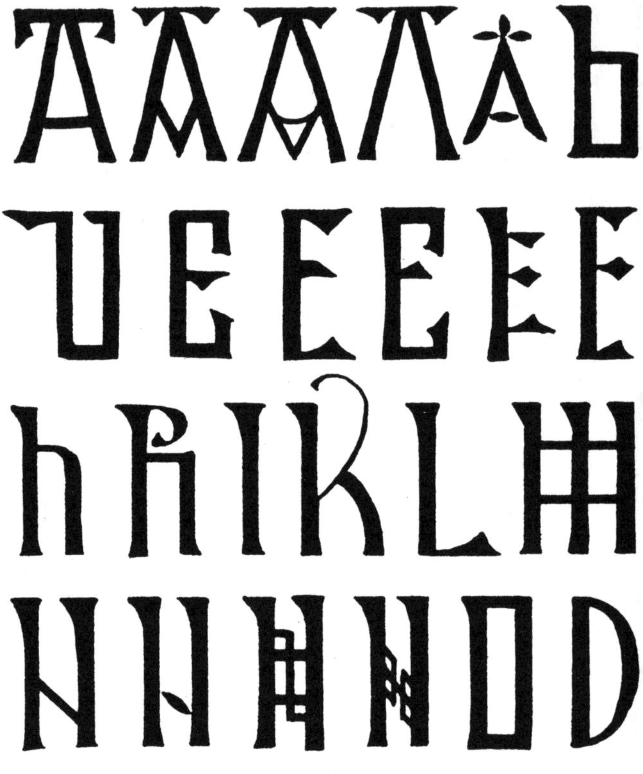

61. IRISH MS. FROM THE

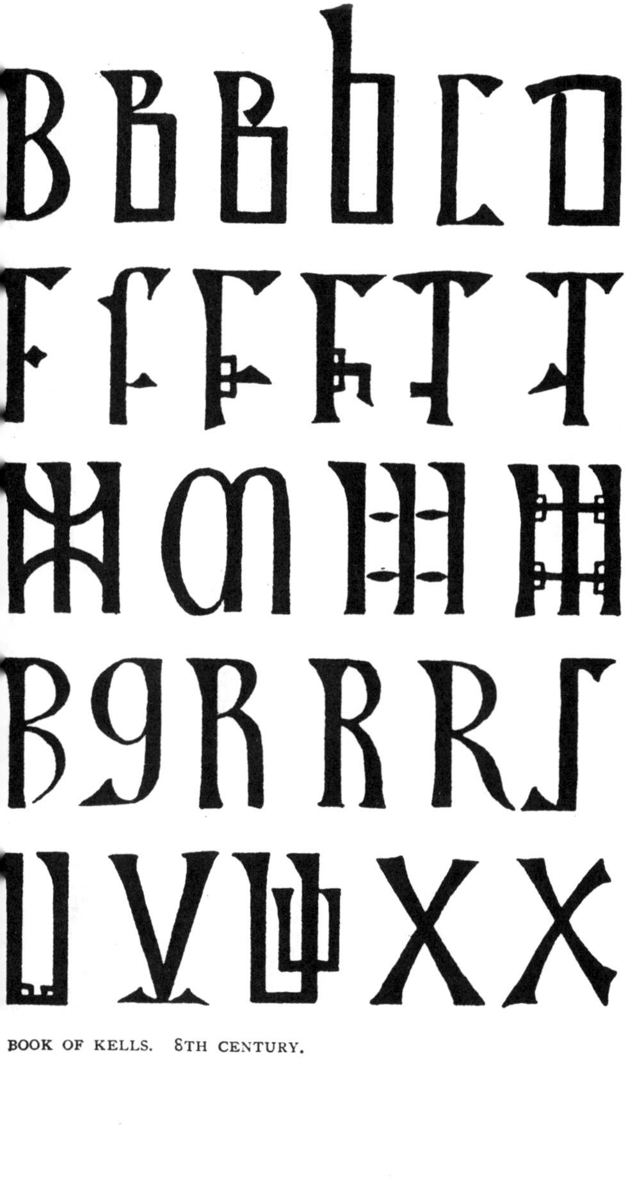

BOOK OF KELLS. 8TH CENTURY.

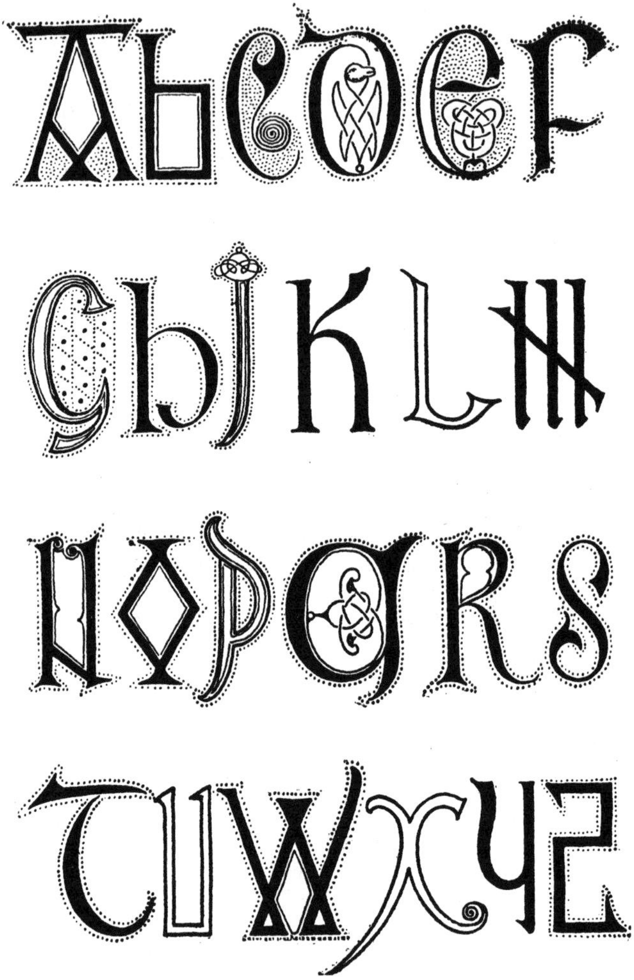

62. ANGLO-SAXON MSS. 8TH AND 9TH CENTURIES.

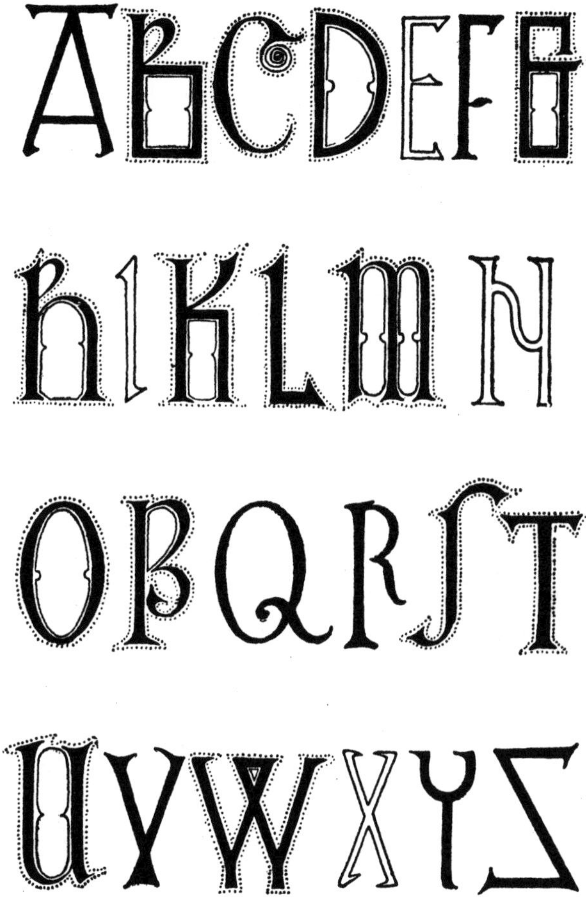

63. ANGLO-SAXON MSS. 8TH AND 9TH CENTURIES.

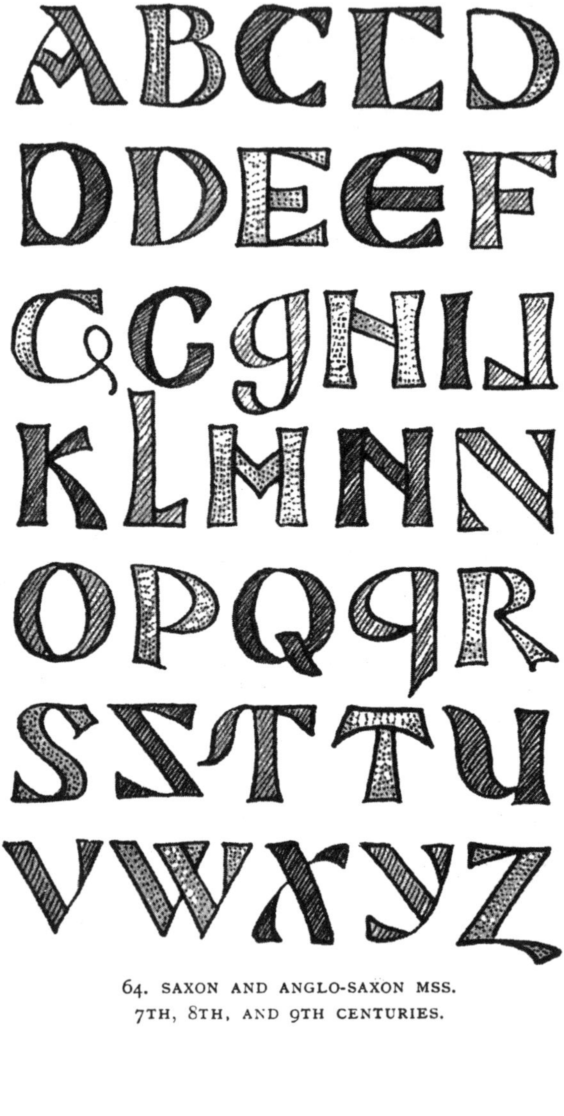

64. SAXON AND ANGLO-SAXON MSS.
7TH, 8TH, AND 9TH CENTURIES.

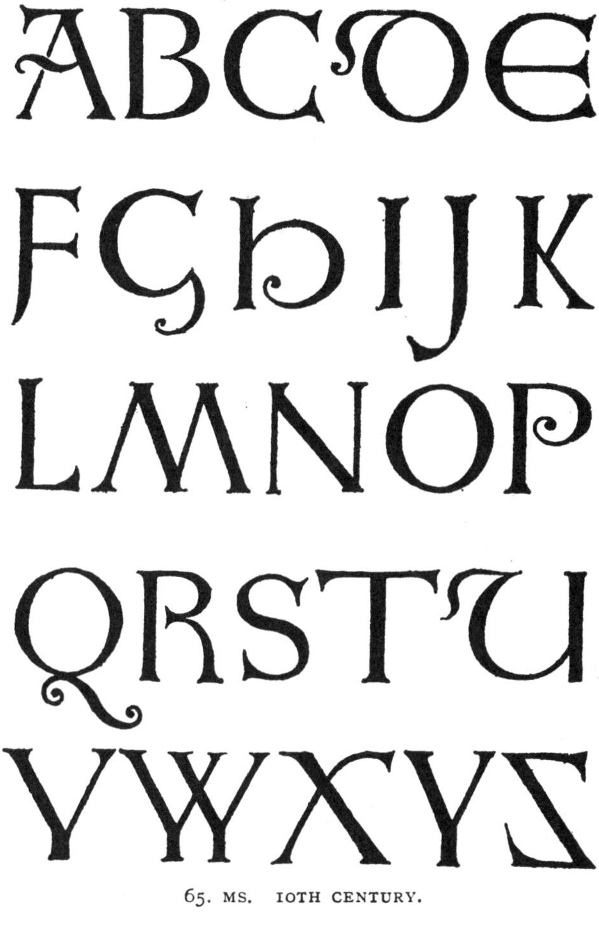

65. MS. 10TH CENTURY.

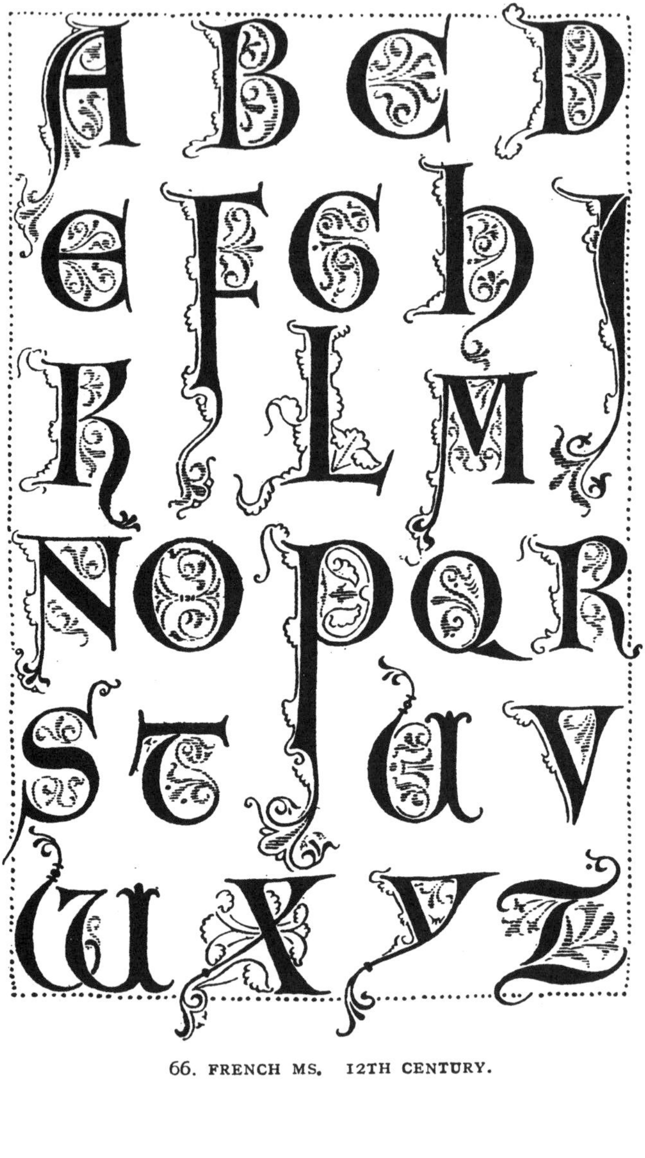

66. FRENCH MS. 12TH CENTURY.

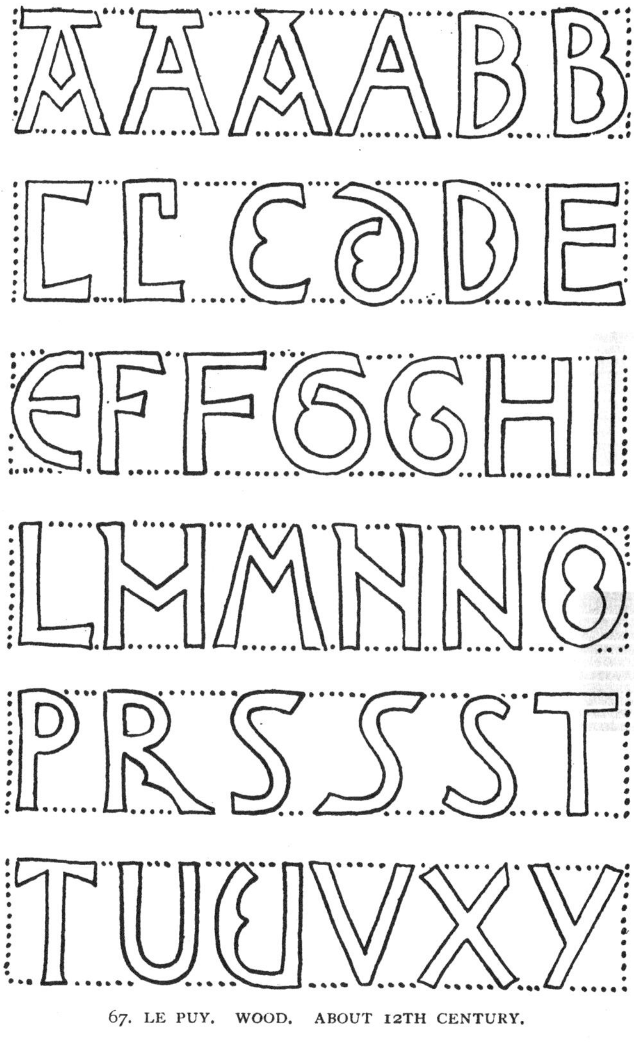

67. LE PUY. WOOD. ABOUT 12TH CENTURY.

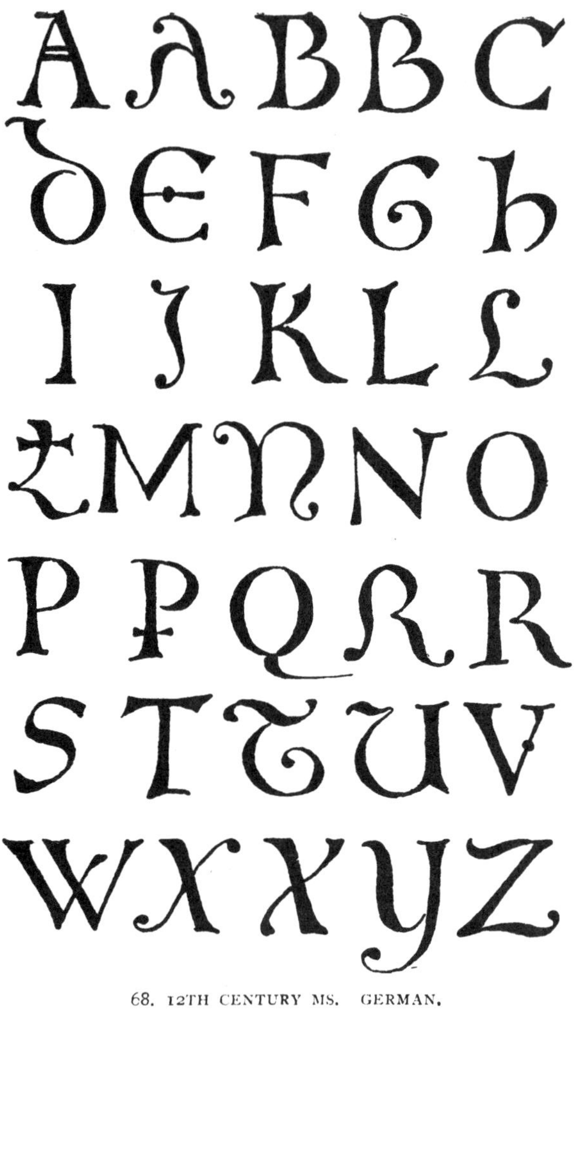

68. 12TH CENTURY MS. GERMAN.

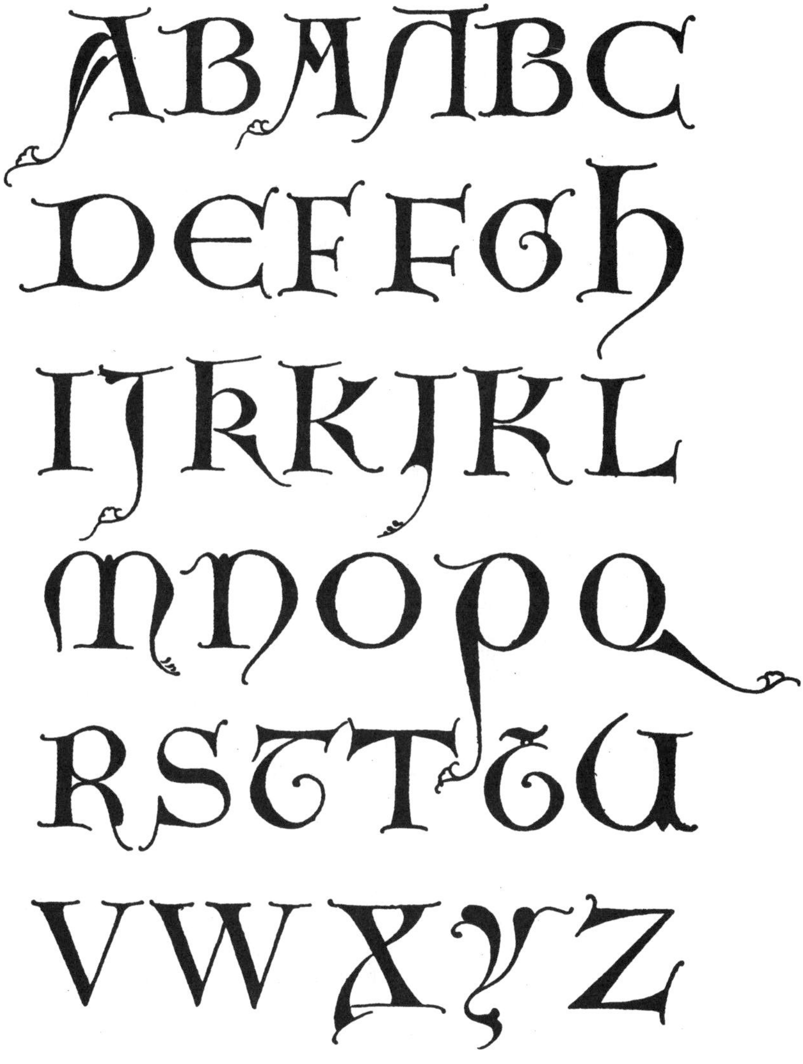

69. END OF 12TH CENTURY MSS. ENGLISH.

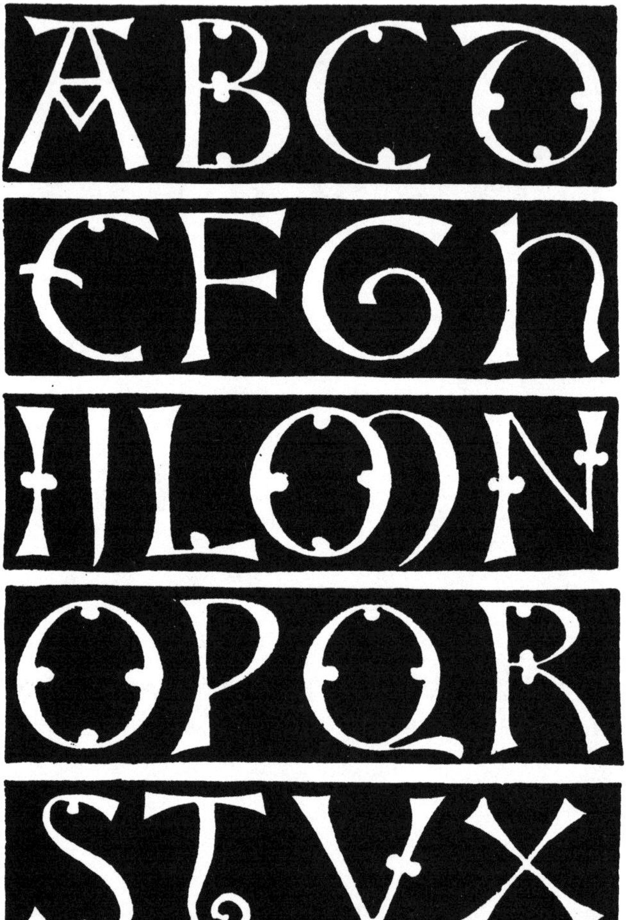

70. 12TH CENTURY. LISBJERG, DENMARK. GILT LETTERS ON TRANSPARENT BROWN.

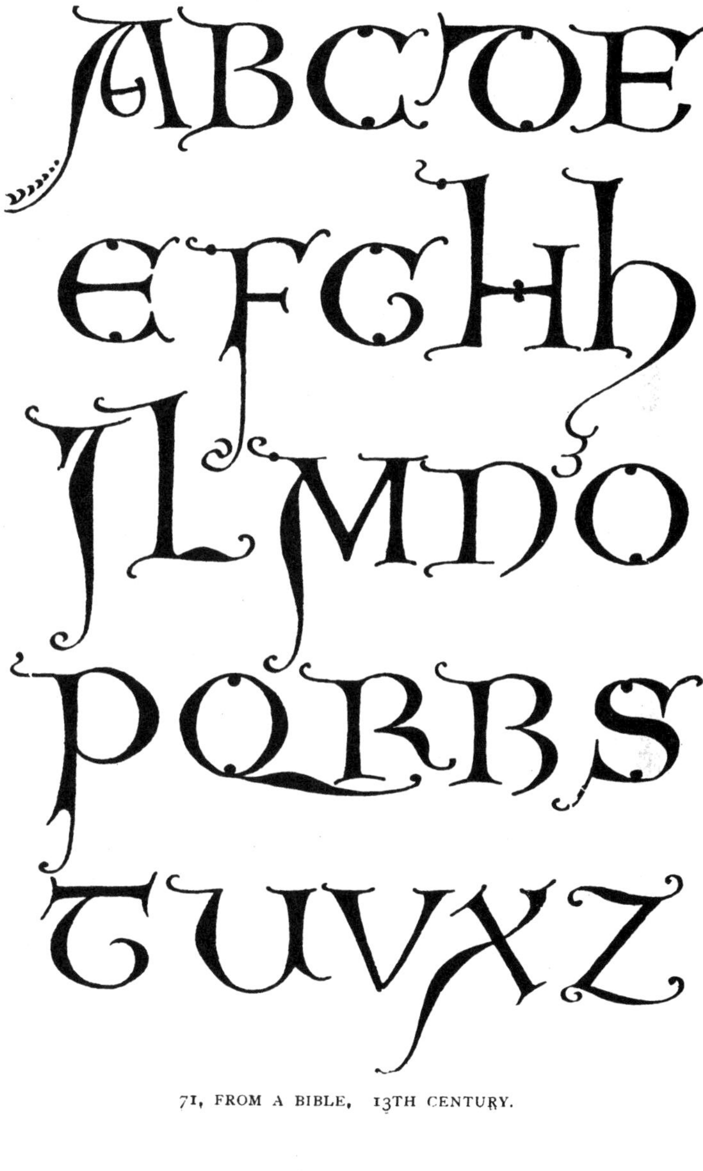

71, FROM A BIBLE, 13TH CENTURY.

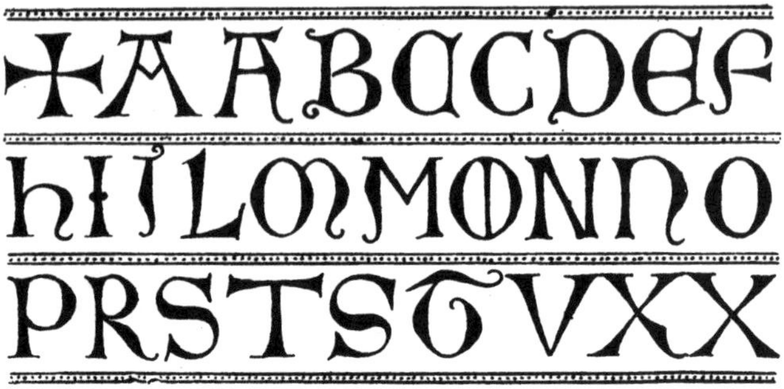

72. FROM A GERMAN BELL. 1270.

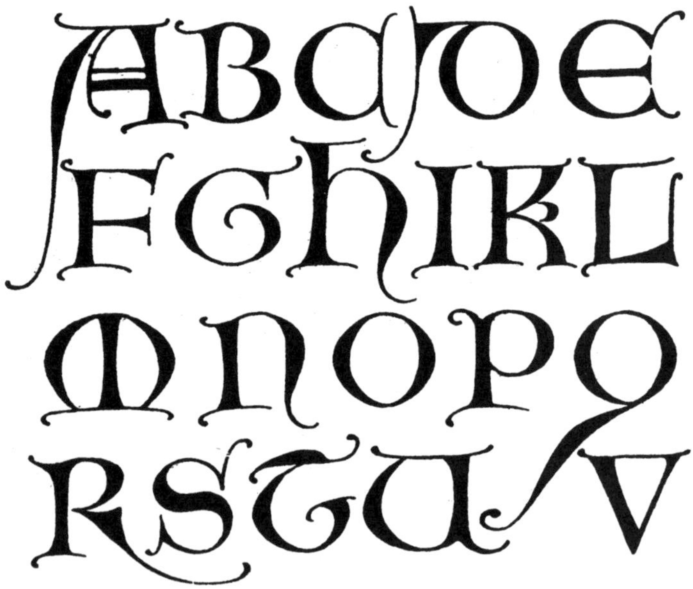

73. FROM A PSALTER, 13TH CENTURY.

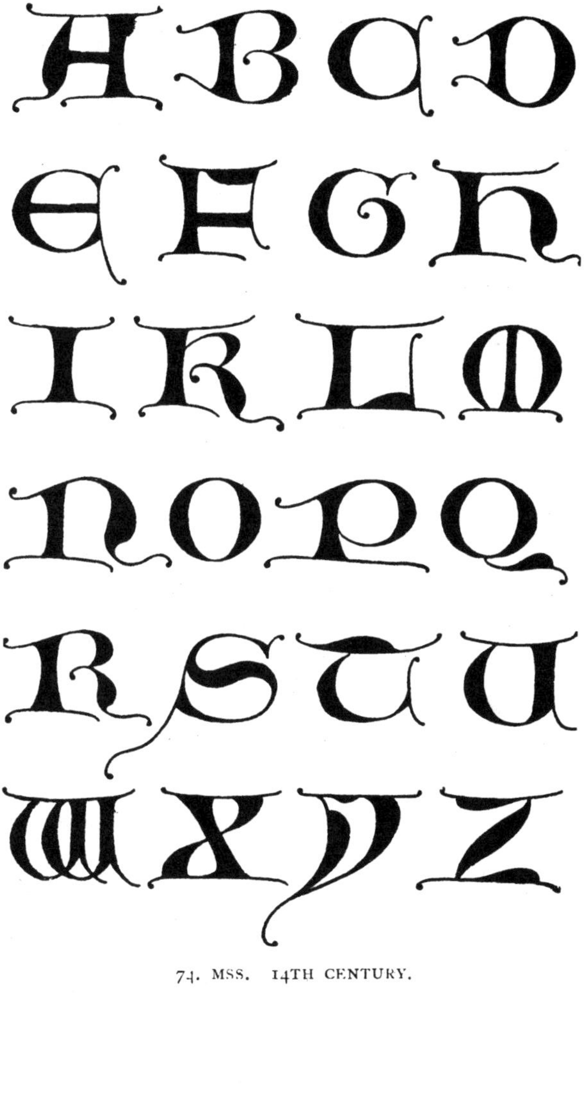

74. MSS. 14TH CENTURY.

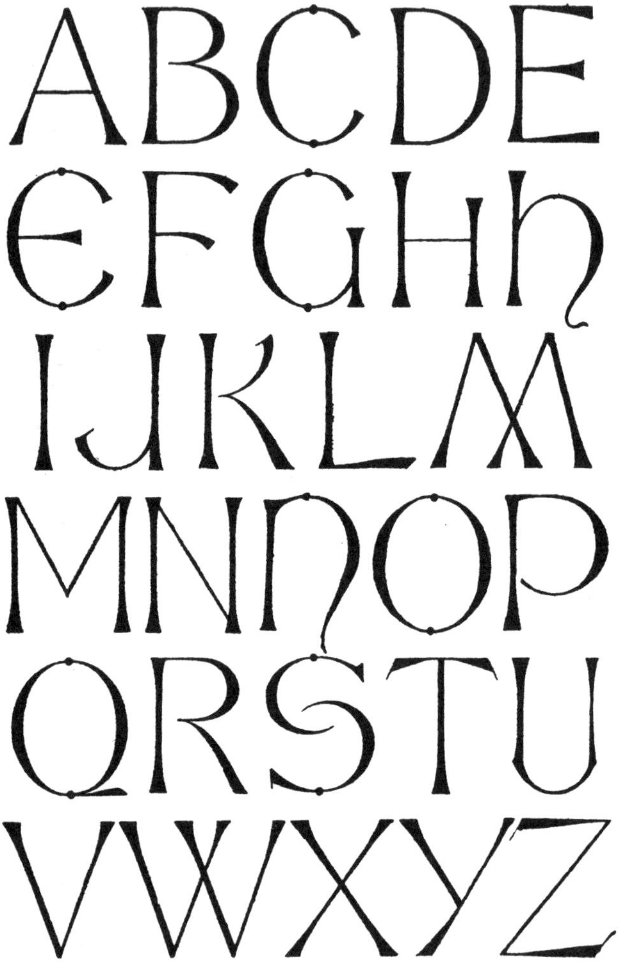

75. ITALIAN. 14TH CENTURY.

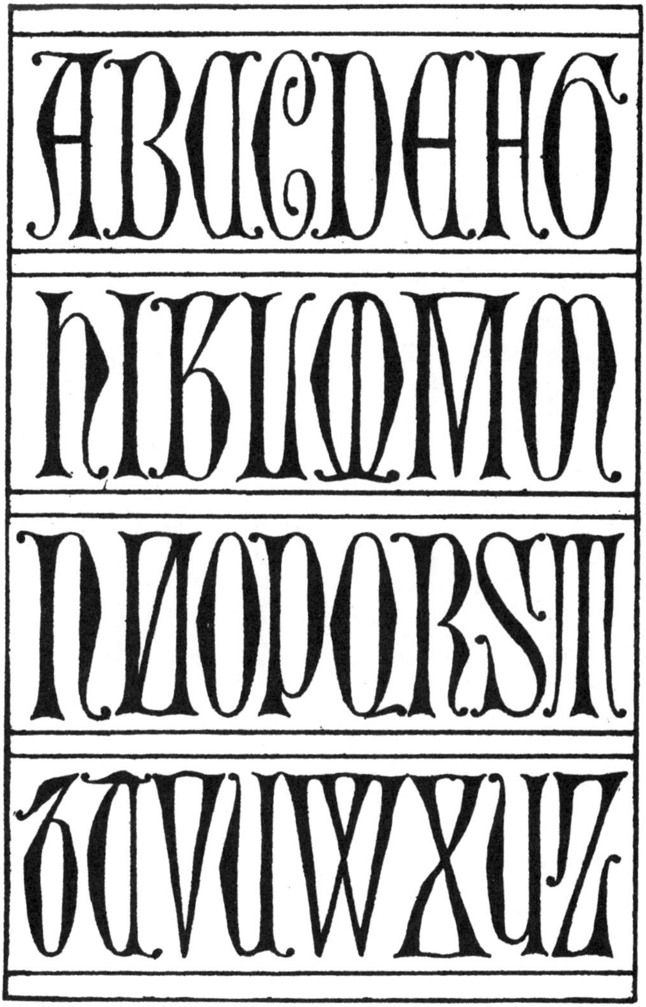

76. INCISED GOTHIC CAPITALS. ABOUT 1350.

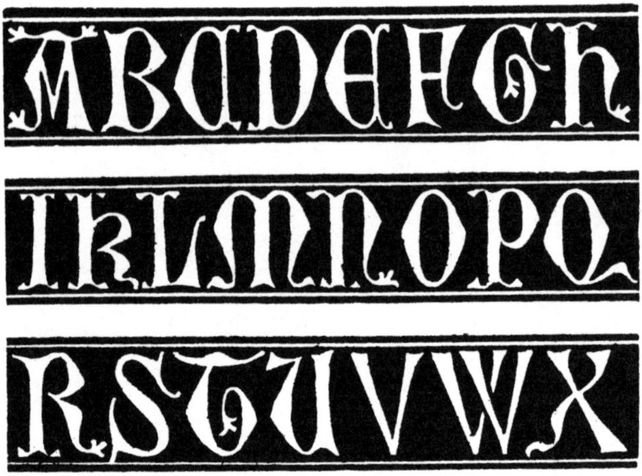

77. FROM A BRASS. NORDHAUSEN. 1397.

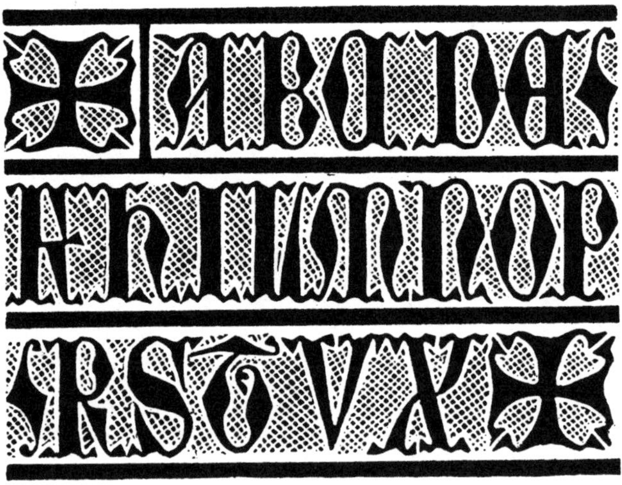

78. FROM A BRASS. NORDHAUSEN. 1395.

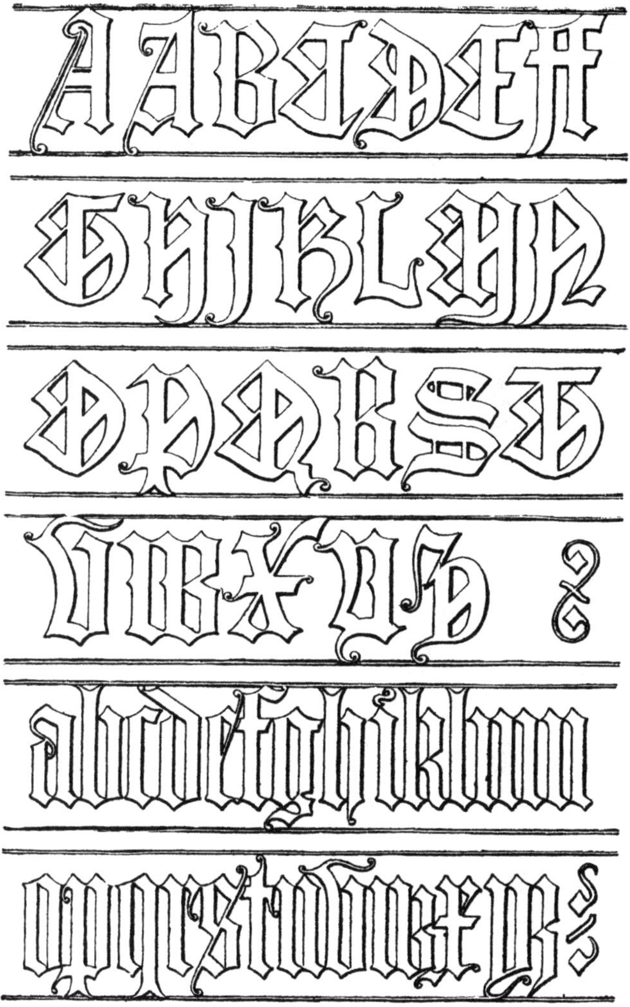

79. STONE. WESTMINSTER ABBEY. ABOUT 1400.

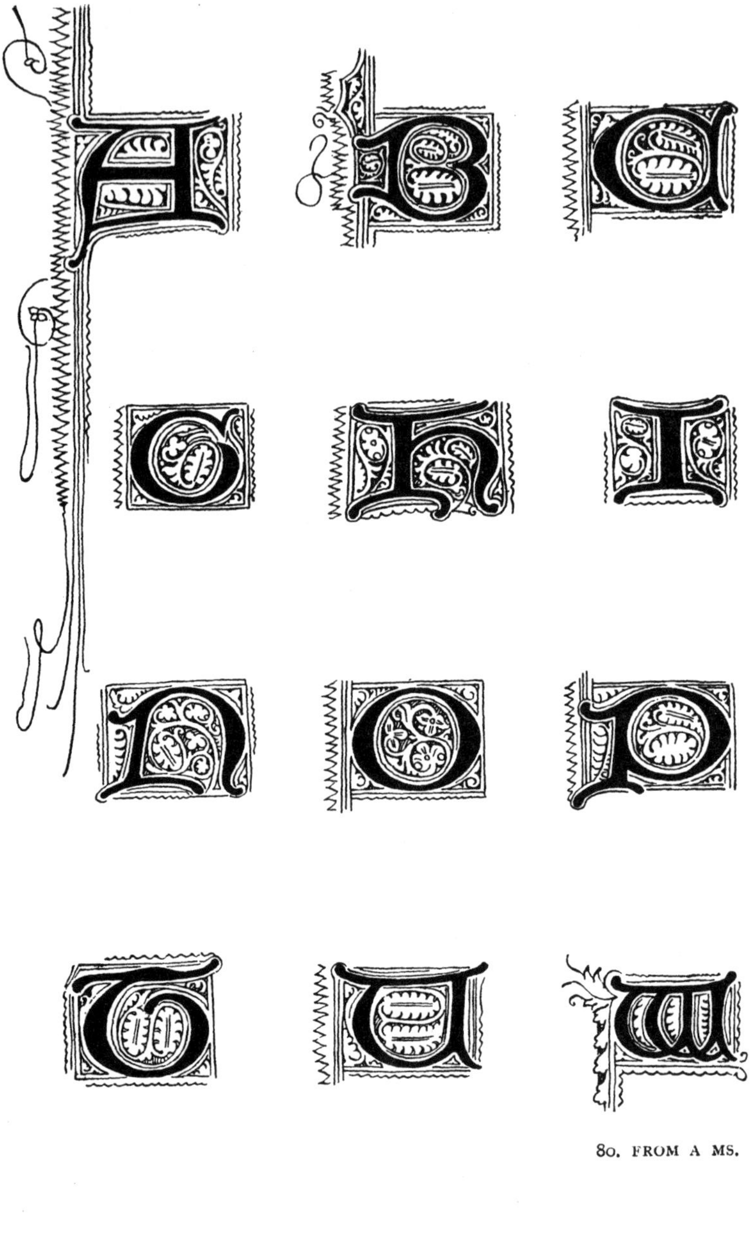

80. FROM A MS.

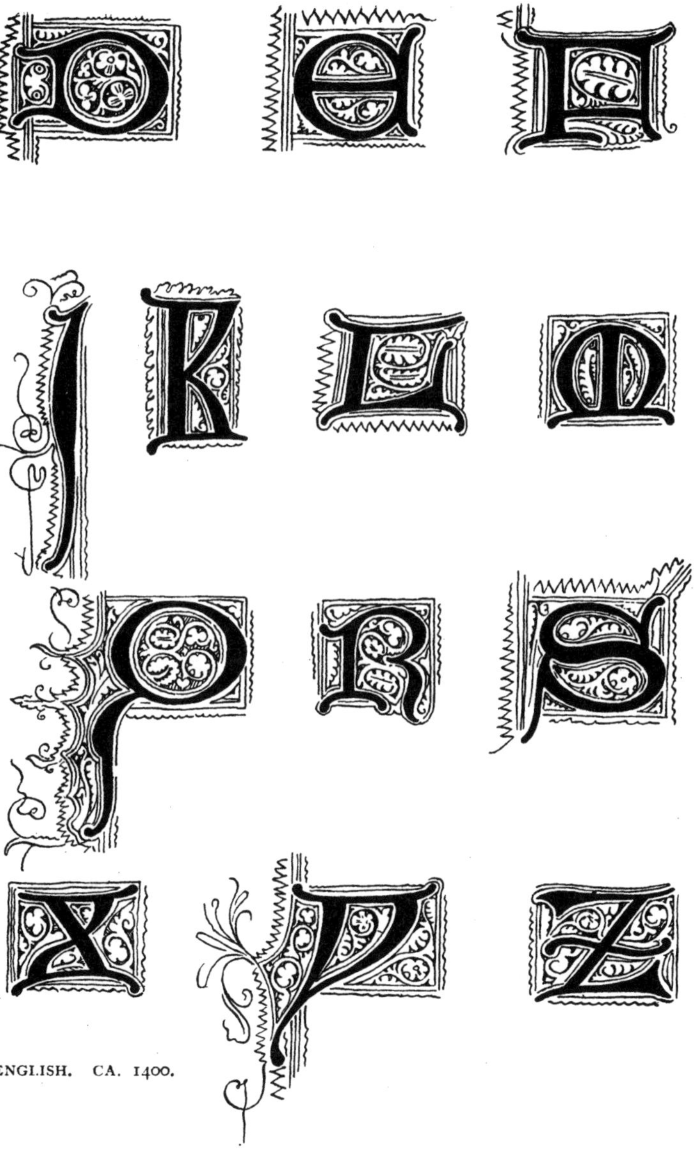

ENGLISH. CA. 1400.

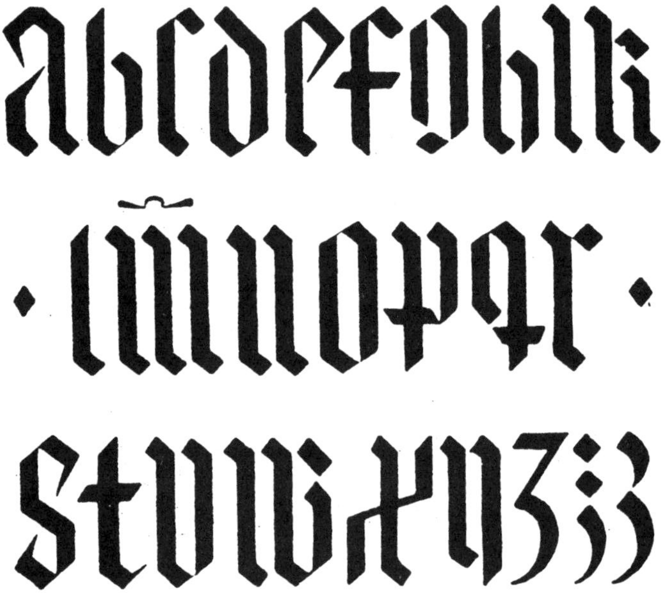

81. INCISED AND FILLED WITH CEMENT. PRATO. 1410.

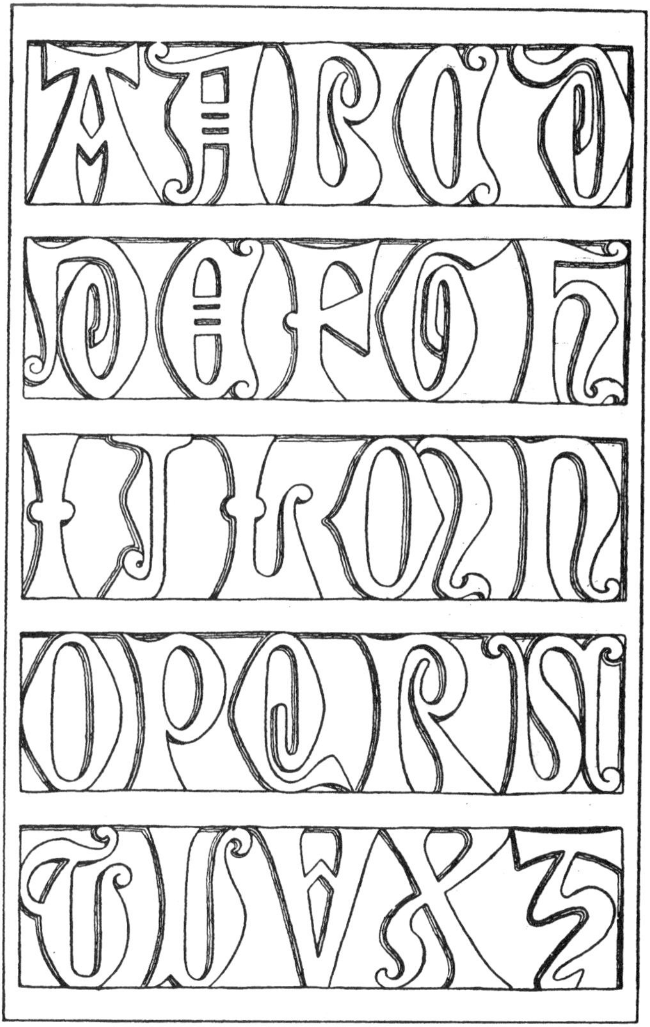

82. CARVED IN STONE. SPANISH.

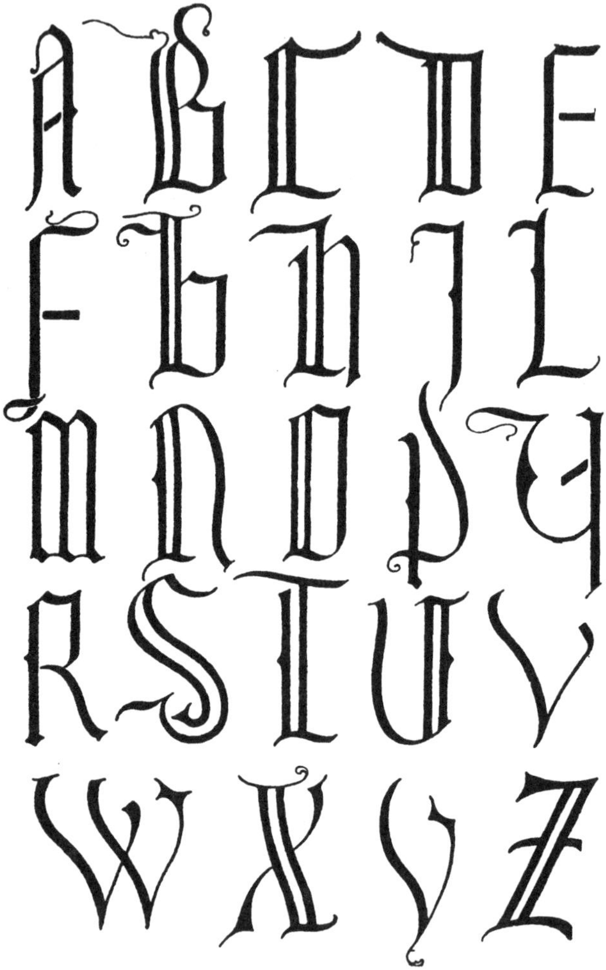

83. 1420 MS.

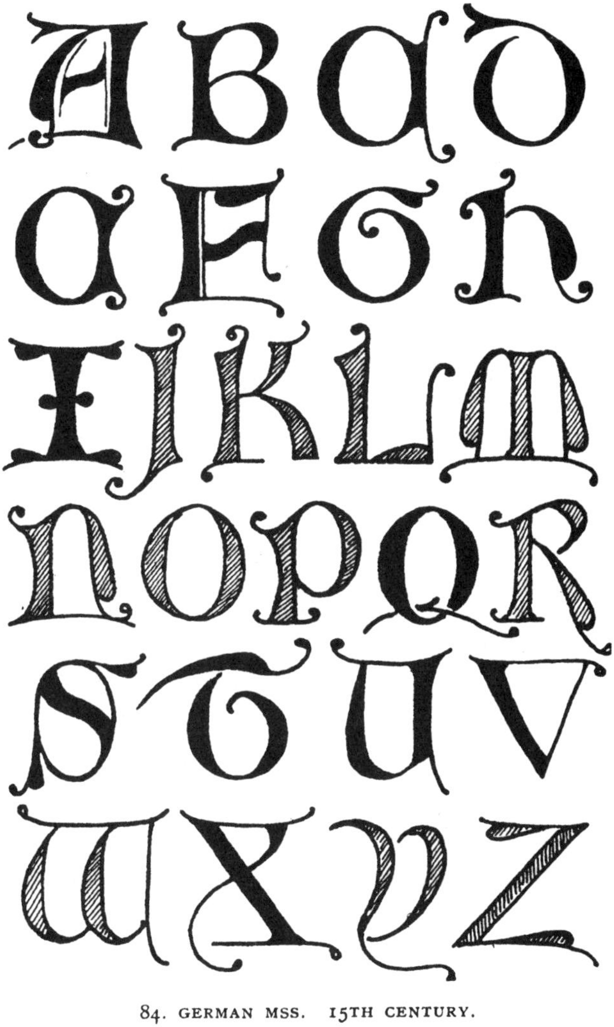

84. GERMAN MSS. 15TH CENTURY.

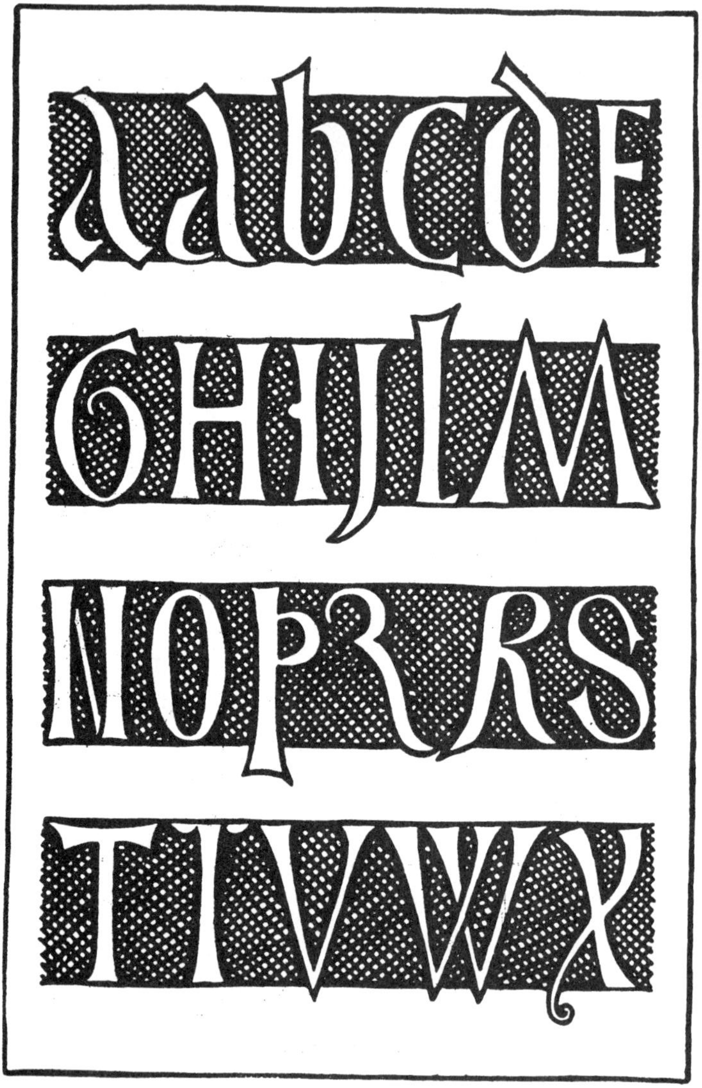

85. ENGRAVED ON BRASS. BAMBERG. 1464.

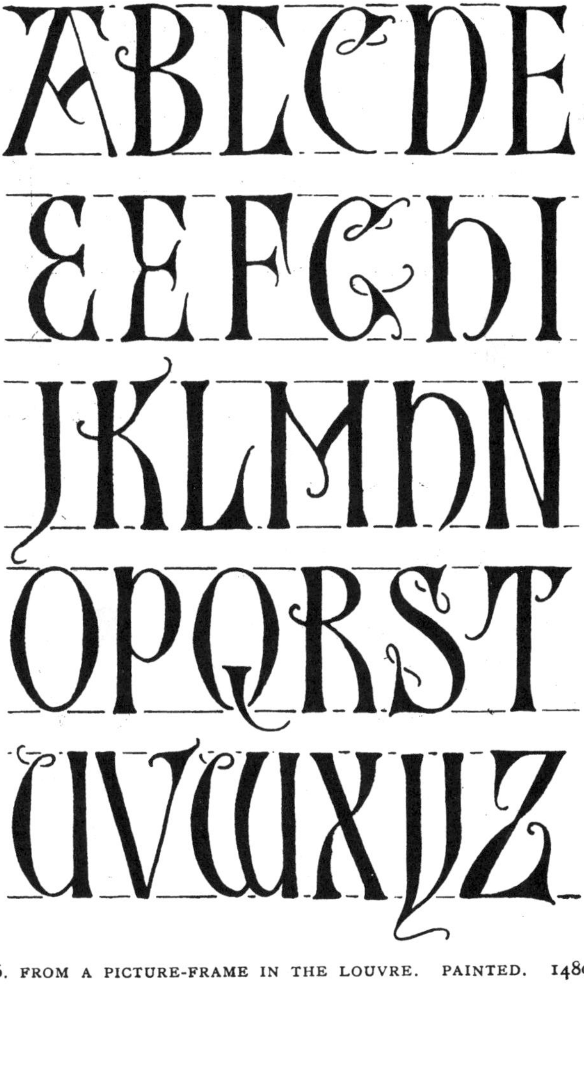

86. FROM A PICTURE-FRAME IN THE LOUVRE. PAINTED. 1480.

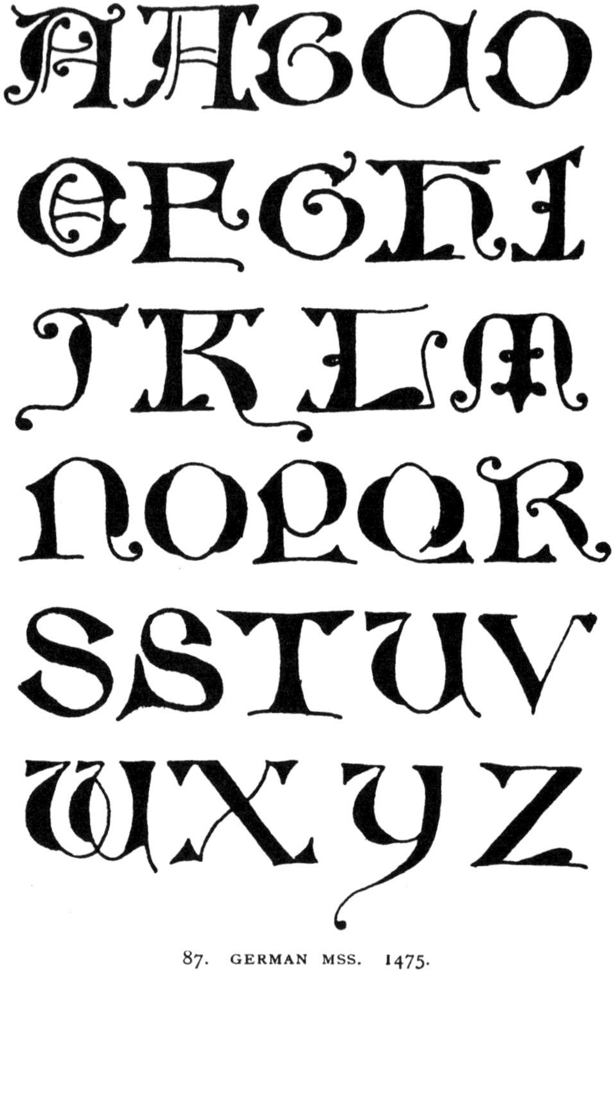

87. GERMAN MSS. 1475.

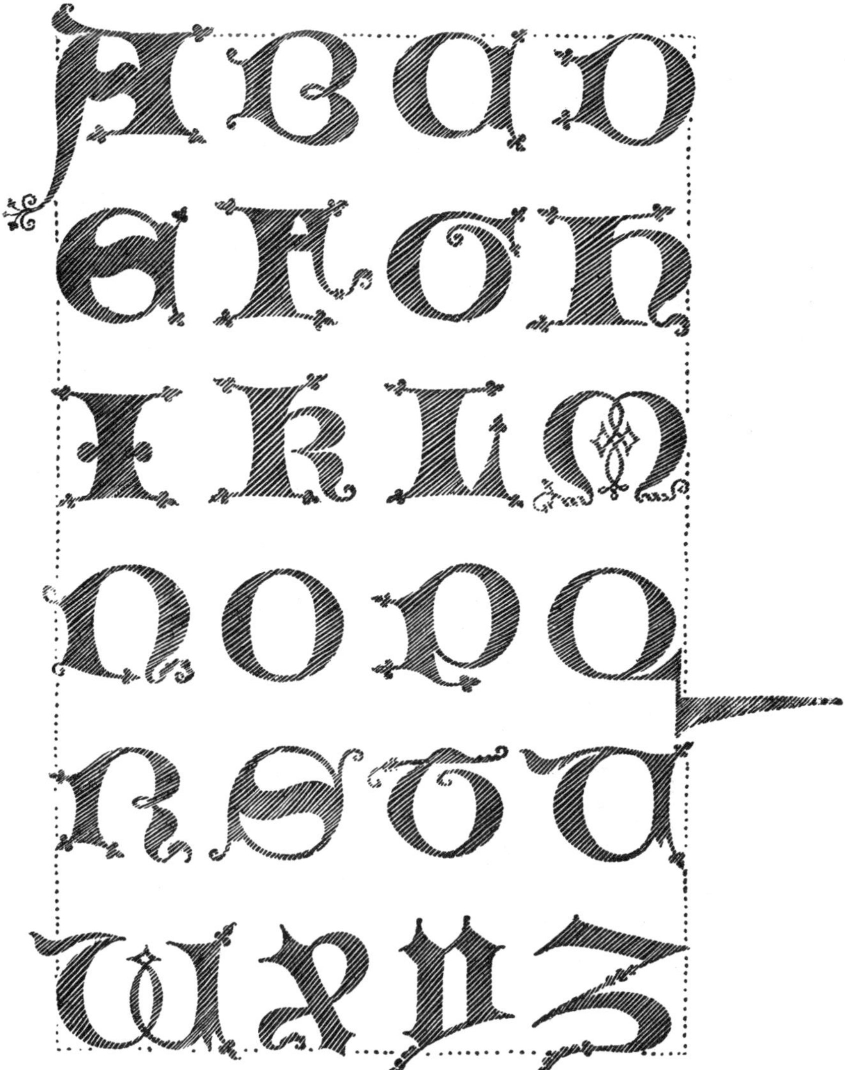

88. MS. ABOUT 1475.

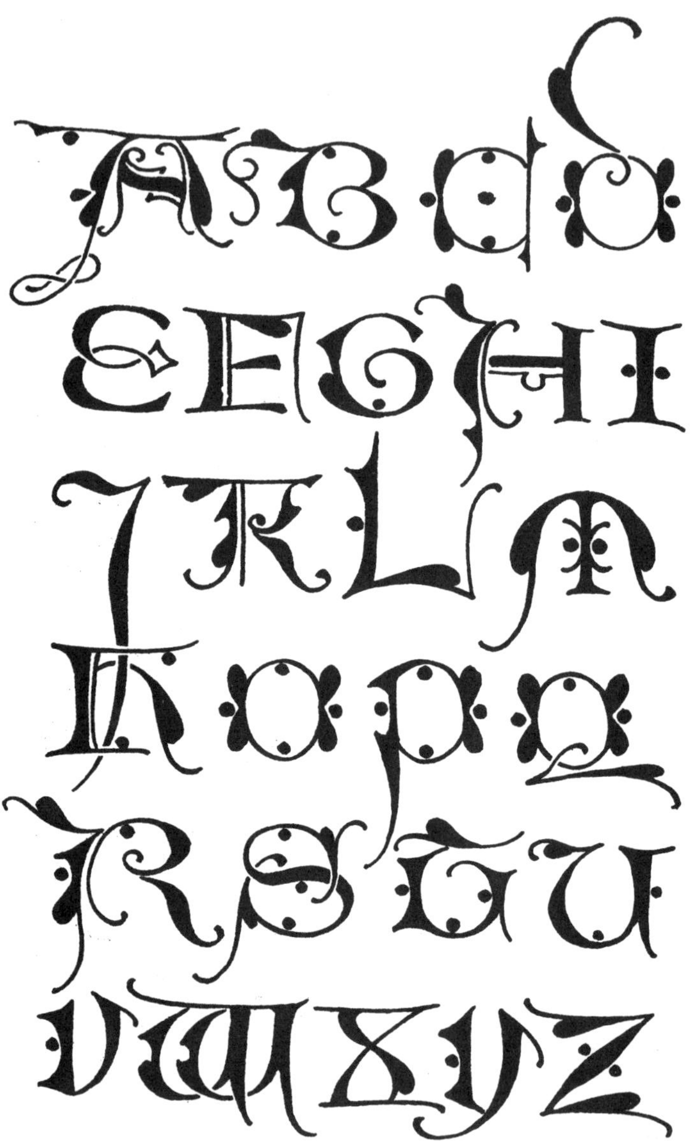

89. PAINTED INITIALS. CA. 1480.

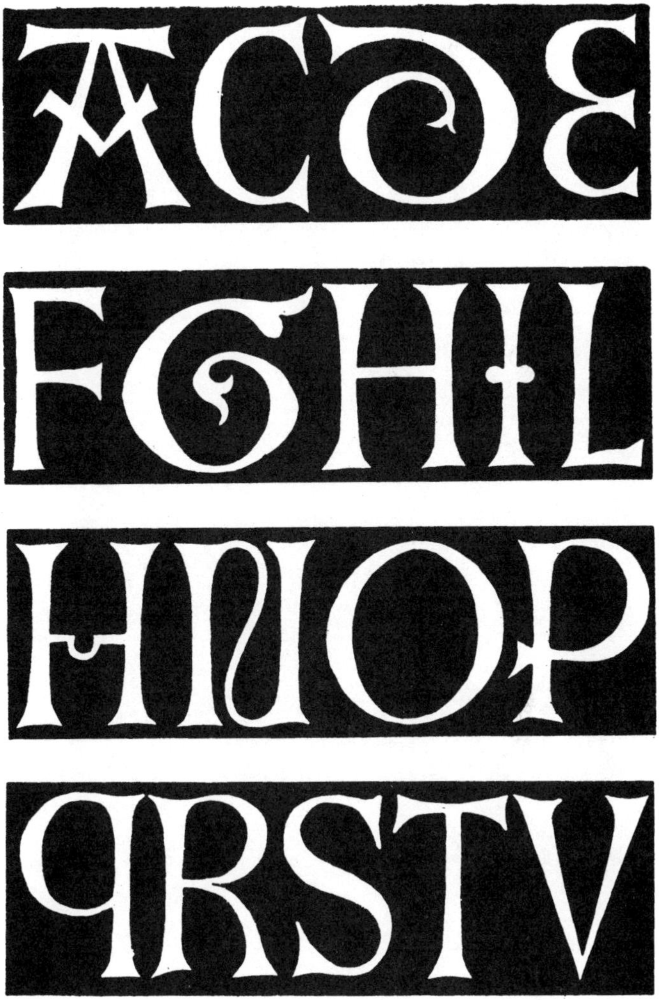

90. INCISED IN MARBLE. GERMAN. 1482.

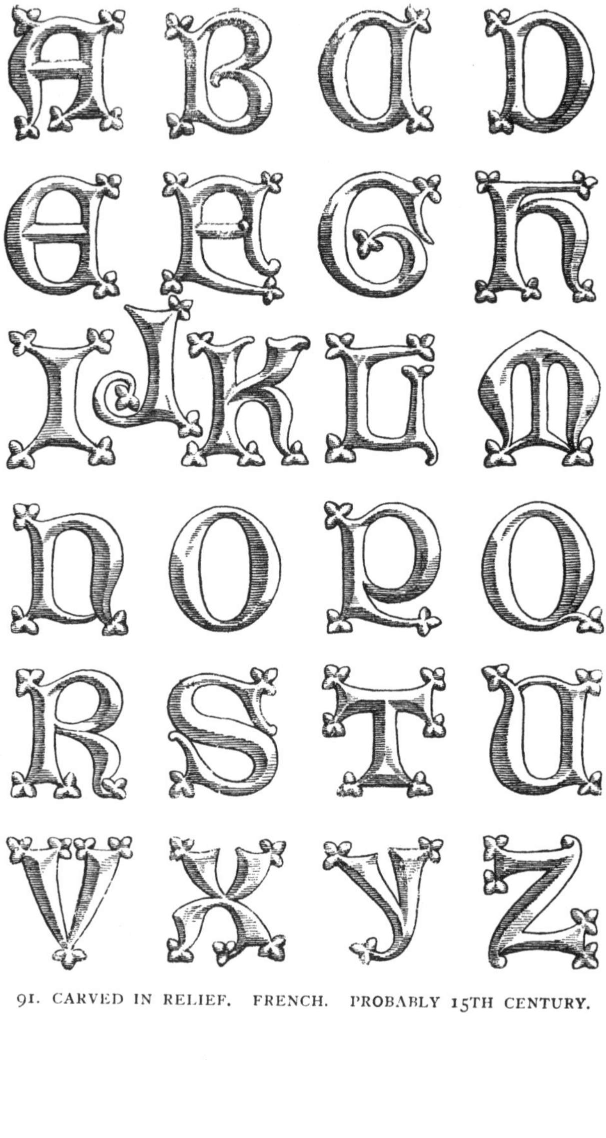

91. CARVED IN RELIEF. FRENCH. PROBABLY 15TH CENTURY.

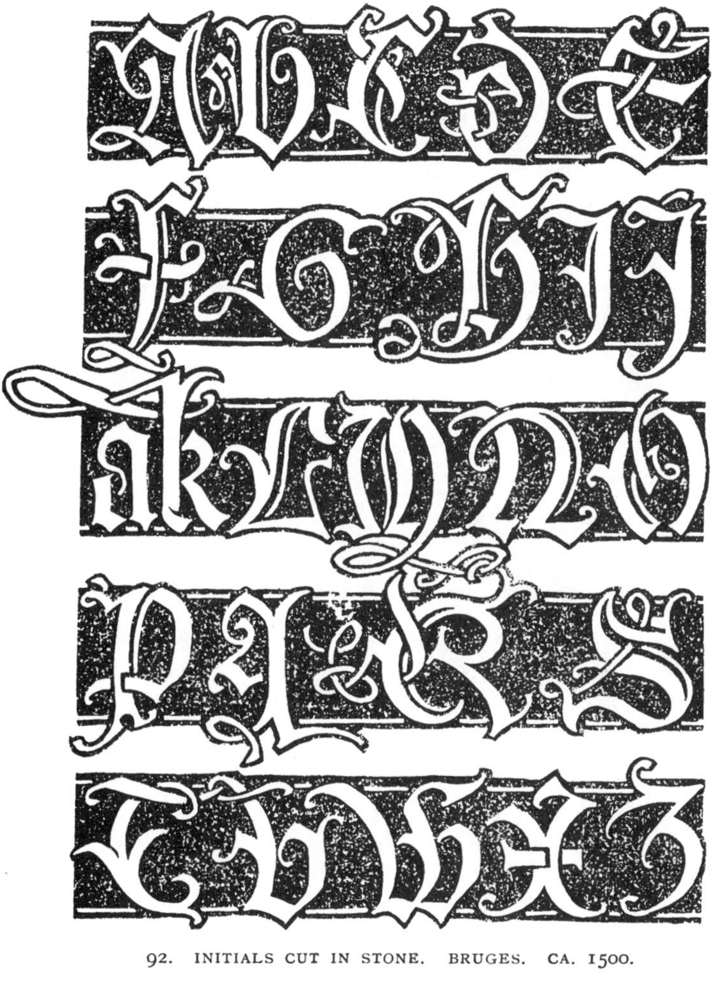

92. INITIALS CUT IN STONE. BRUGES. CA. 1500.

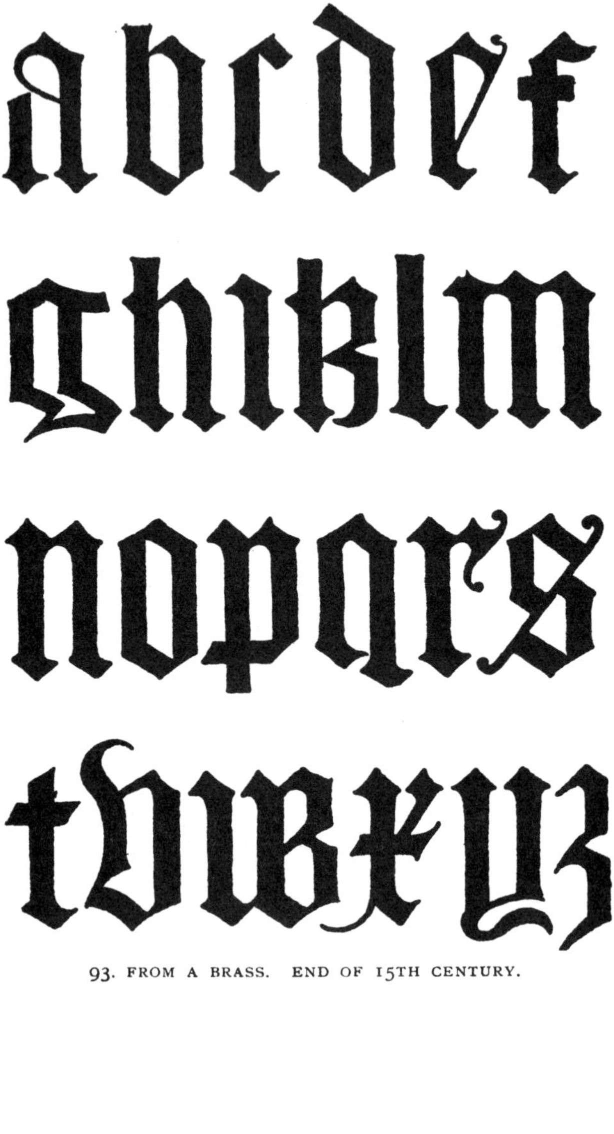

93. FROM A BRASS. END OF 15TH CENTURY.

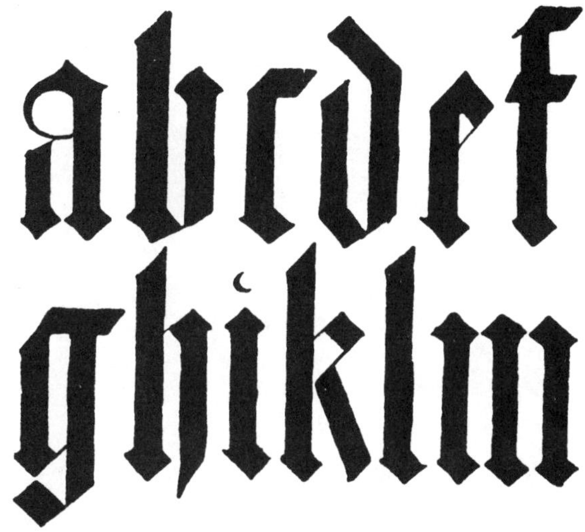

94. FROM A BRASS. END OF 15TH CENTURY.

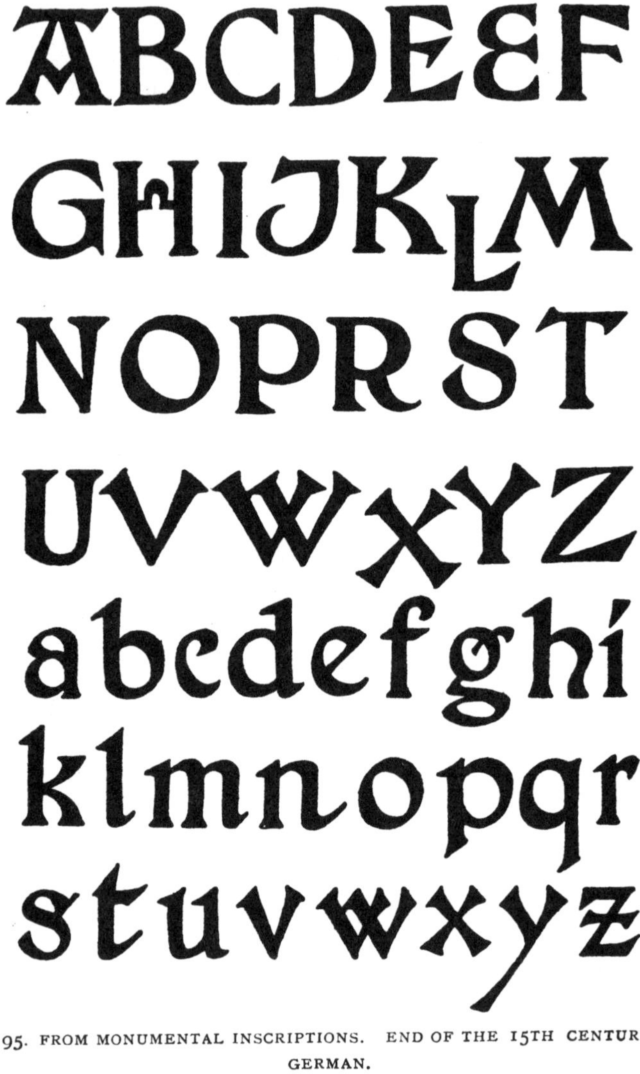

95. FROM MONUMENTAL INSCRIPTIONS. END OF THE 15TH CENTURY GERMAN.

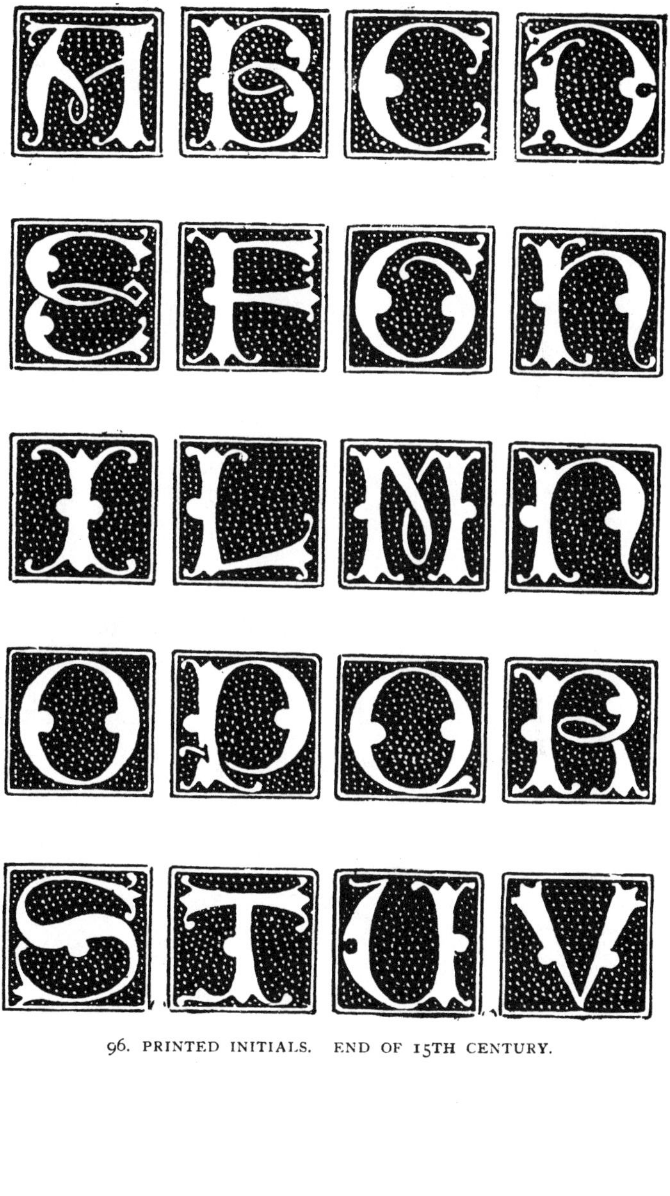

96. PRINTED INITIALS. END OF 15TH CENTURY.

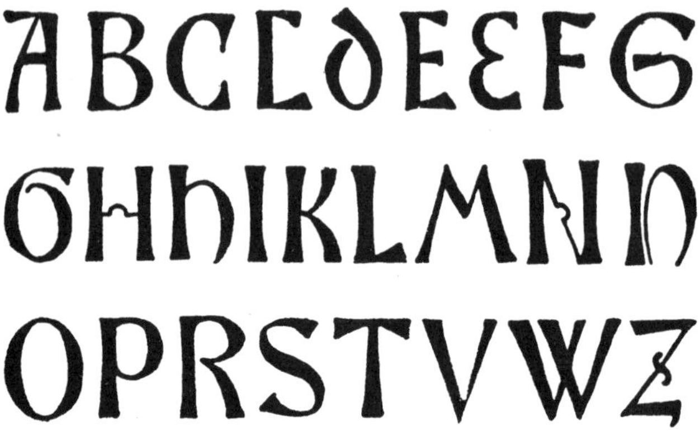

97. FROM A BRASS. MEISSEN, 1500.

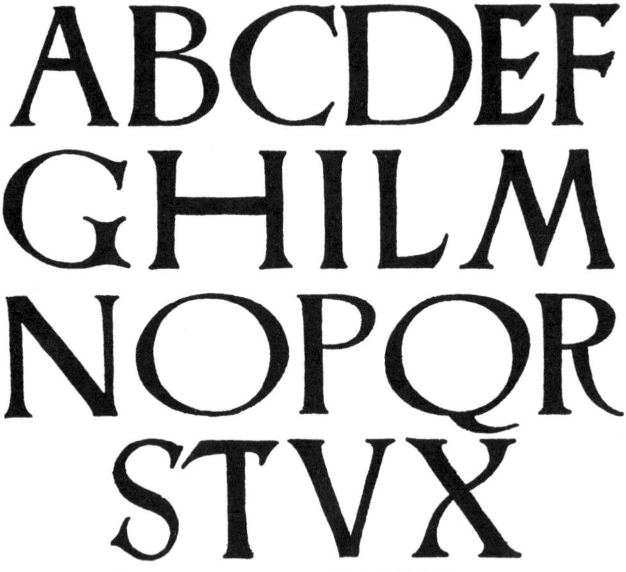

98. FROM BRONZE BY PETER VISCHER. 1495.

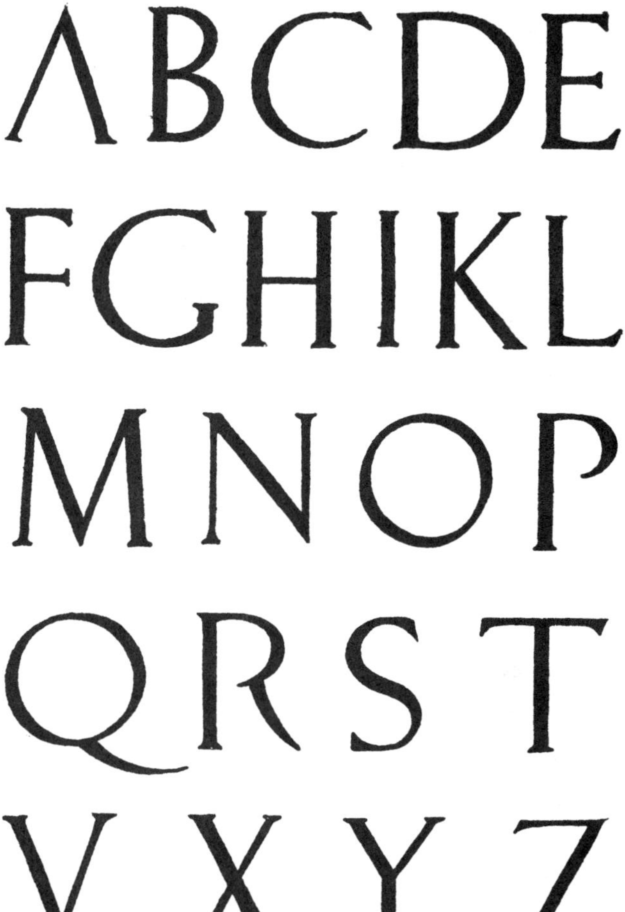

99. INCISED. ITALIAN RENAISSANCE. S. CROCE, FLORENCE.

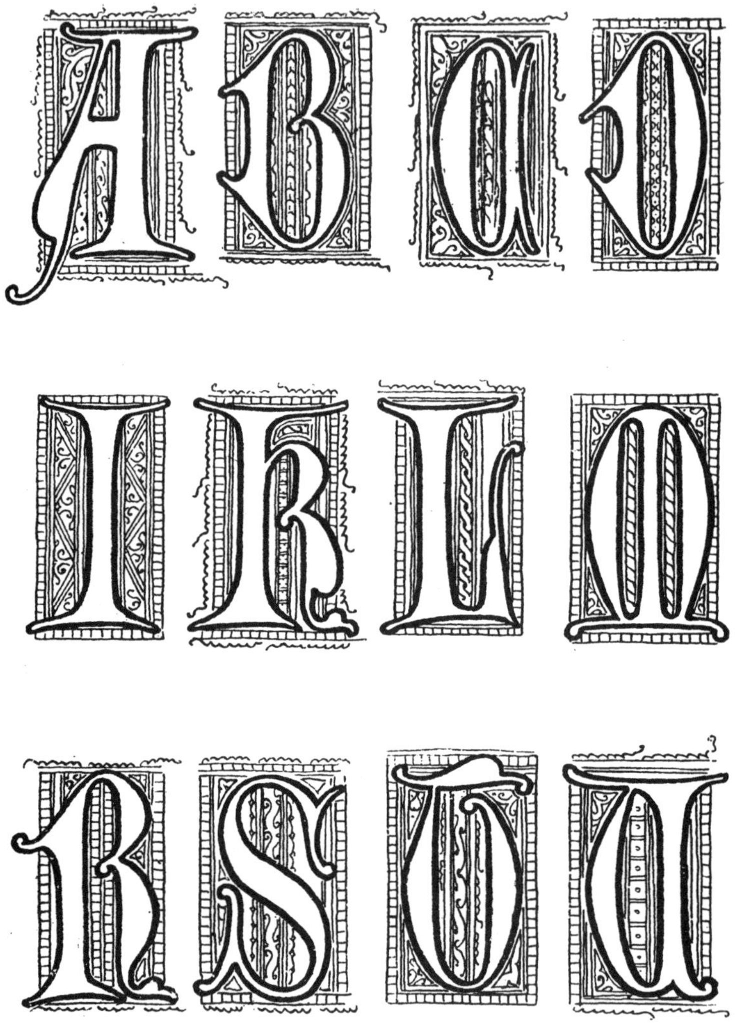

100. FROM A MANUSCRIPT

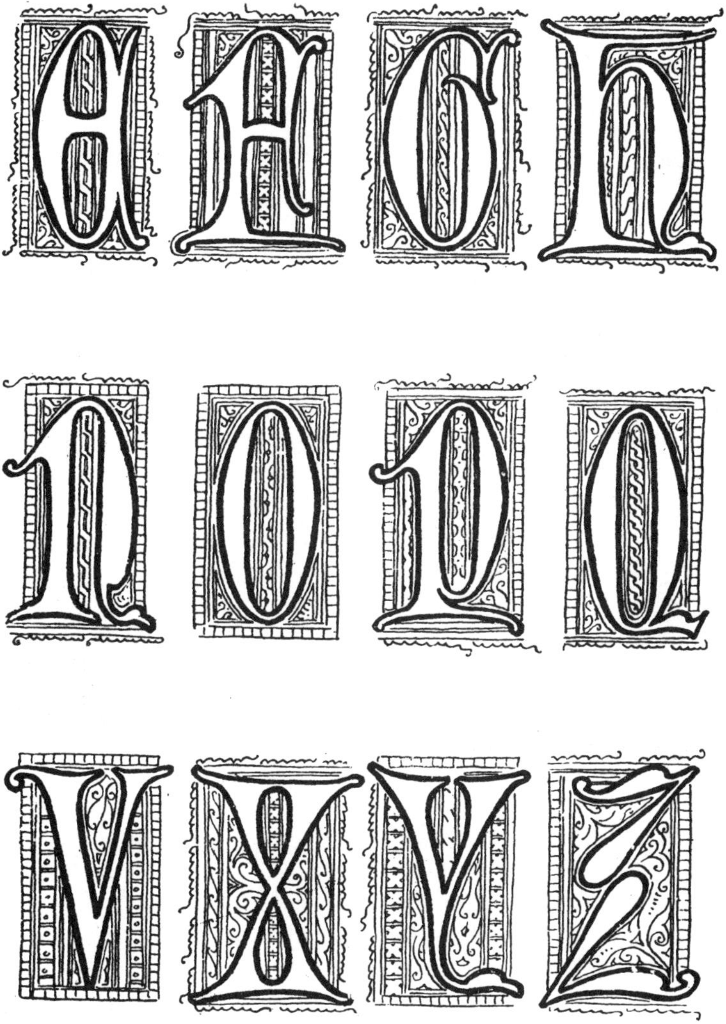

OF THE 16TH CENTURY.

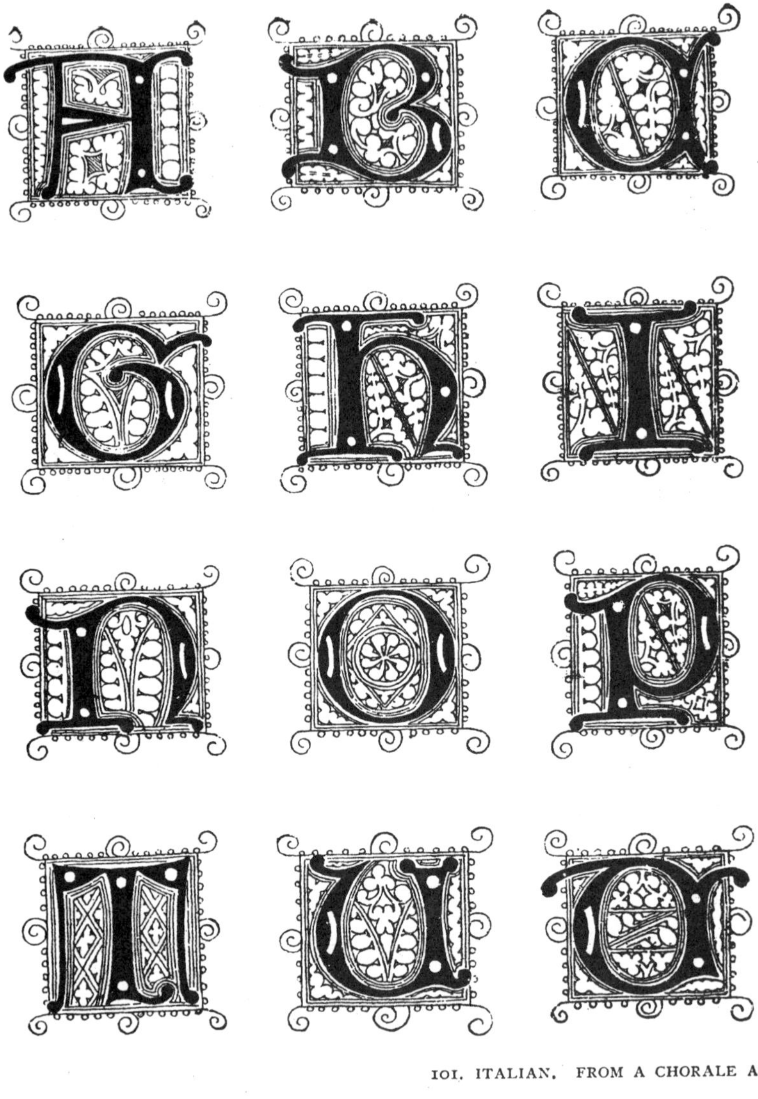

101. ITALIAN. FROM A CHORALE AT

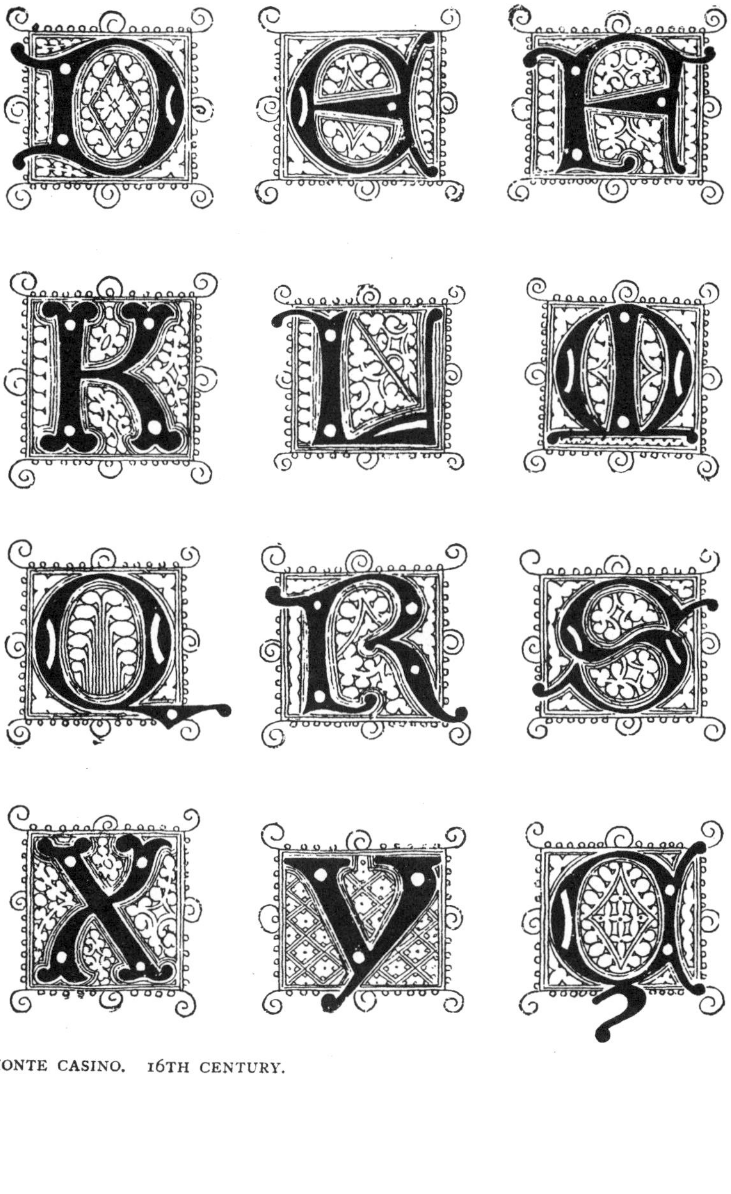

MONTE CASINO. 16TH CENTURY.

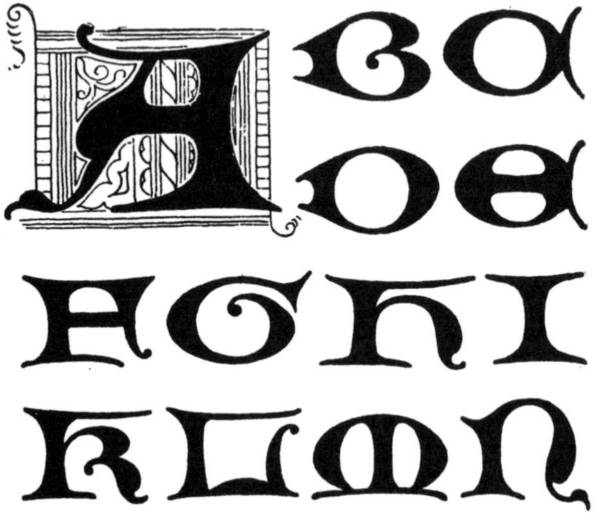

102. GOTHIC. 16TH CENTURY.

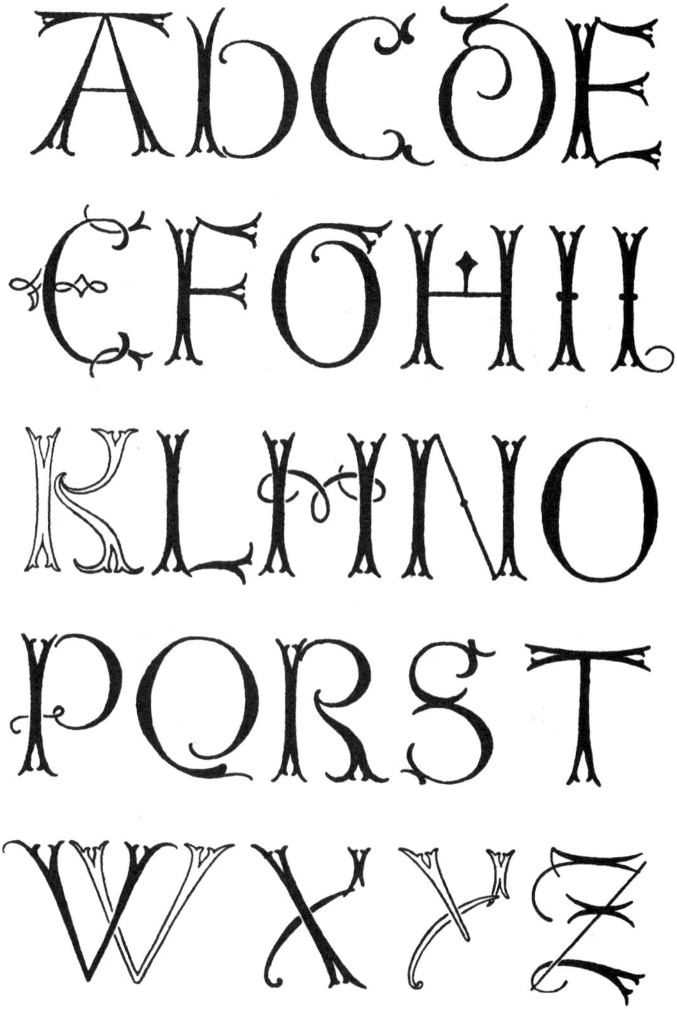

103. PAINTED. FLEMISH. EARLY 16TH CENTURY.

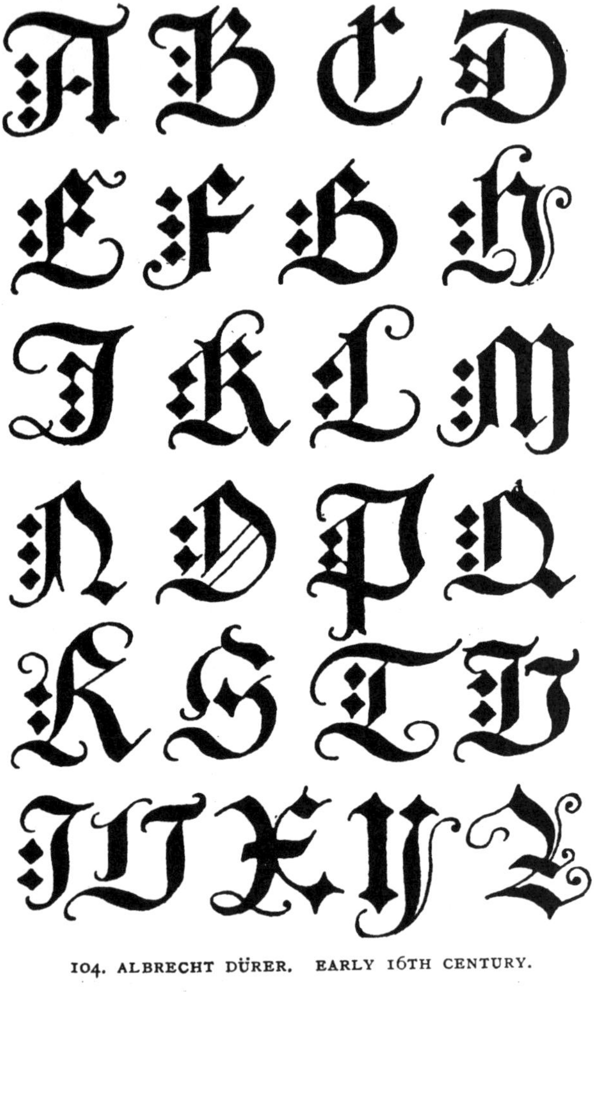

104. ALBRECHT DÜRER. EARLY 16TH CENTURY.

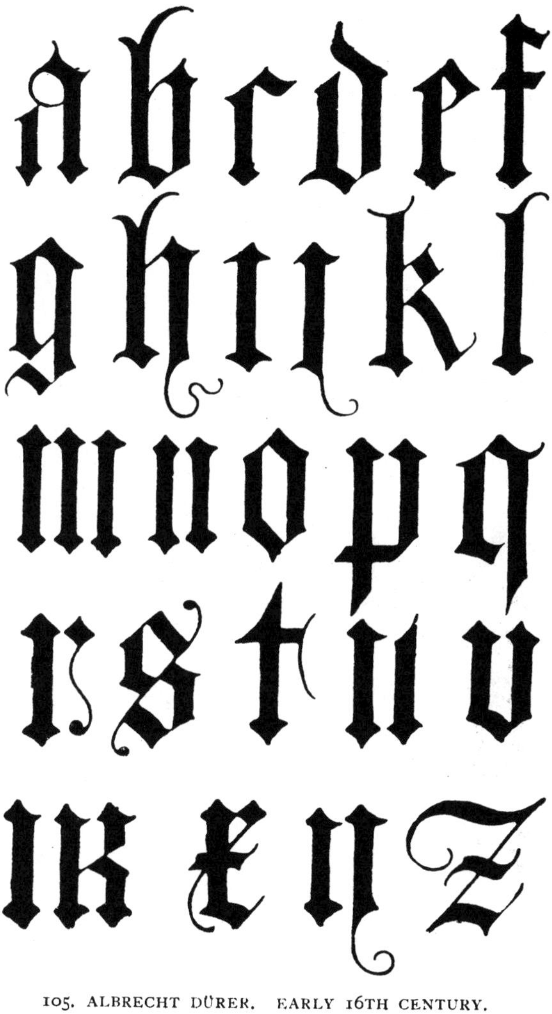

105. ALBRECHT DÜRER. EARLY 16TH CENTURY.

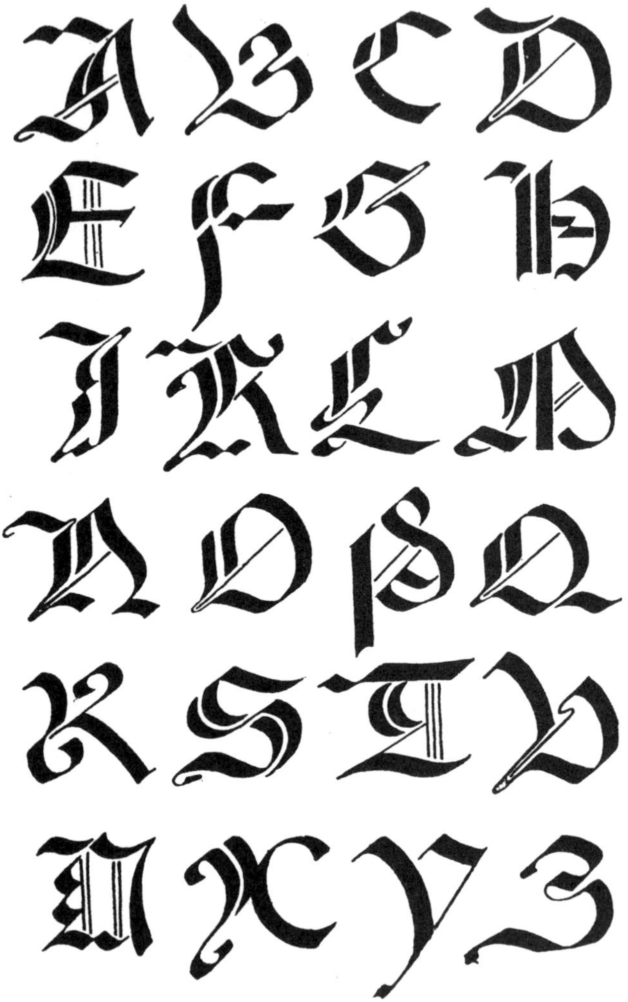

106. ITALIAN MSS. 15TH AND 16TH CENTURIES.

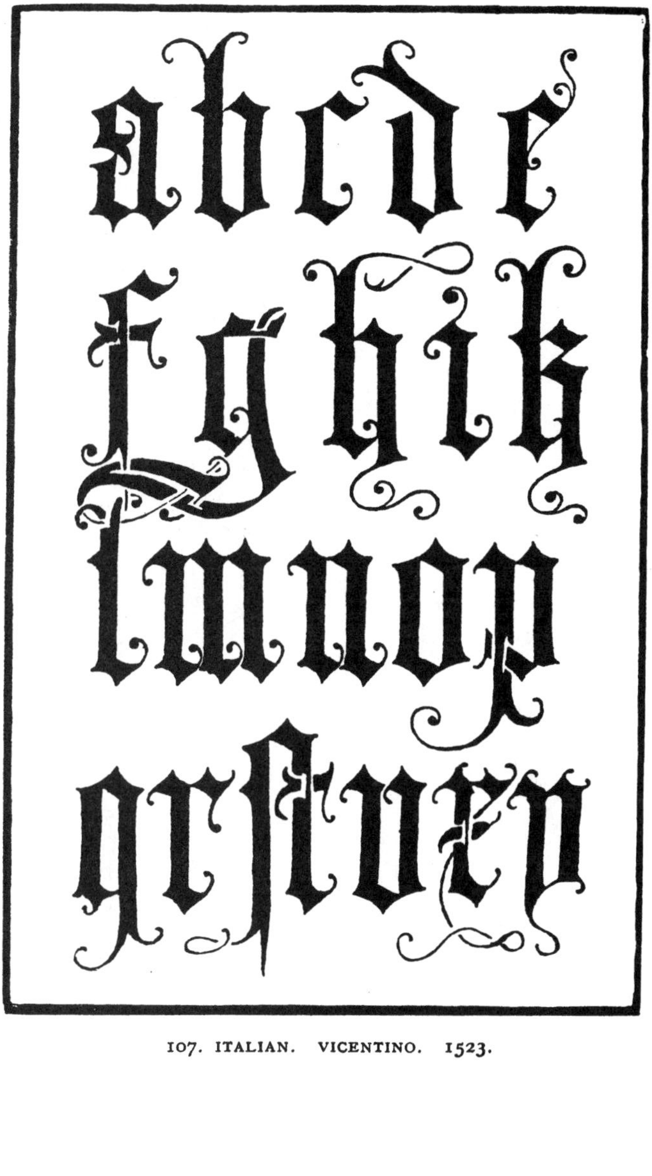

107. ITALIAN. VICENTINO. 1523.

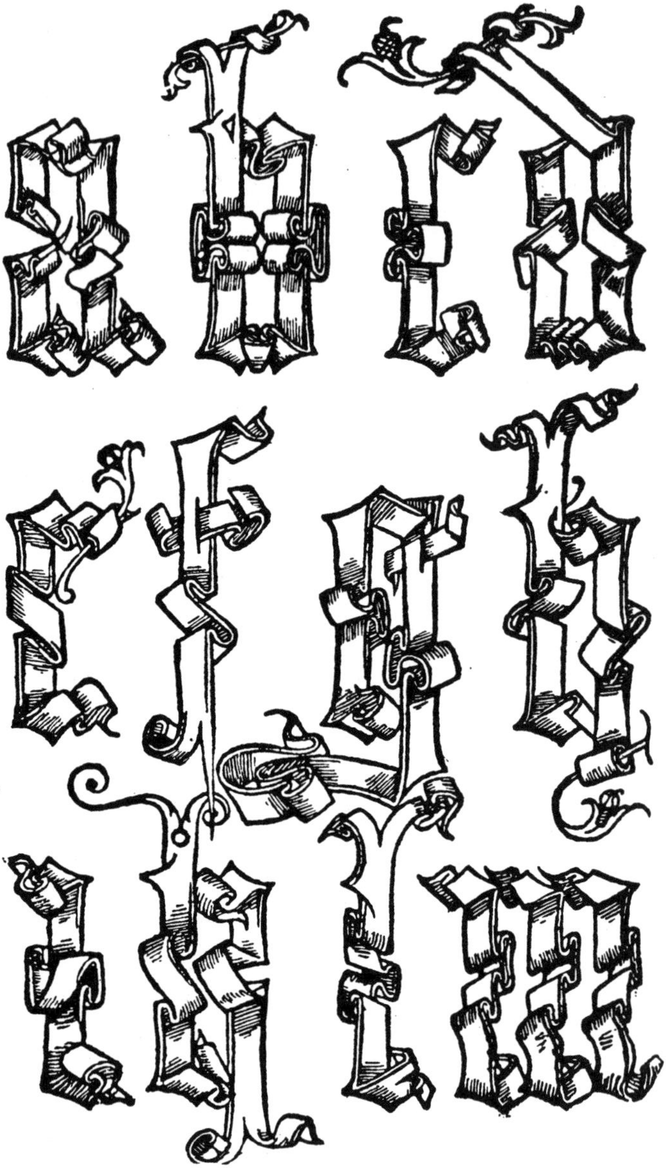

108. ITALIAN. LUDOVICO

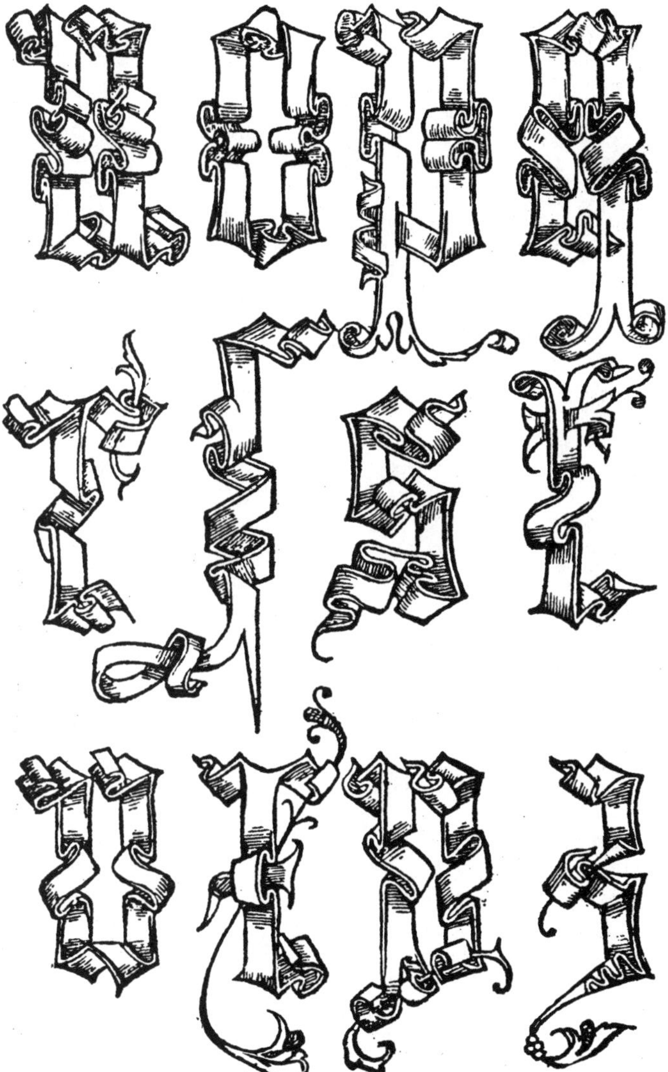

VICENTINO. 1523.

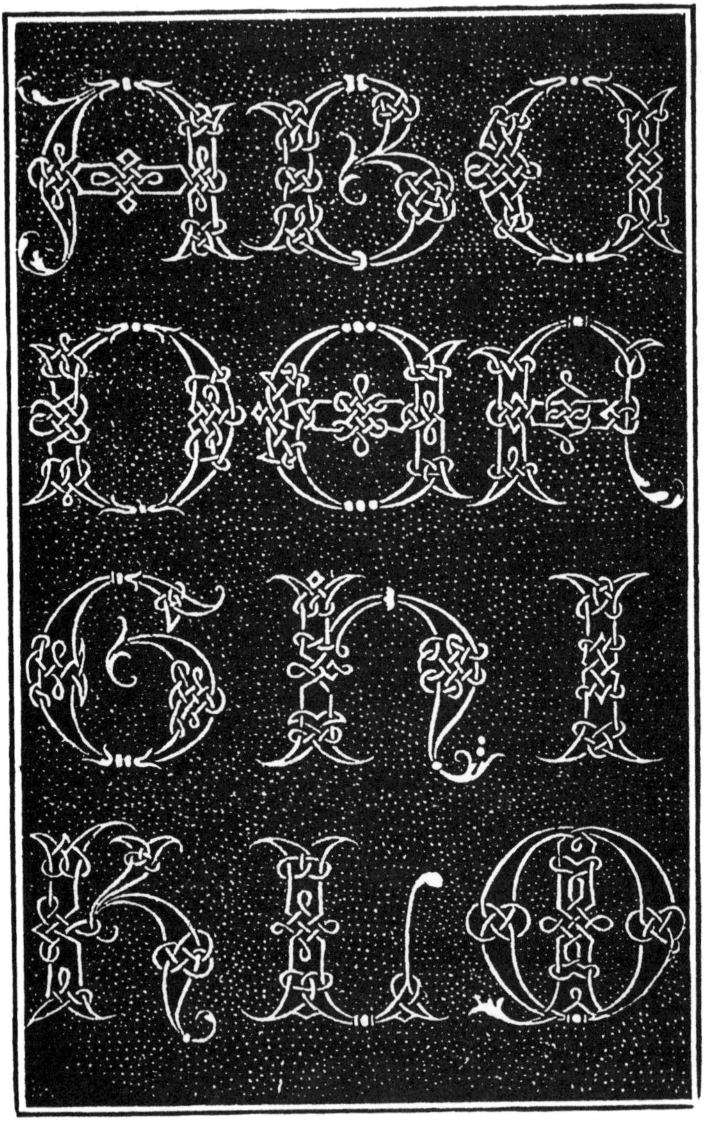

109. ITALIAN. LUDOVICO

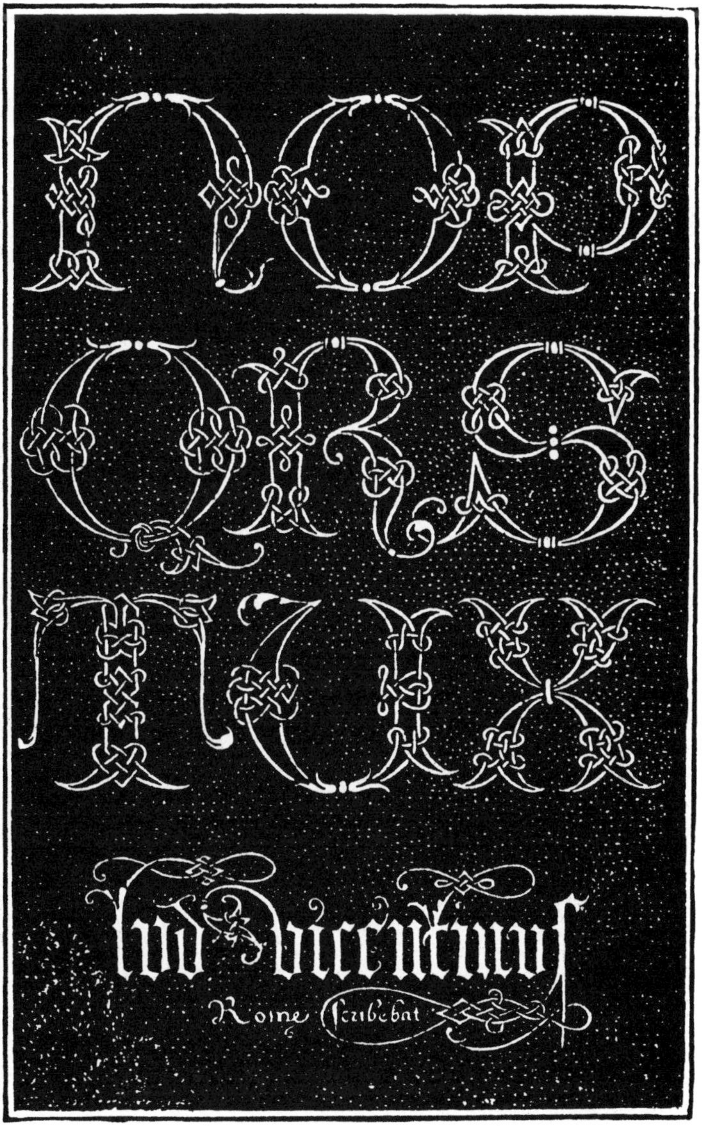

VICENTINO. 1523.

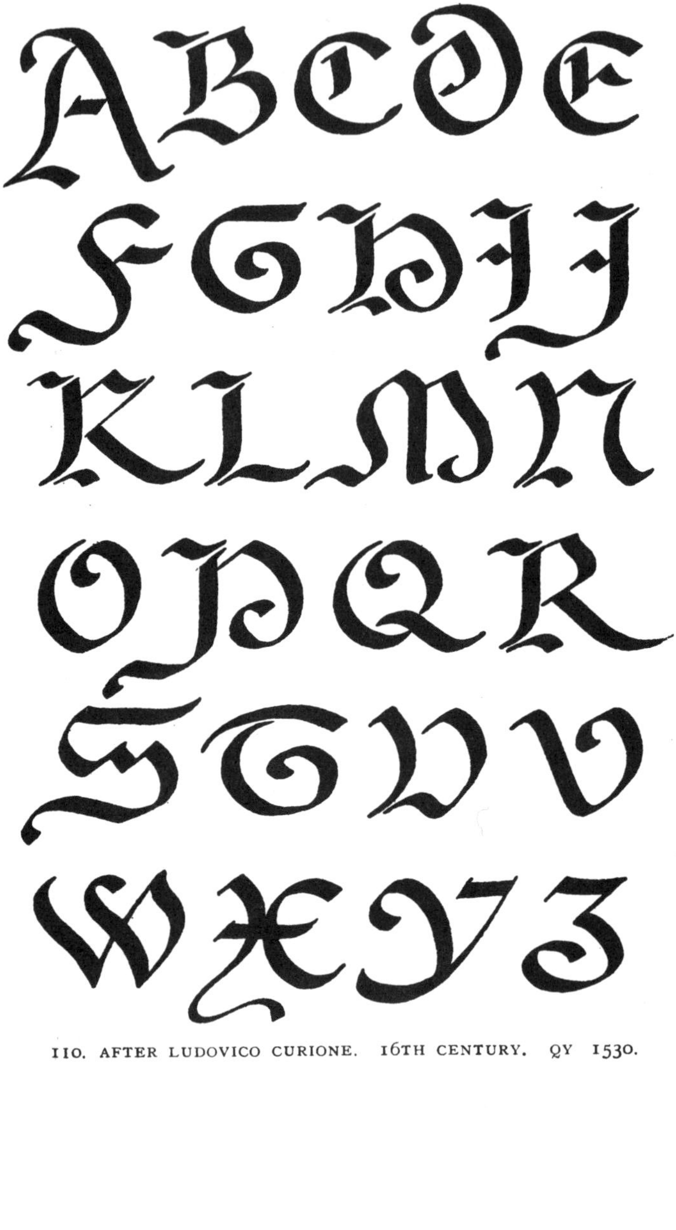

110. AFTER LUDOVICO CURIONE. 16TH CENTURY. QY 1530.

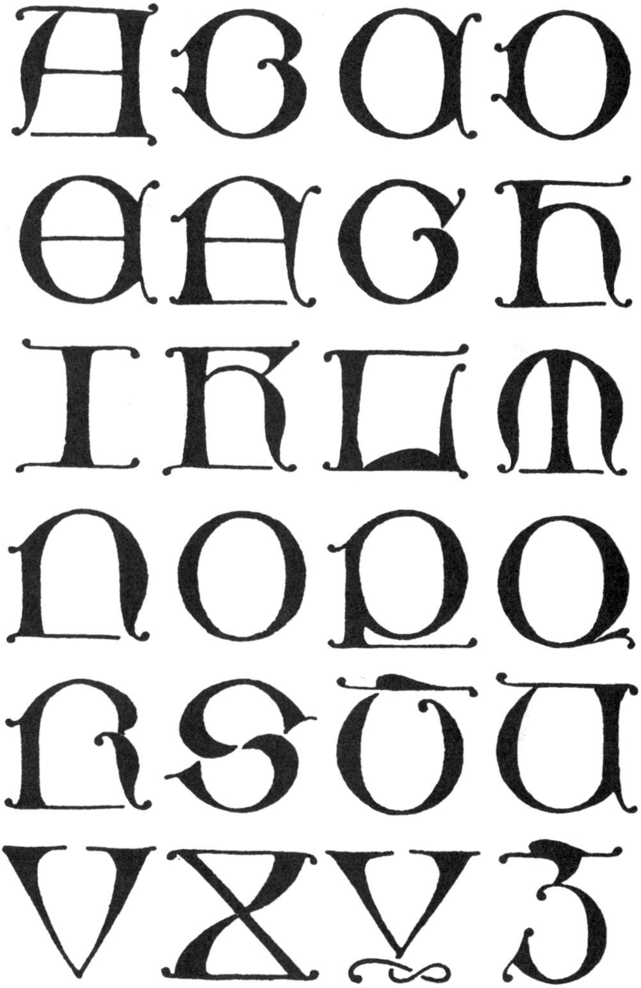

III. SPANISH. JUAN YCIAR. FIRST HALF OF THE 16TH CENTURY.

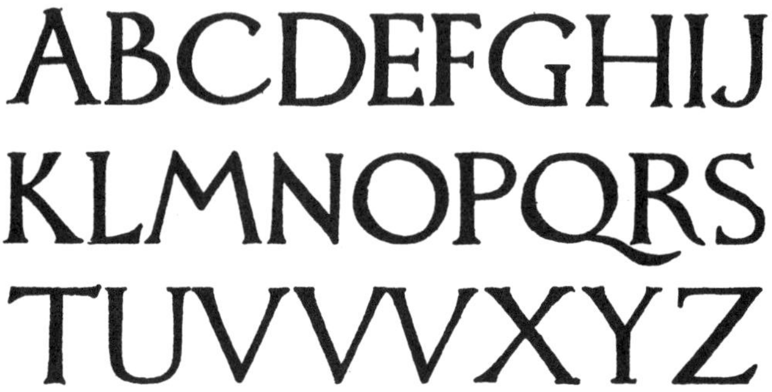

112. INCISED. FLORENTINE. 15TH CENTURY.

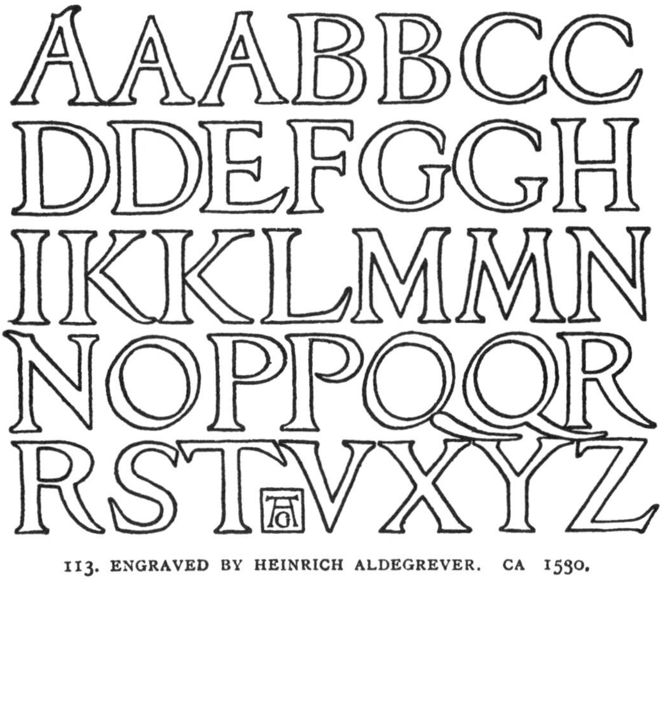

113. ENGRAVED BY HEINRICH ALDEGREVER. CA 1530.

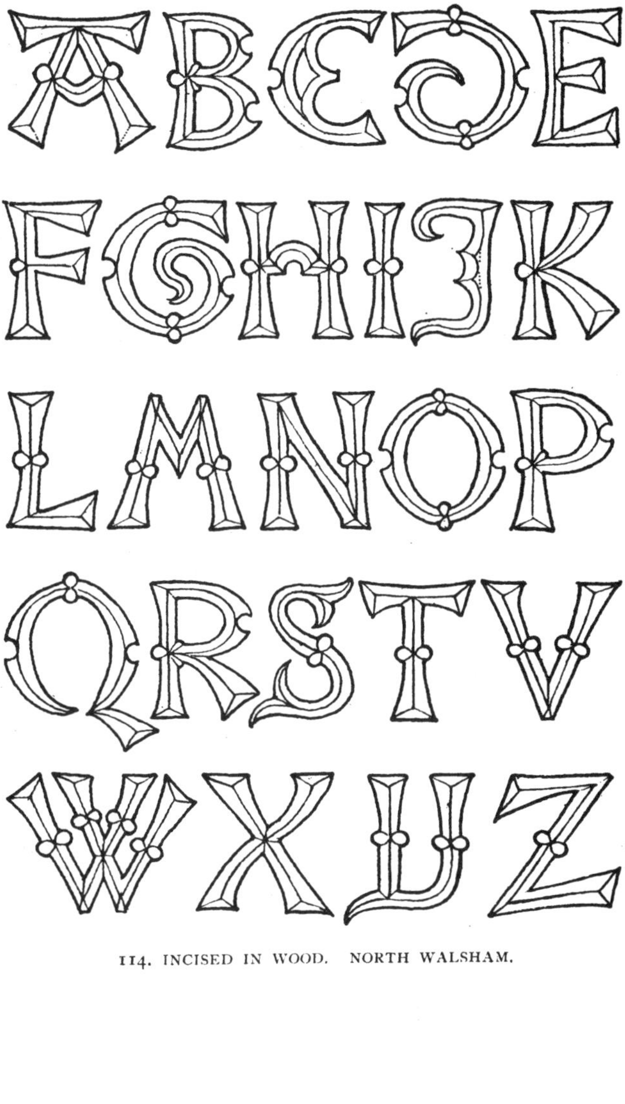

114. INCISED IN WOOD. NORTH WALSHAM.

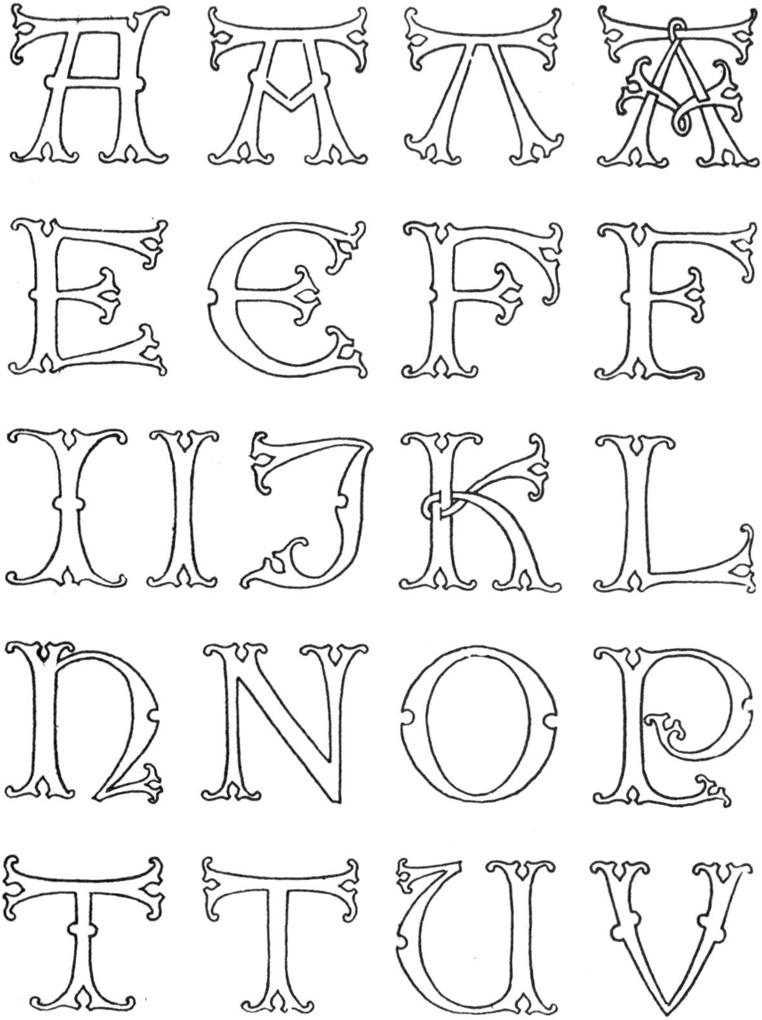

115. QUASI-

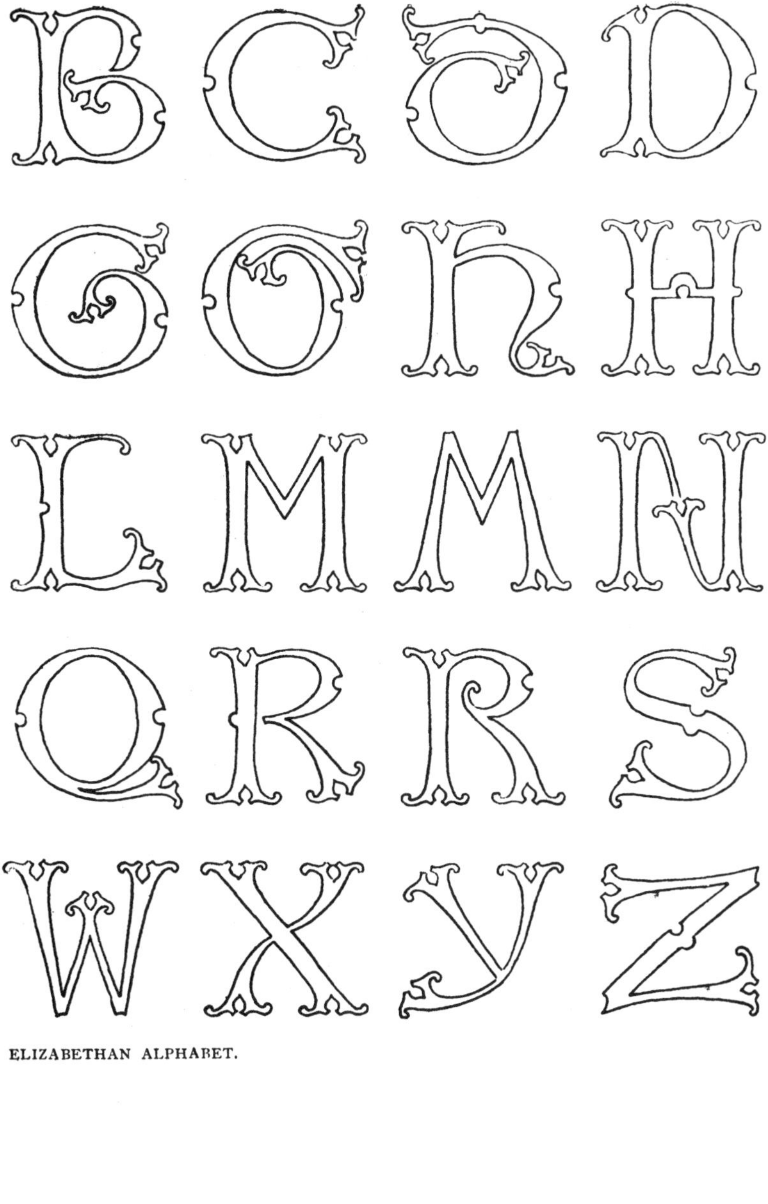

ELIZABETHAN ALPHABET.

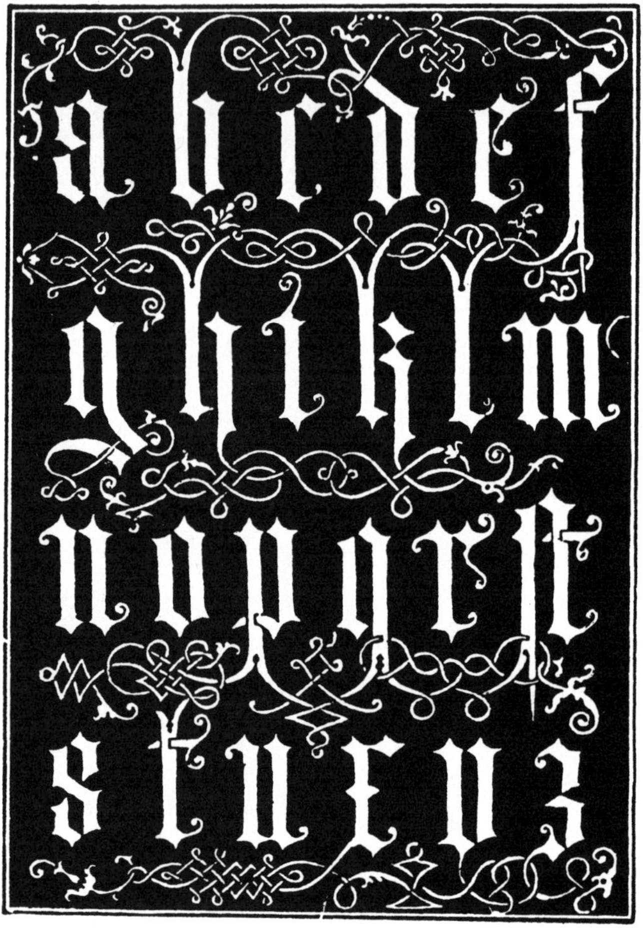

116. ITALIAN. PALATINO. 1546.

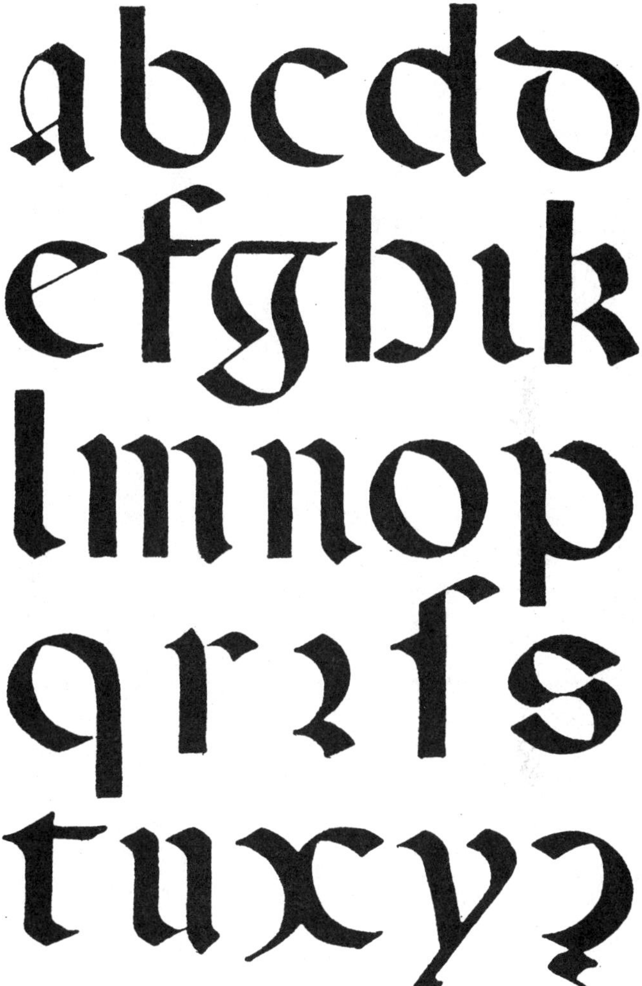

117. ITALIAN. VESPASIANO. 1556.

ABC

GHI

NOP

TVW

118. ITALIAN. SERLIO.

D E F

K L M

Q R S

X Y Z

16TH CENTURY.

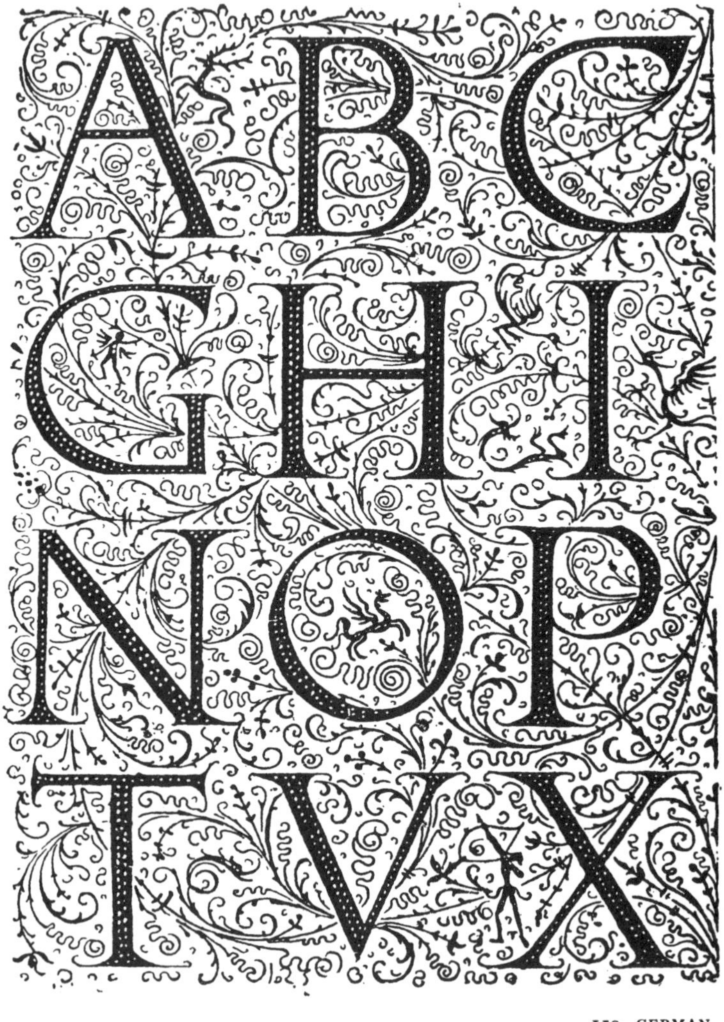

119. GERMAN.

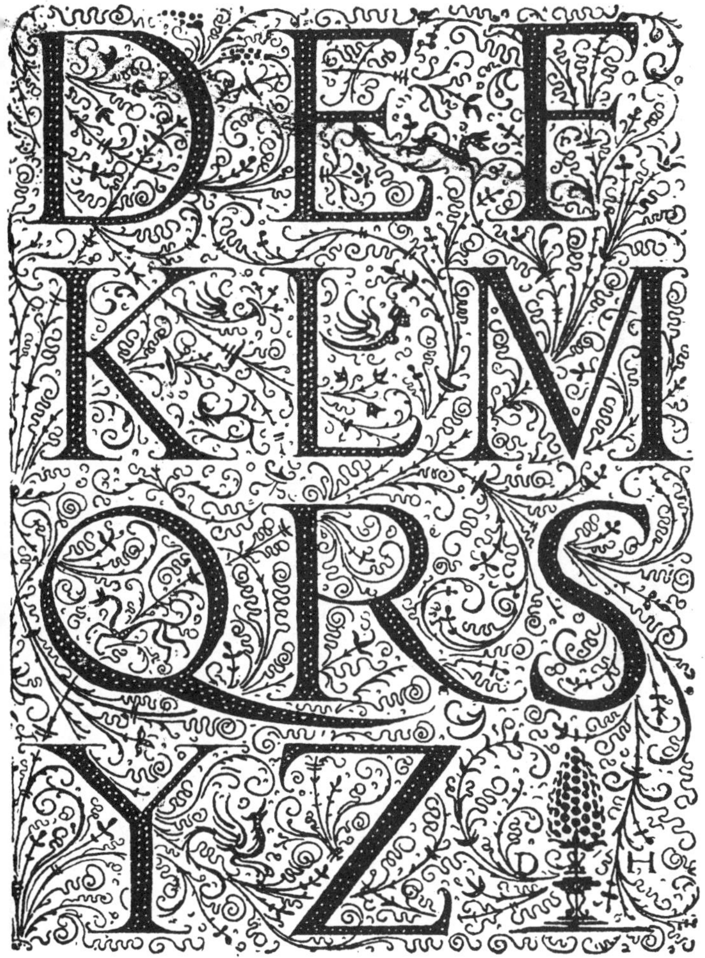

HOPFER. 1549.

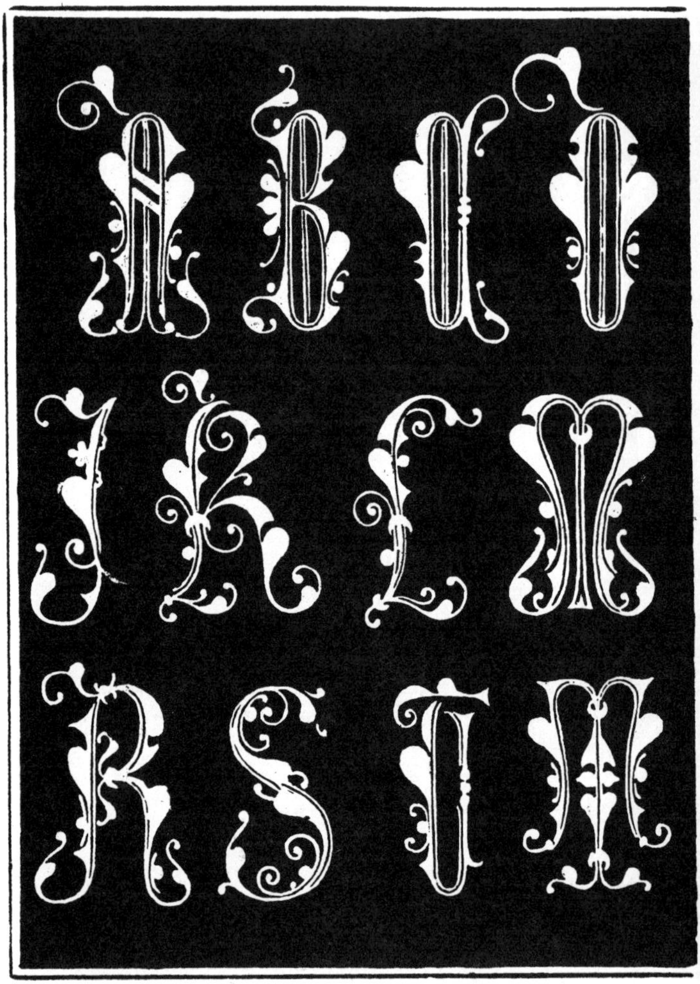

120. ITALIAN.

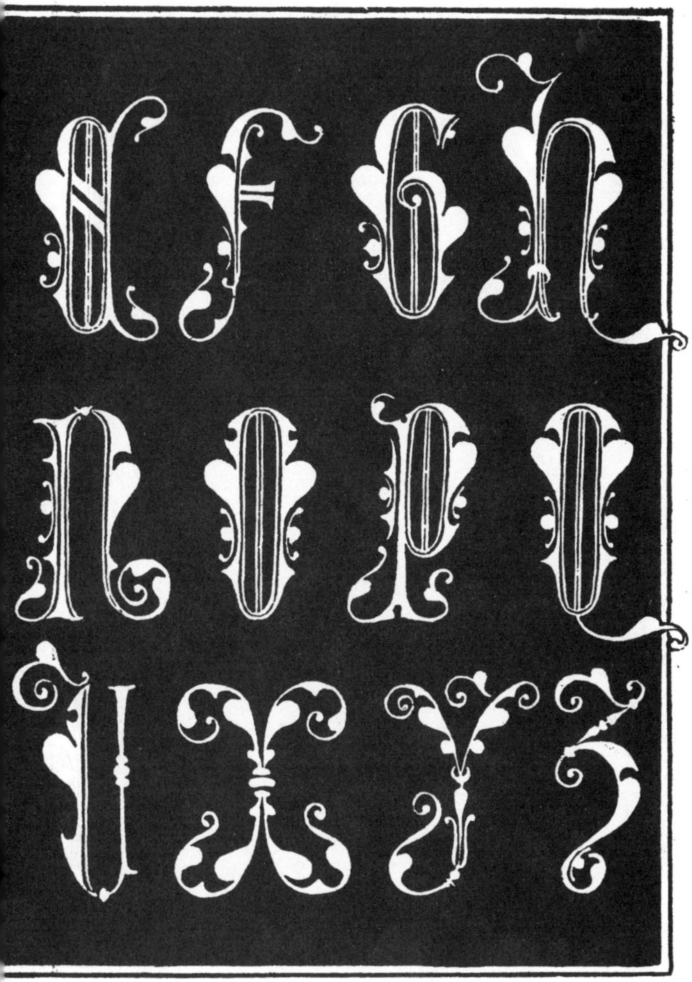

. F. CRESCI. 1570.

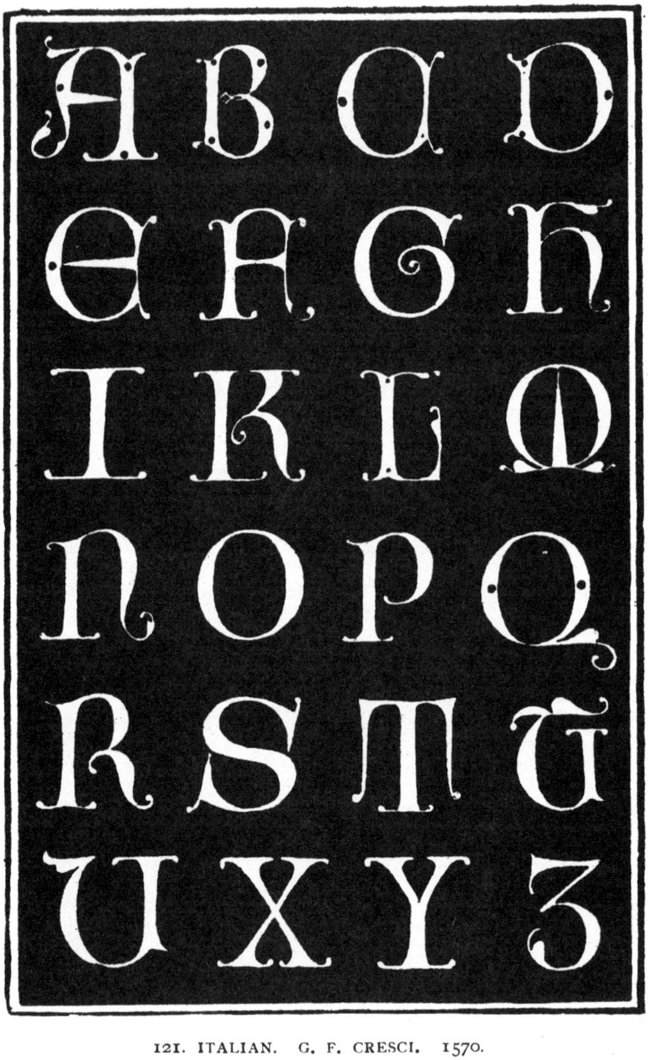

121. ITALIAN. G. F. CRESCI. 1570.

Aabc
defgh
ilmno
pqrst
uxyz

122. ITALIAN. G. F. CRESCI. 1570.

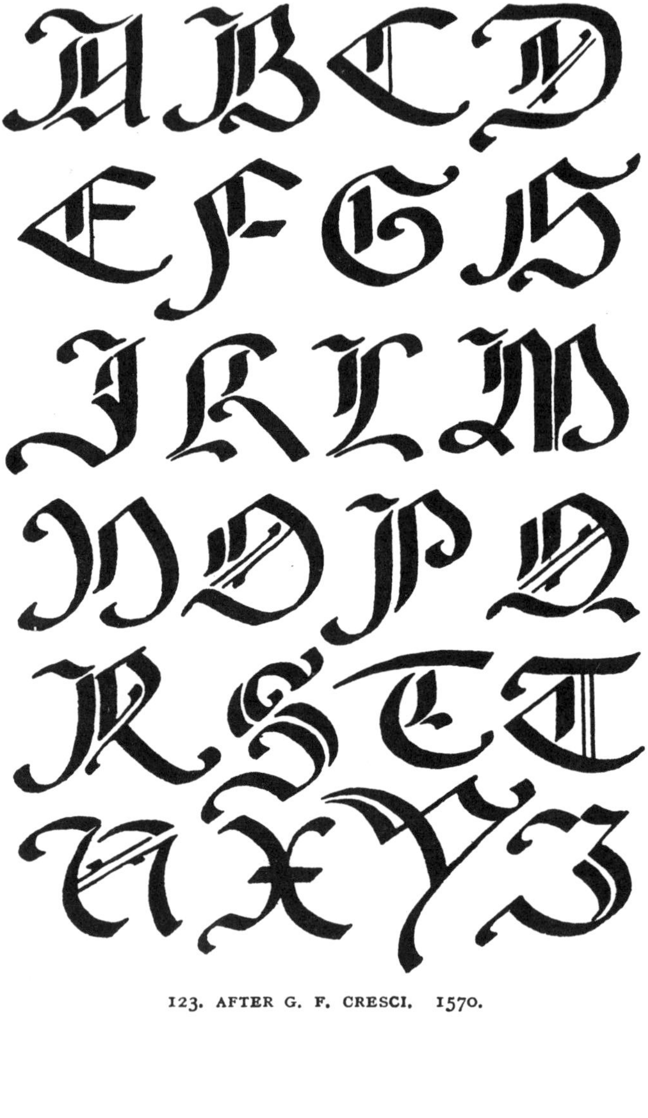

123. AFTER G. F. CRESCI. 1570.

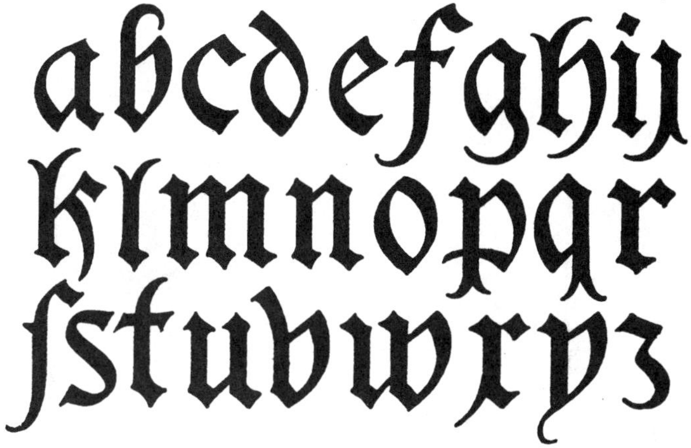

124. INCISED. FLEMISH. 1579.

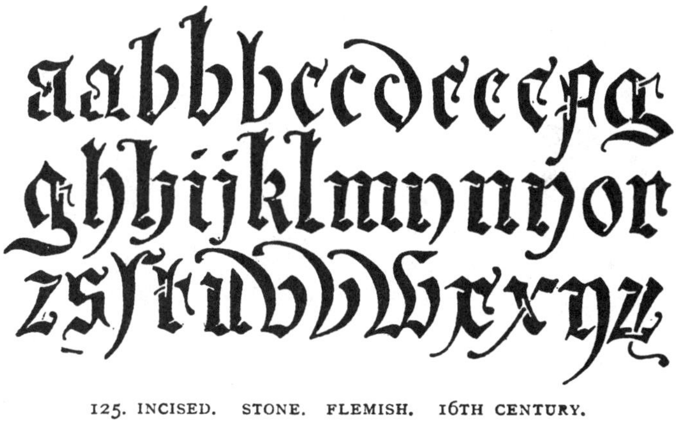

125. INCISED. STONE. FLEMISH. 16TH CENTURY.

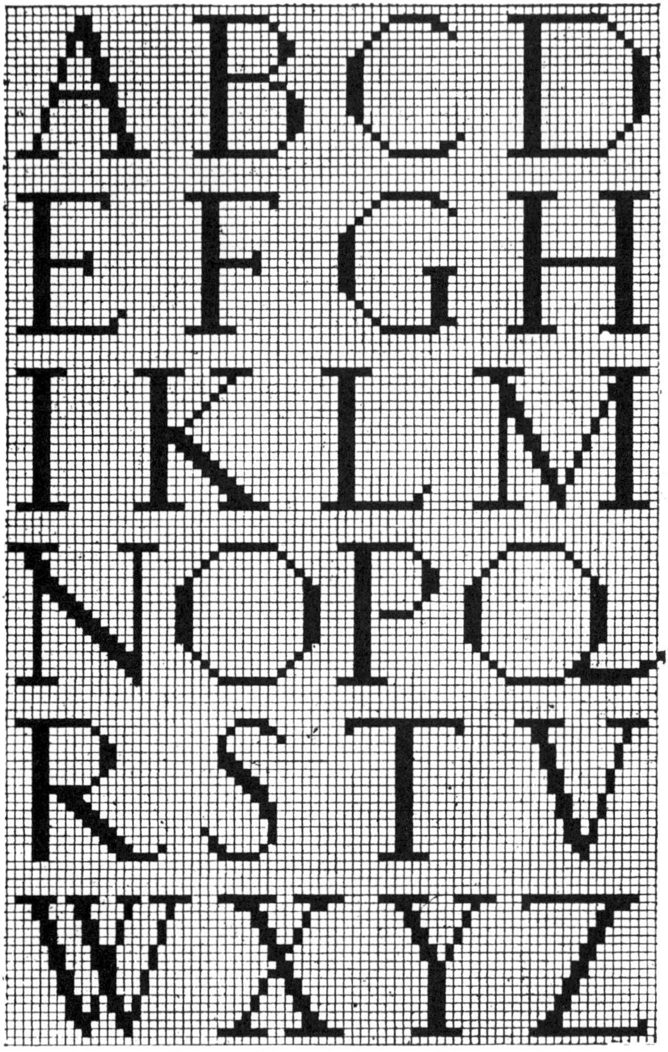

126. FROM THE LACE-BOOK OF GIOVANNI OSTAVS. 1590.

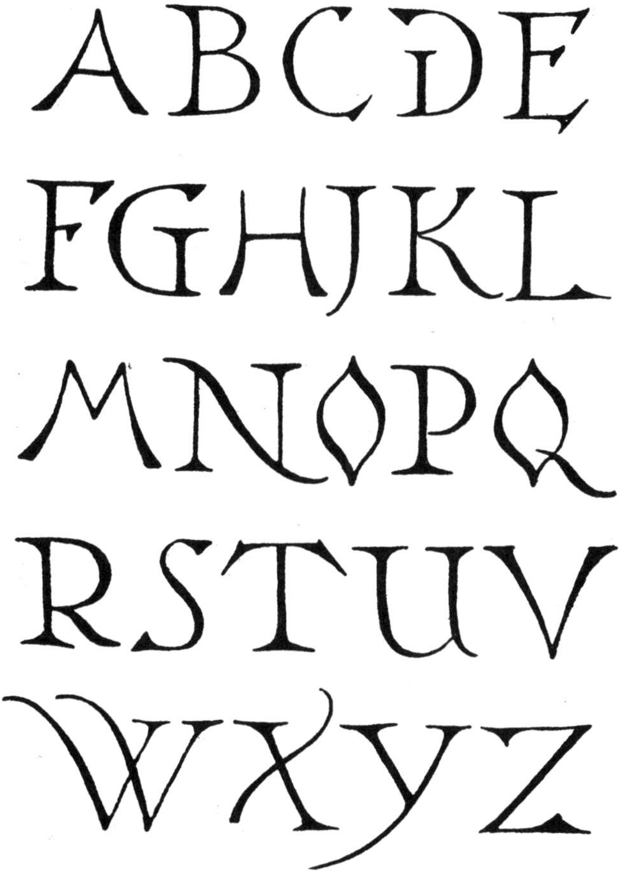

127. STONE. BINGEN. 1576, 1598, 1618.

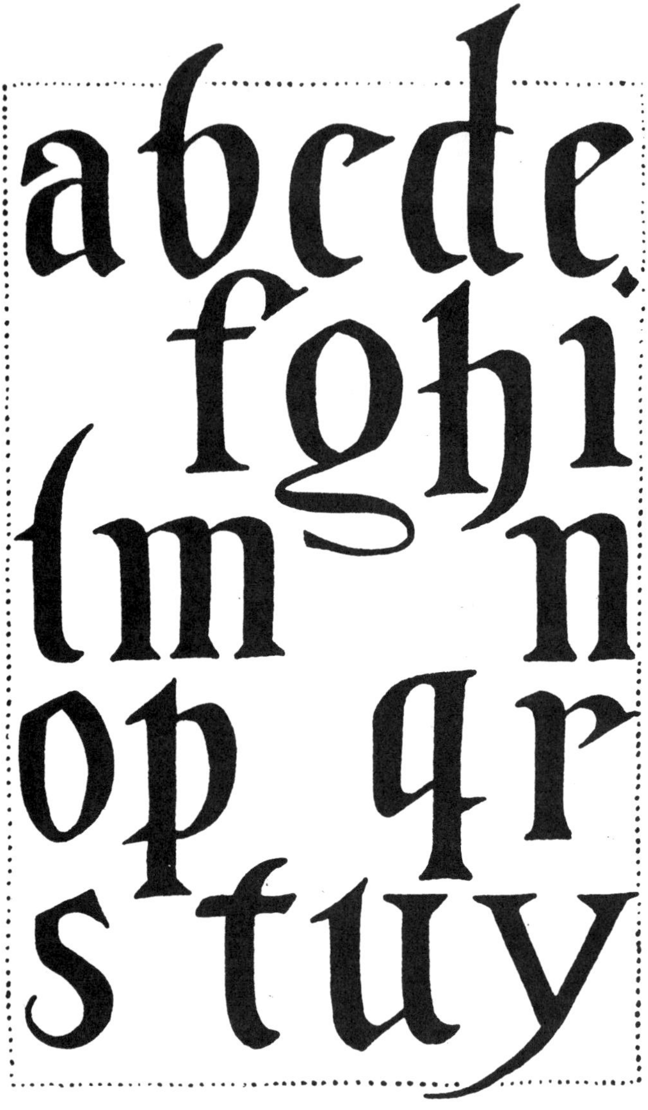

128. BRASS. BAMBERG. 1613

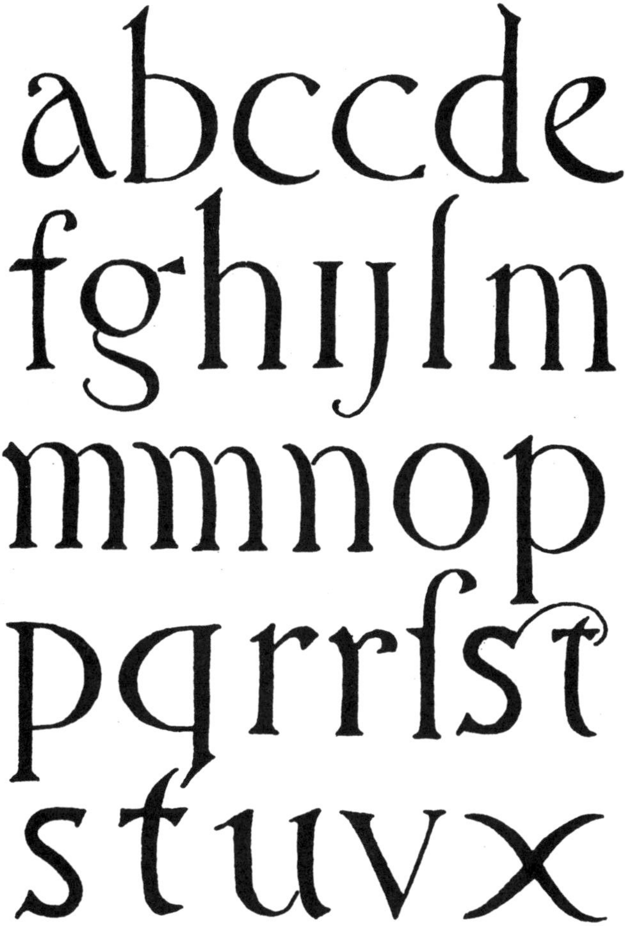

129. SLATE. WÜRZBURG. 1617.

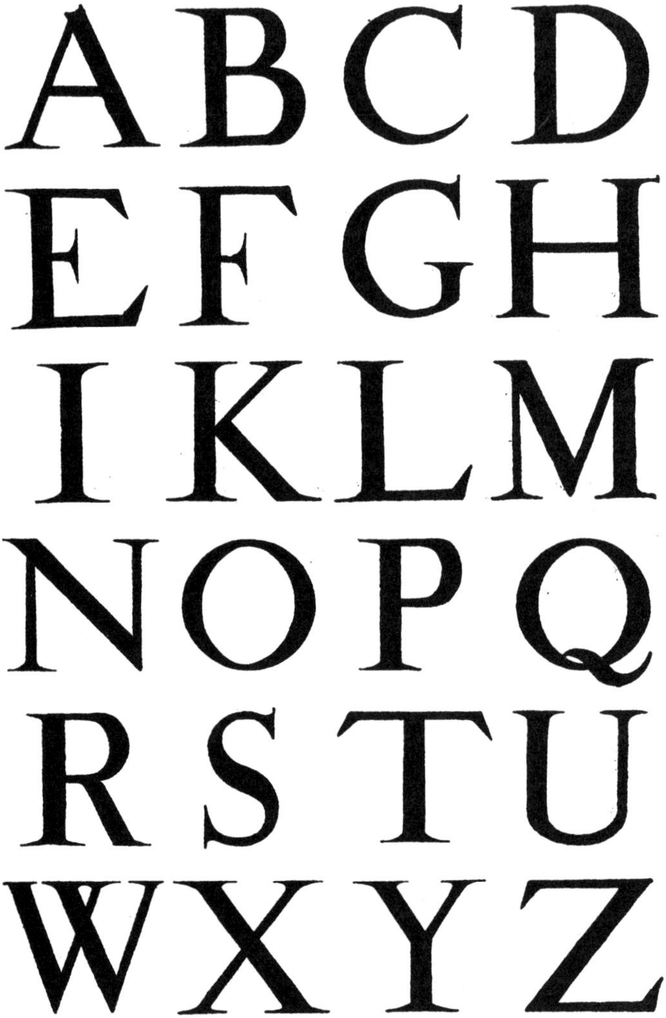

130. PENMANSHIP. 17TH CENTURY.

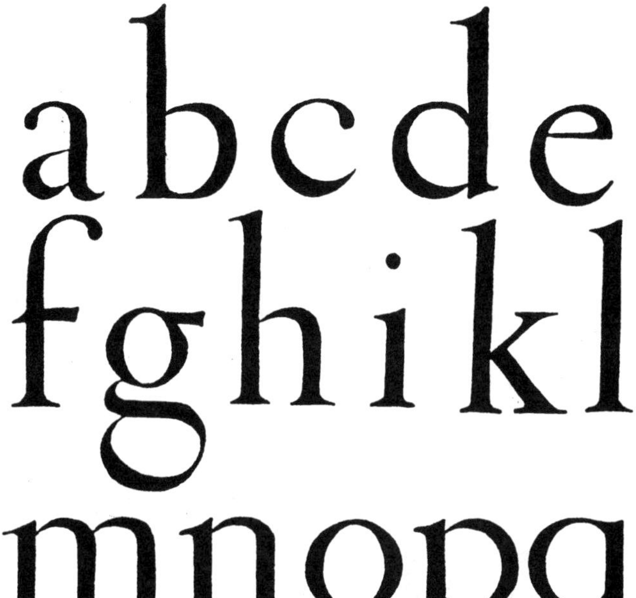

131. PENMANSHIP. 17TH CENTURY.

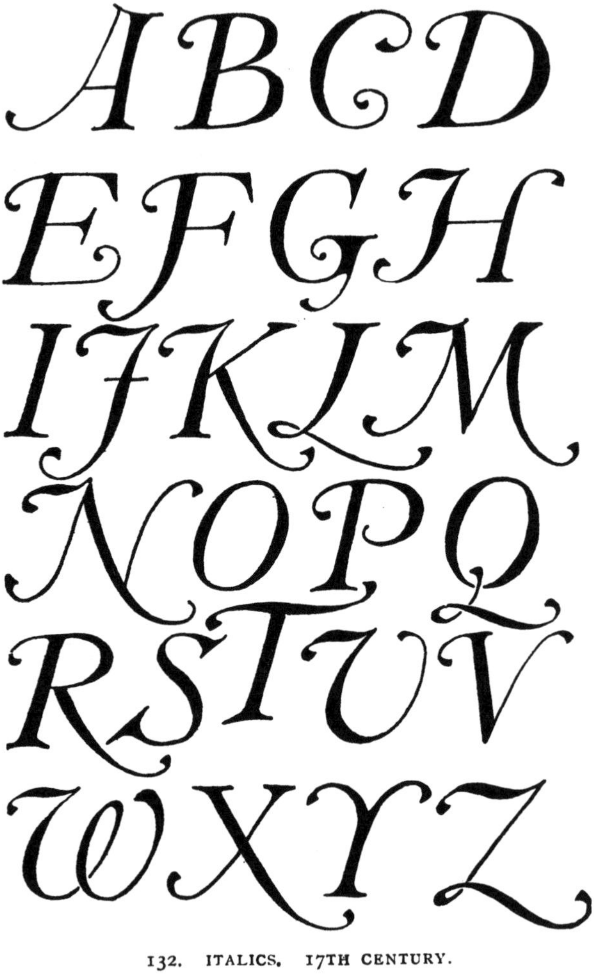

132. ITALICS. 17TH CENTURY.

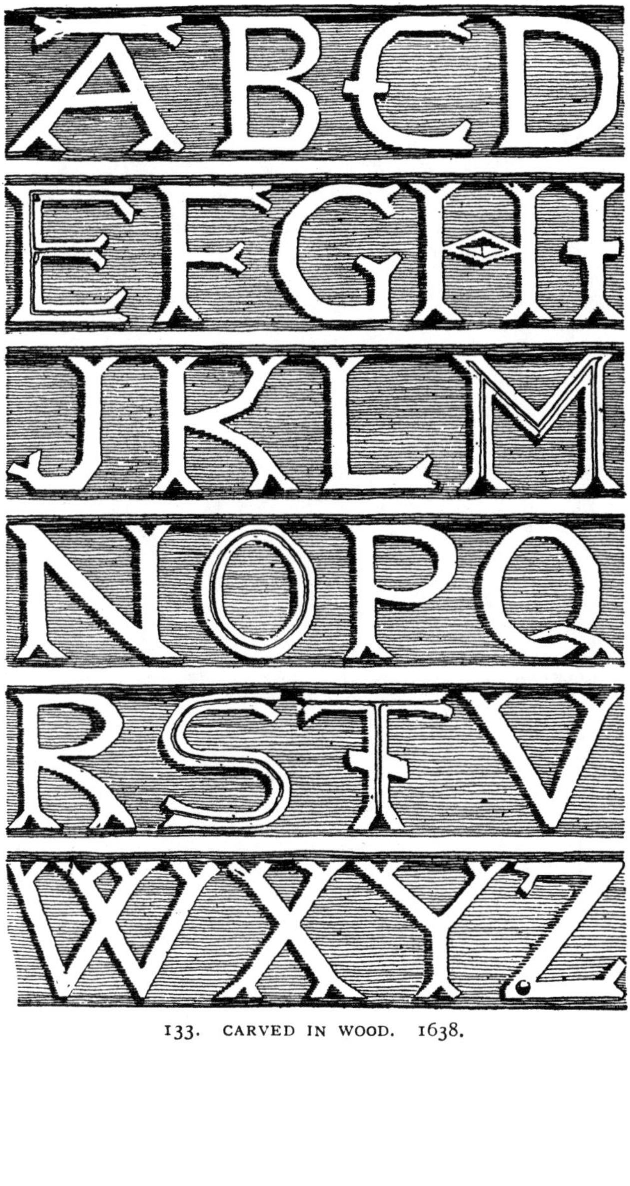

133. CARVED IN WOOD. 1638.

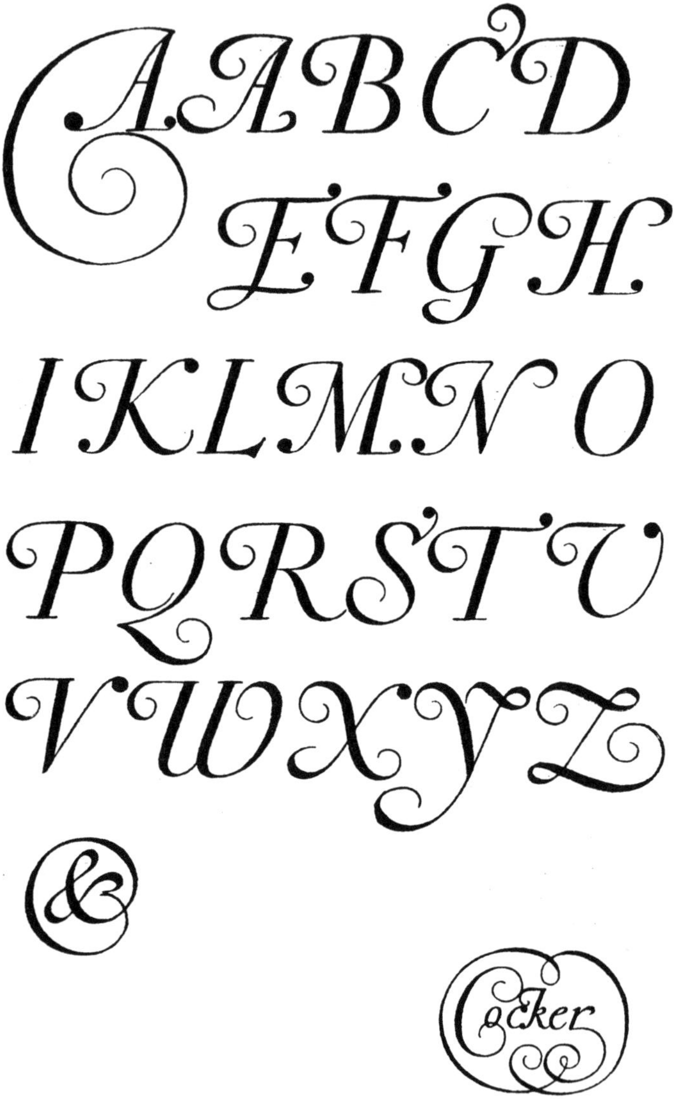

134. PENMANSHIP. E. COCKER. 1660.

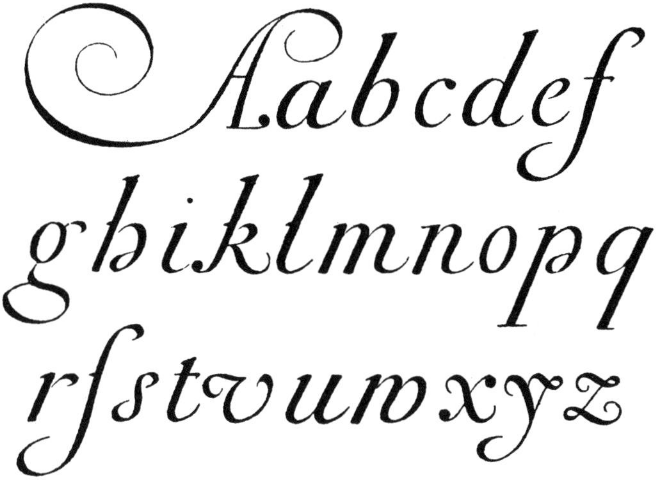

135. PENMANSHIP. E. COCKER. 1660.

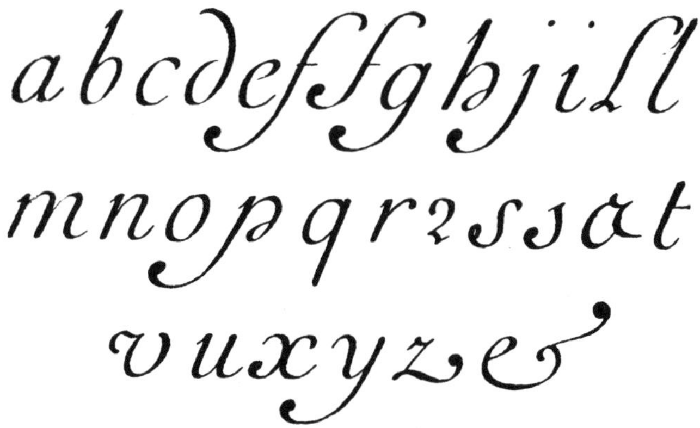

136. PENMANSHIP. LESGRET. 1736.

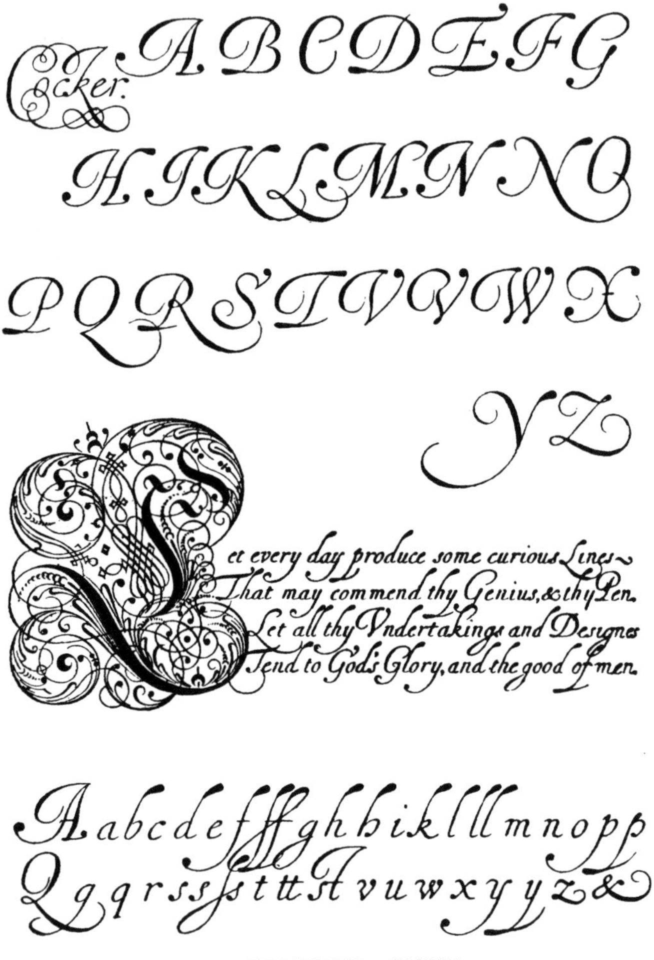

137. PENMANSHIP. COCKER.

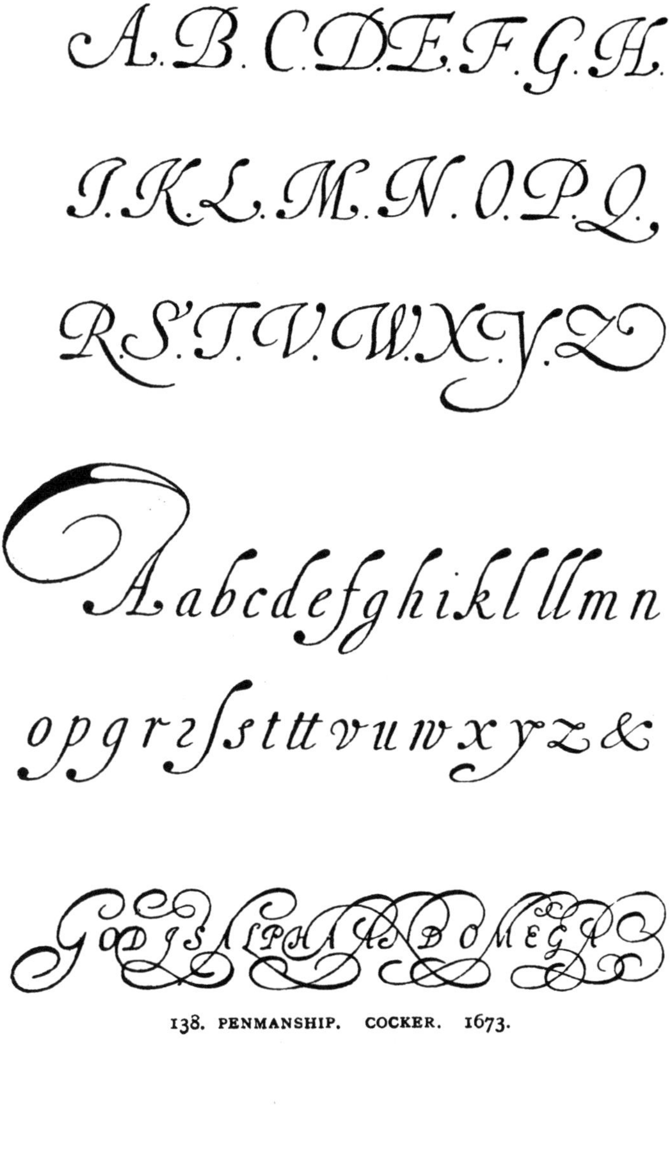

138. PENMANSHIP. COCKER. 1673.

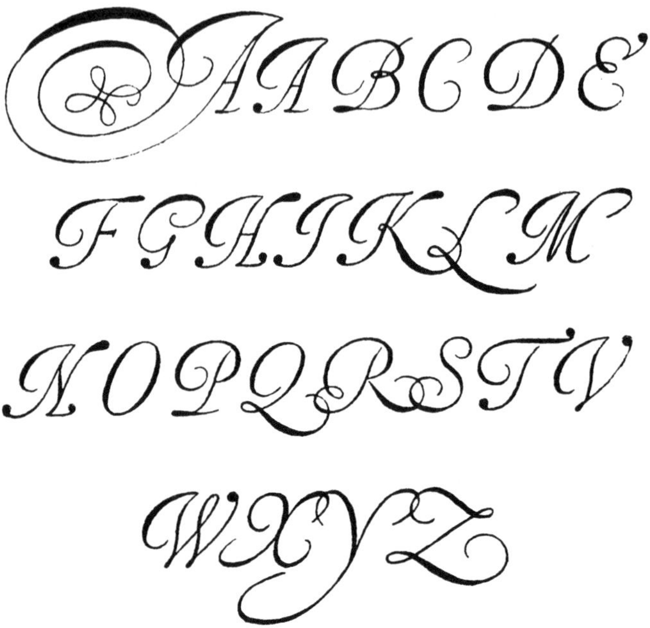

139. PENMANSHIP COCKER. 1673.

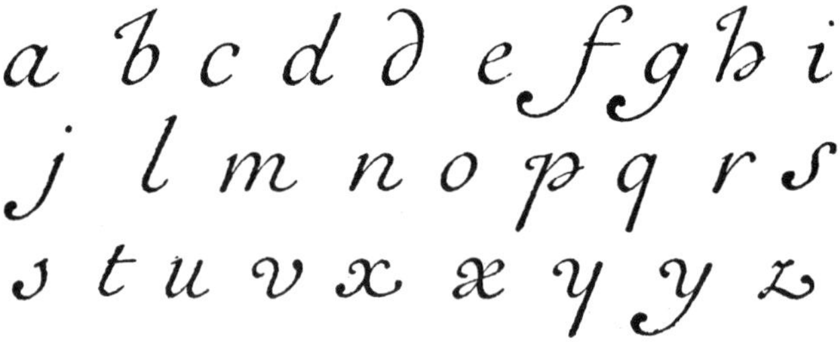

140. PENMANSHIP. MAINGUENEAU. FRENCH.

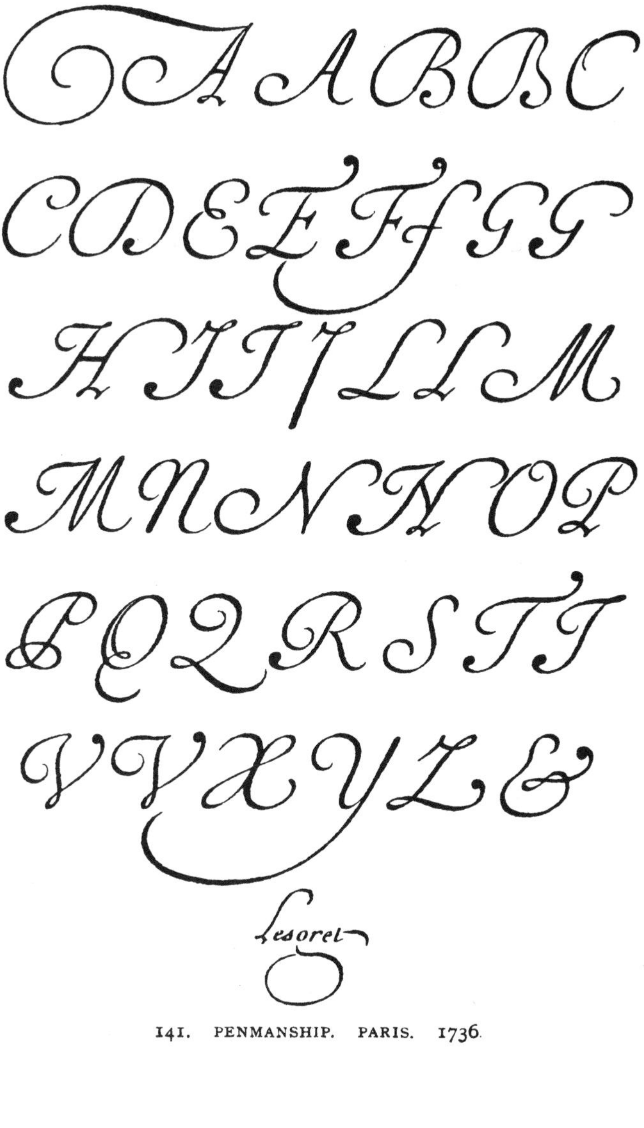

141. PENMANSHIP. PARIS. 1736.

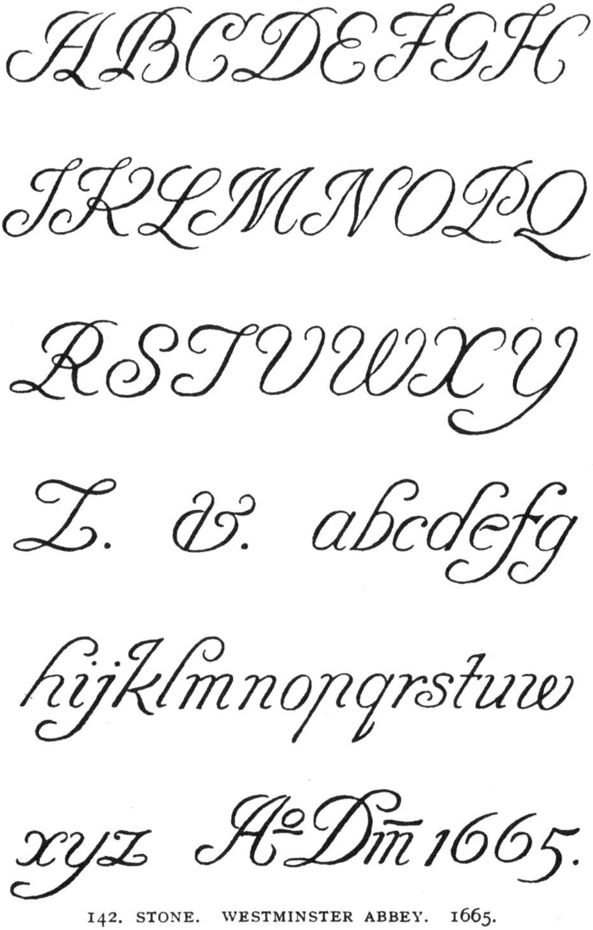

142. STONE. WESTMINSTER ABBEY. 1665.

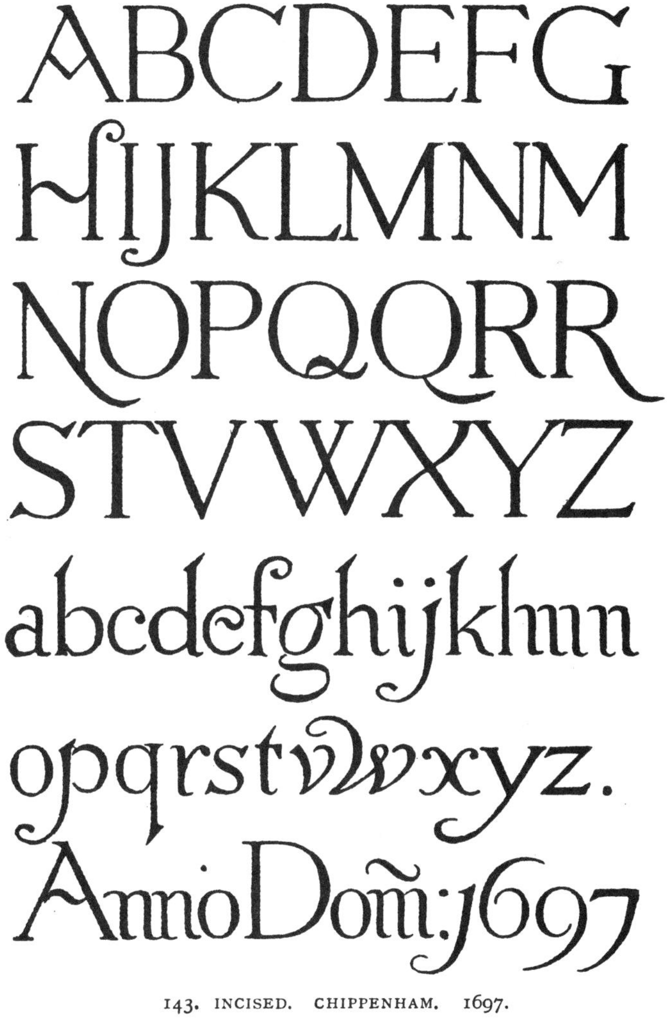

143. INCISED. CHIPPENHAM. 1697.

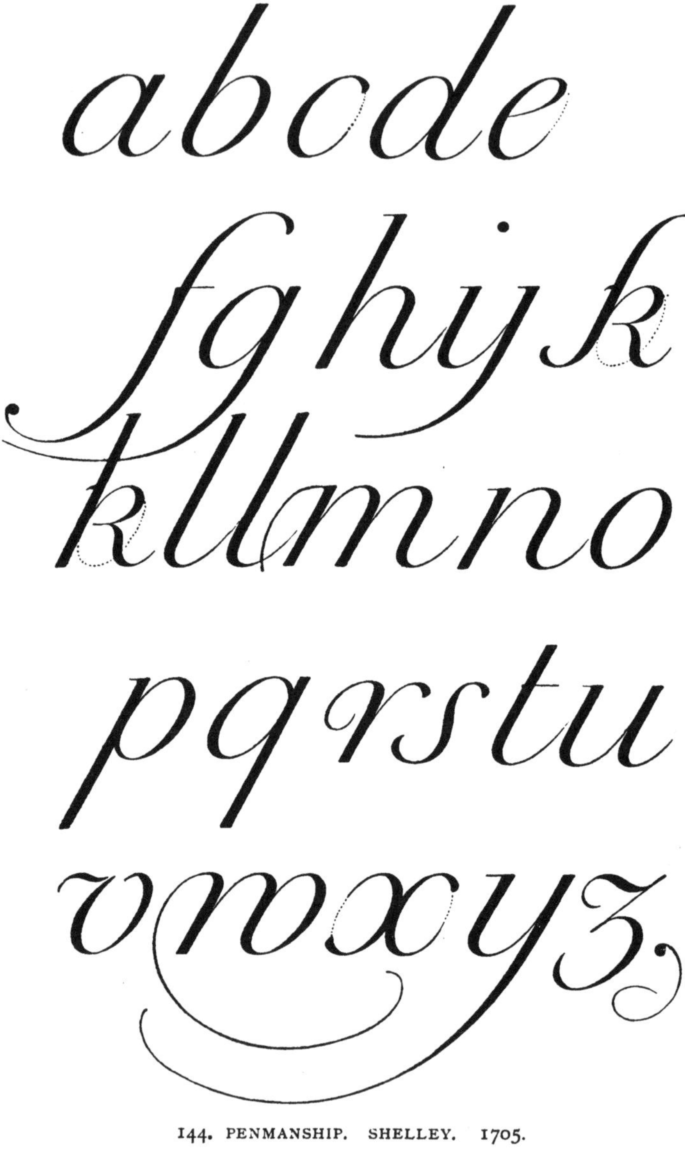

144. PENMANSHIP. SHELLEY. 1705.

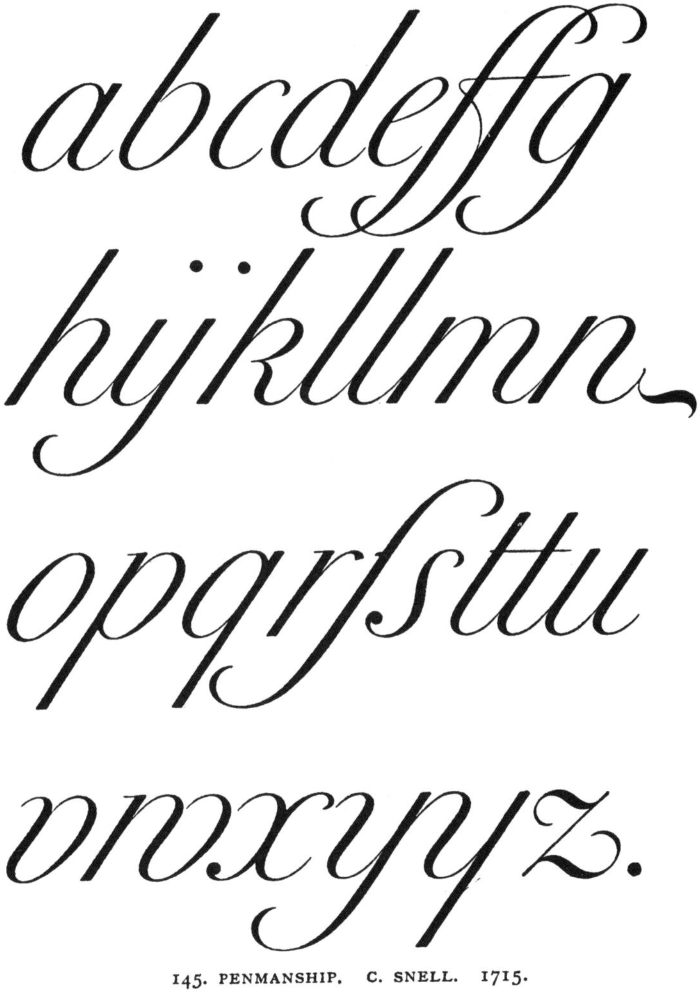

145. PENMANSHIP. C. SNELL. 1715.

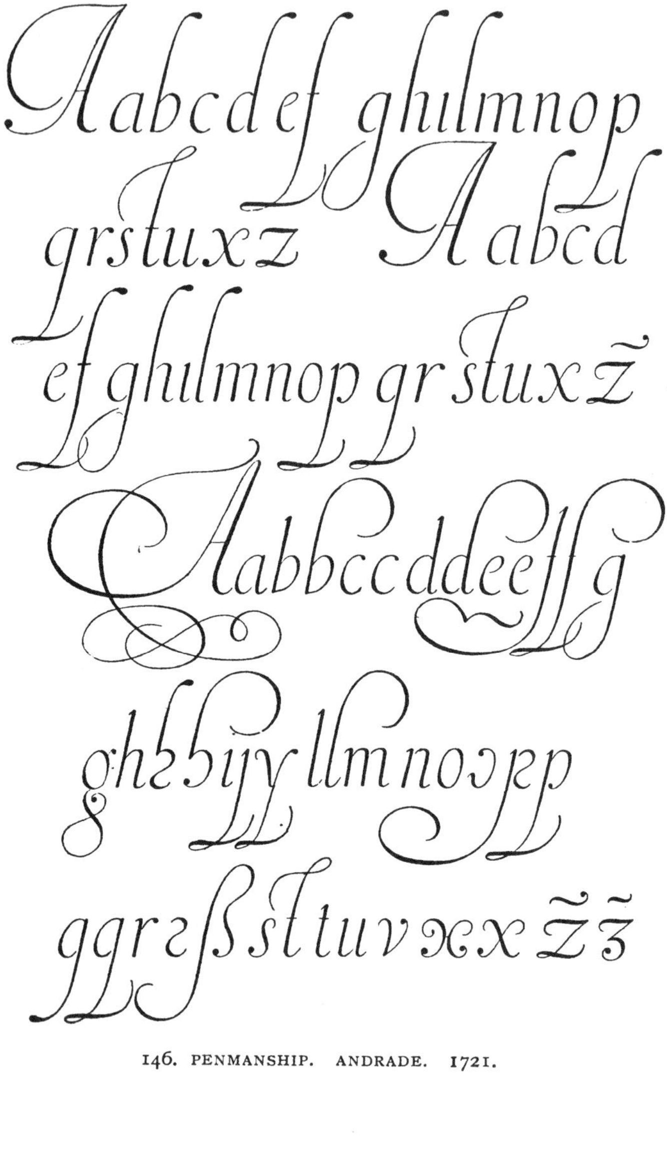

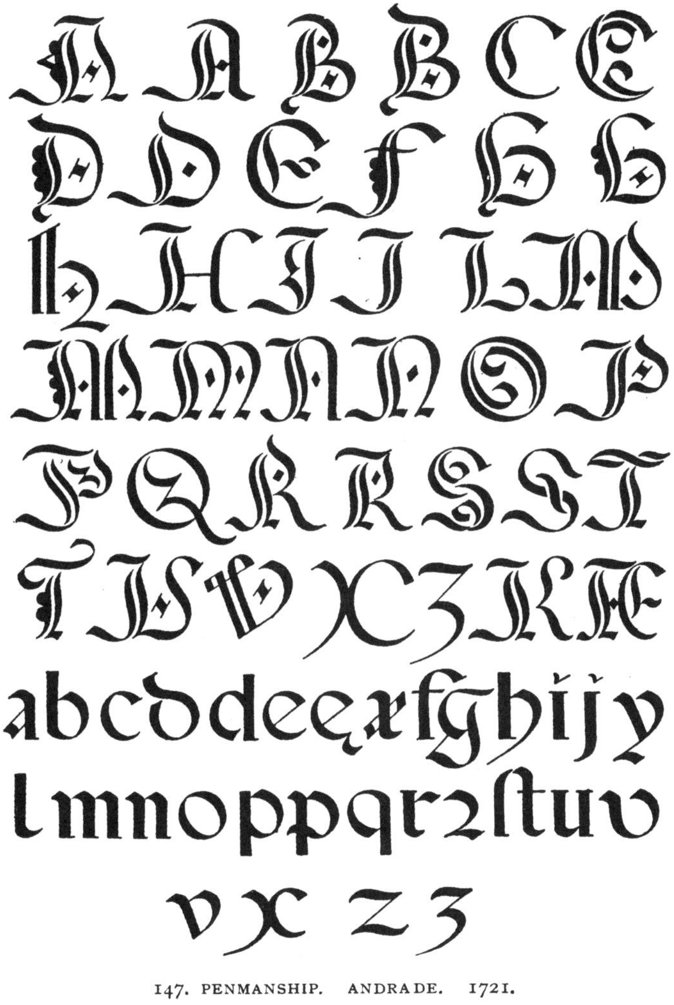

147. PENMANSHIP. ANDRADE. 1721.

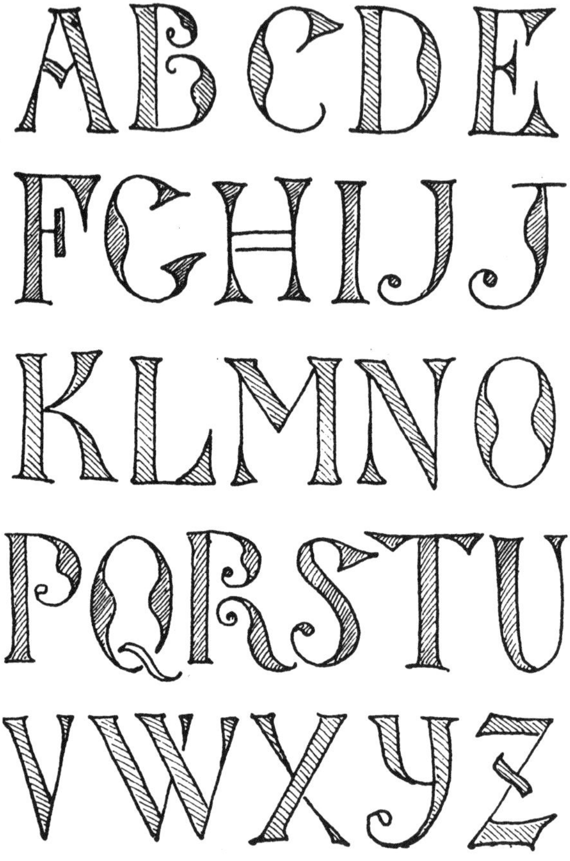

148. PAINTED. GERMAN. 1727.

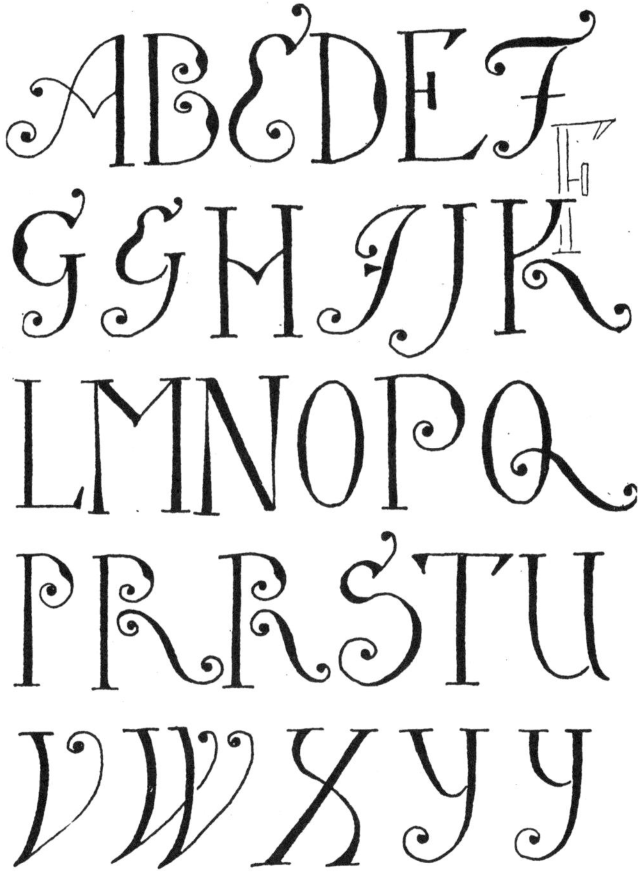

149. PENWORK. GERMAN. J. H. TIEMROTH. 1738-48.

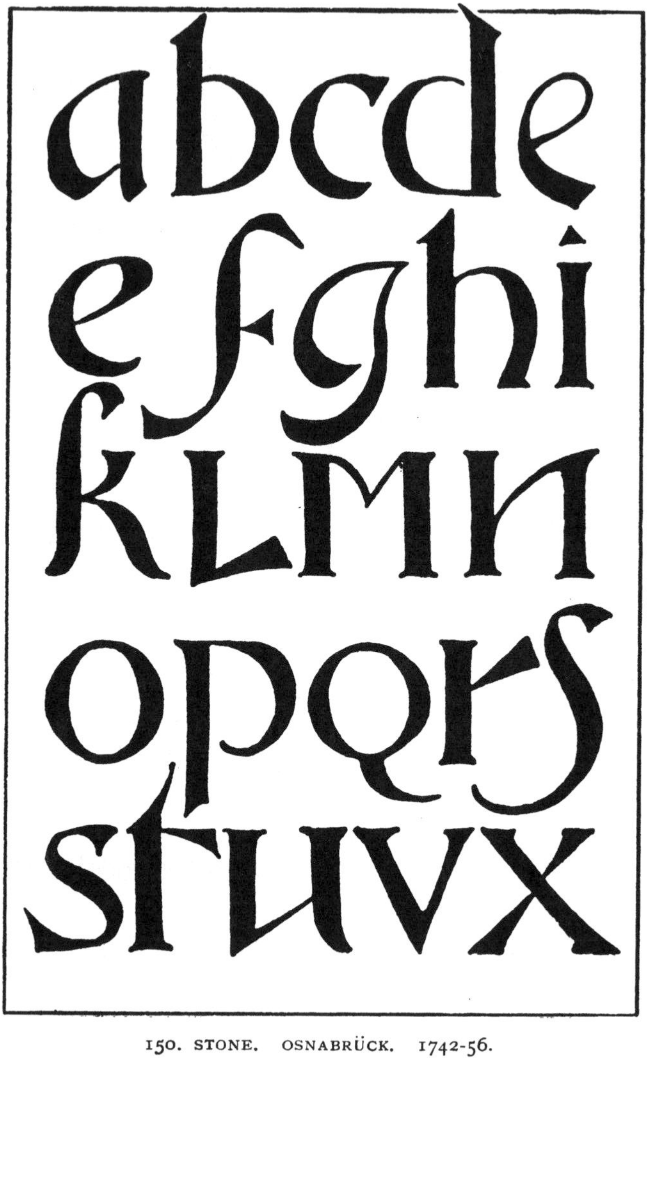

150. STONE. OSNABRÜCK. 1742-56.

151. FRENCH, E. GUICHARD. PERIOD OF LOUIS XV.

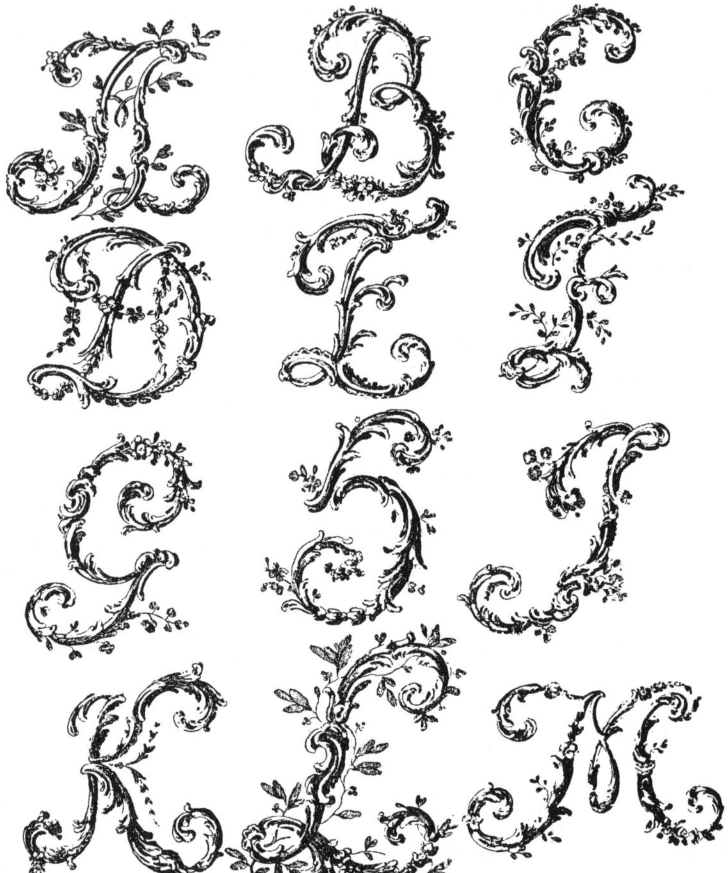

152. FRENCH. LAURENT.

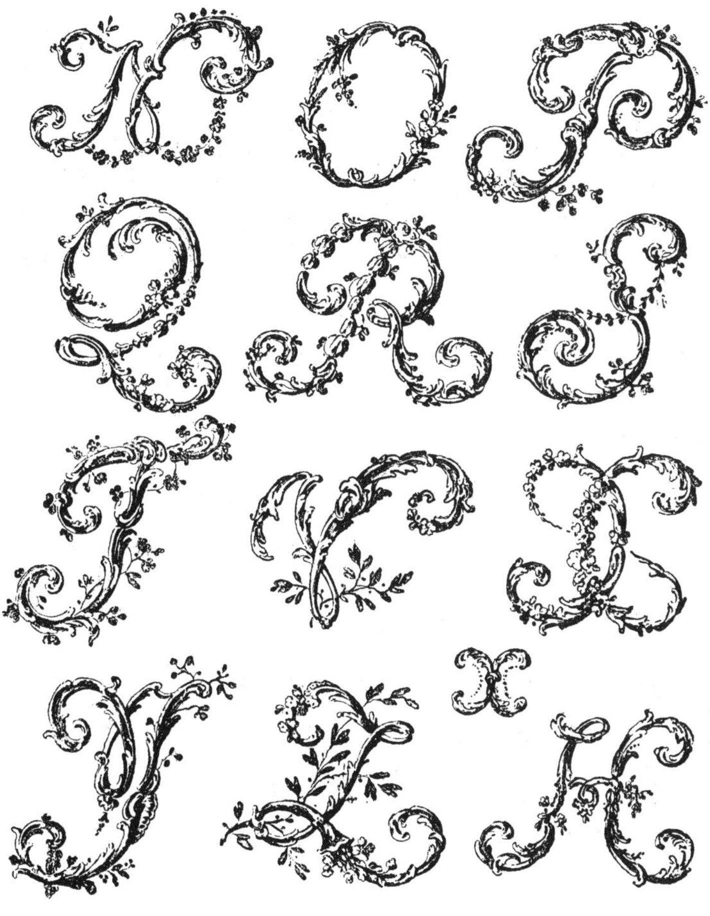

PERIOD OF LOUIS XV.

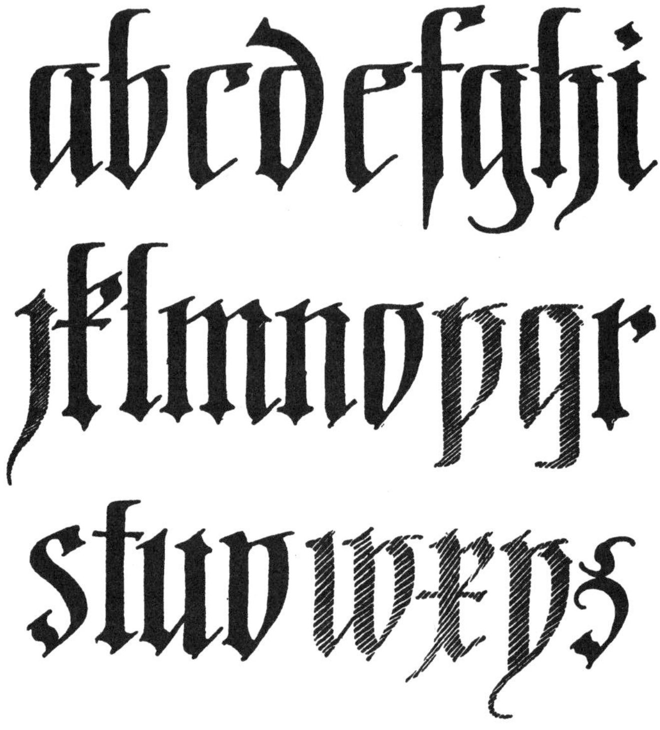

153. ETCHED ON LITHOGRAPHIC STONE. NUREMBERG. 1765-70.

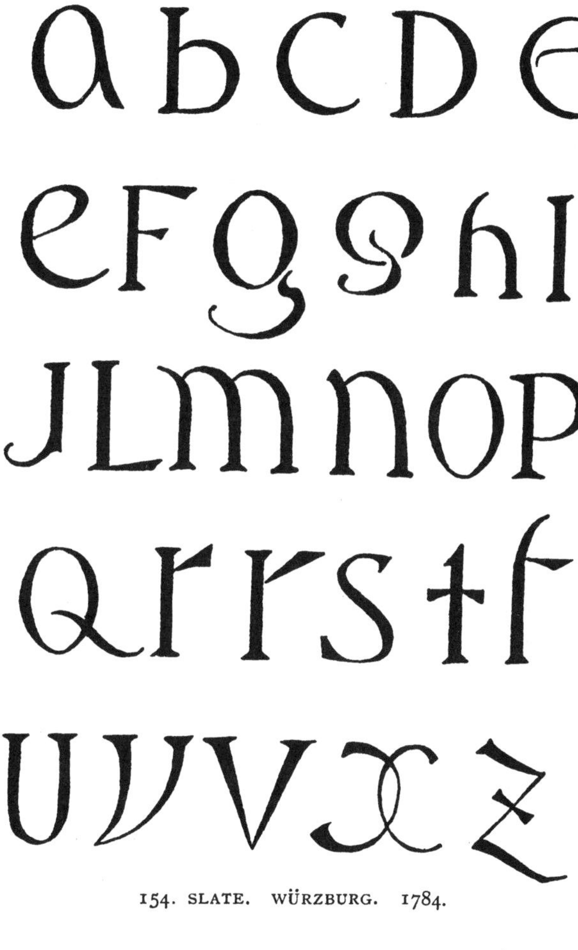

154. SLATE. WÜRZBURG. 1784.

ABCDEFG
HIJKLMN
OPQRSTU
VWXYZ&
12345
67890

155. PRINTED "CASLON" TYPE.

abcdefghijkl

mnopqrstuv

wxyz *ABCD*

EFGHIJKL

MNOPQRS

TUVWXYZ

abcdefghijklmn

opqrstuvwxyz

156. PRINTED "CASLON" TYPE.

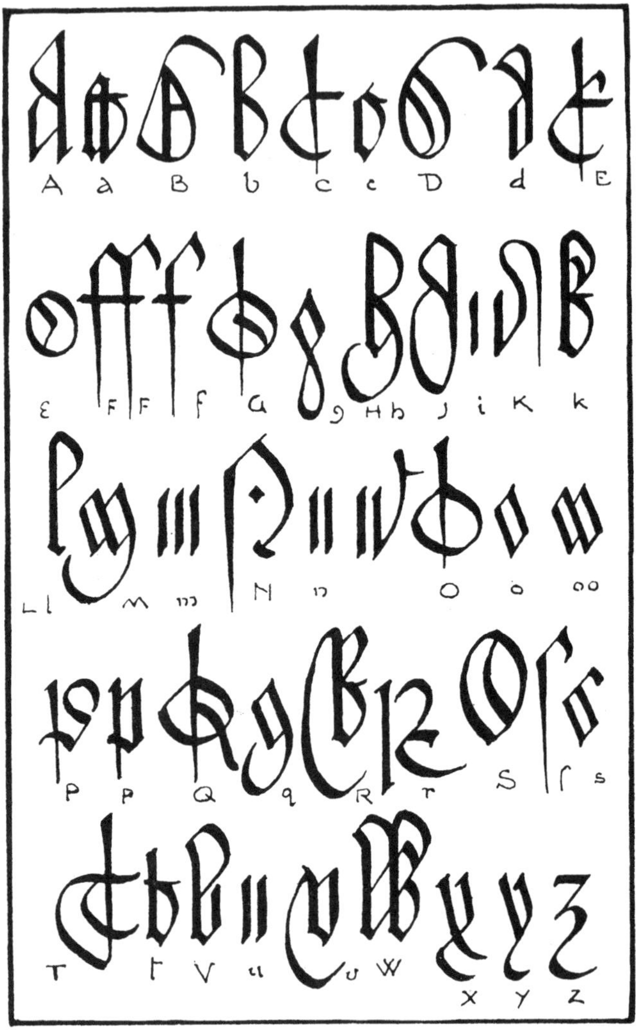

157. ENGLISH COURTHAND. FROM A. WRIGHT'S "COURTHAND RESTORED." 1815.

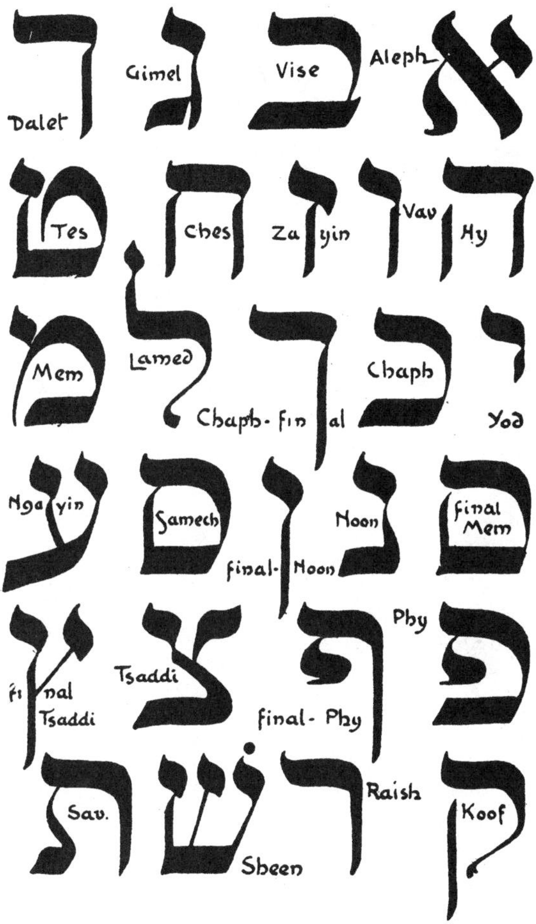

158. HEBREW ALPHABET.

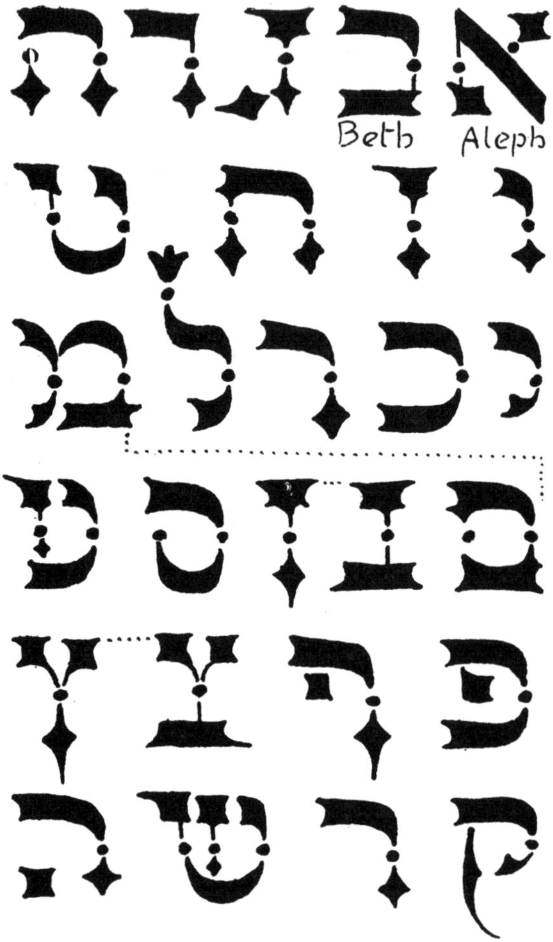

159. HEBREW ALPHABET. FROM SILVESTRE'S PALEGRAPHIE.

MODERN ALPHABETS

SHOWING THE CHARACTER WHICH COMES OF USING PEN, CHISEL, OR WHATEVER IT MAY BE

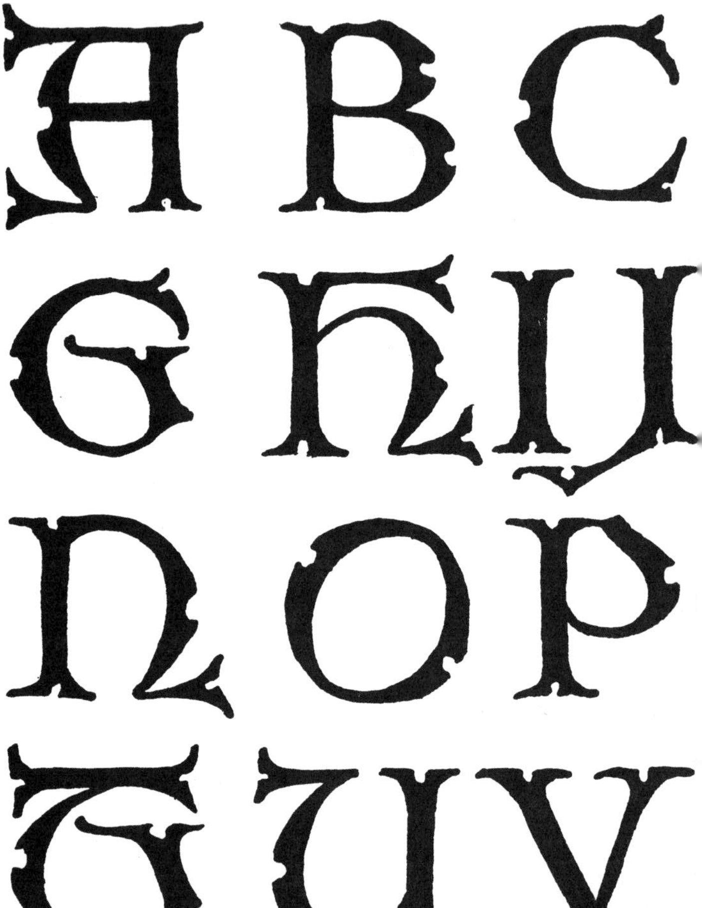

160. PENWORK

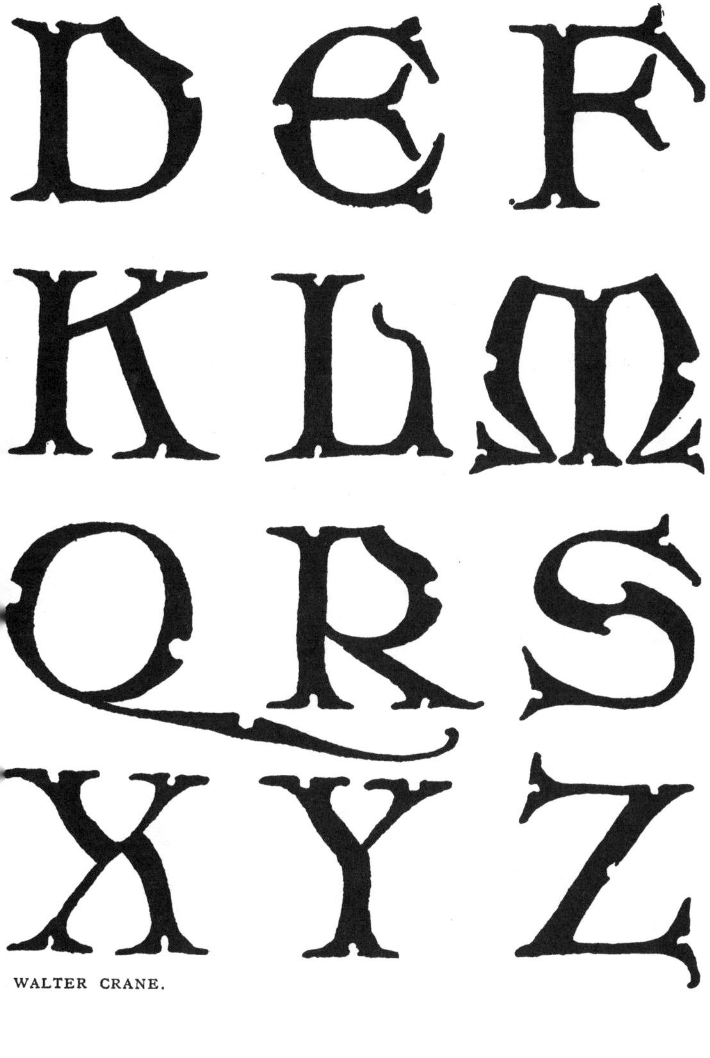

WALTER CRANE.

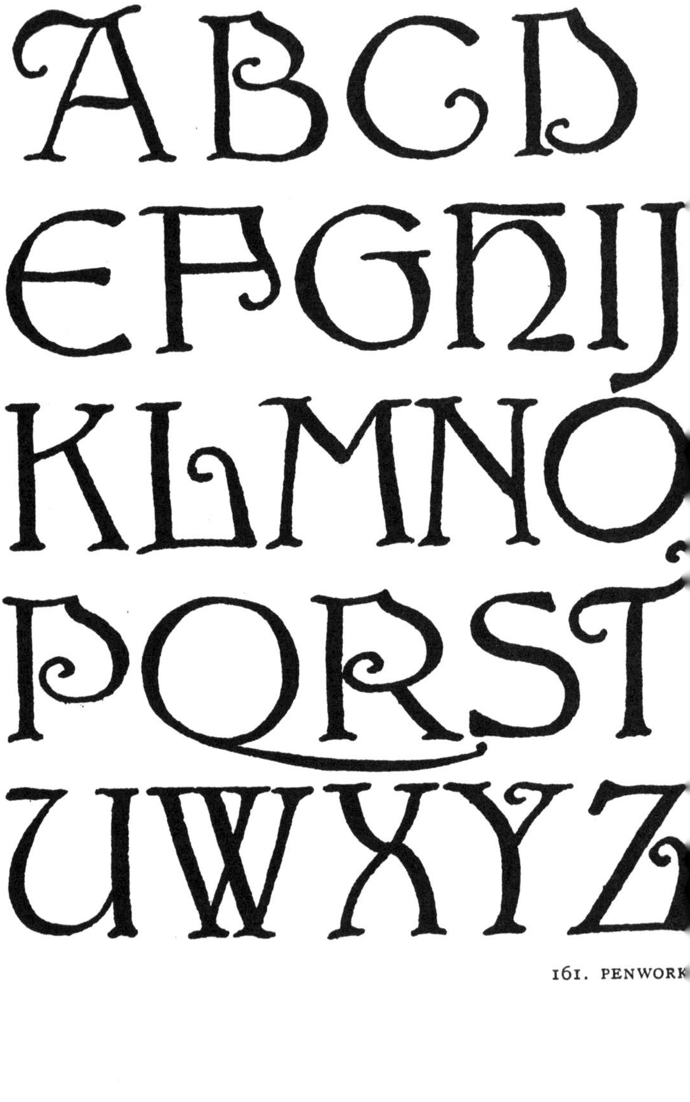

161. PENWORK

a b c d e
f g h i j k
l m n o p
q r s t u v
w x y
z

WALTER CRANE.

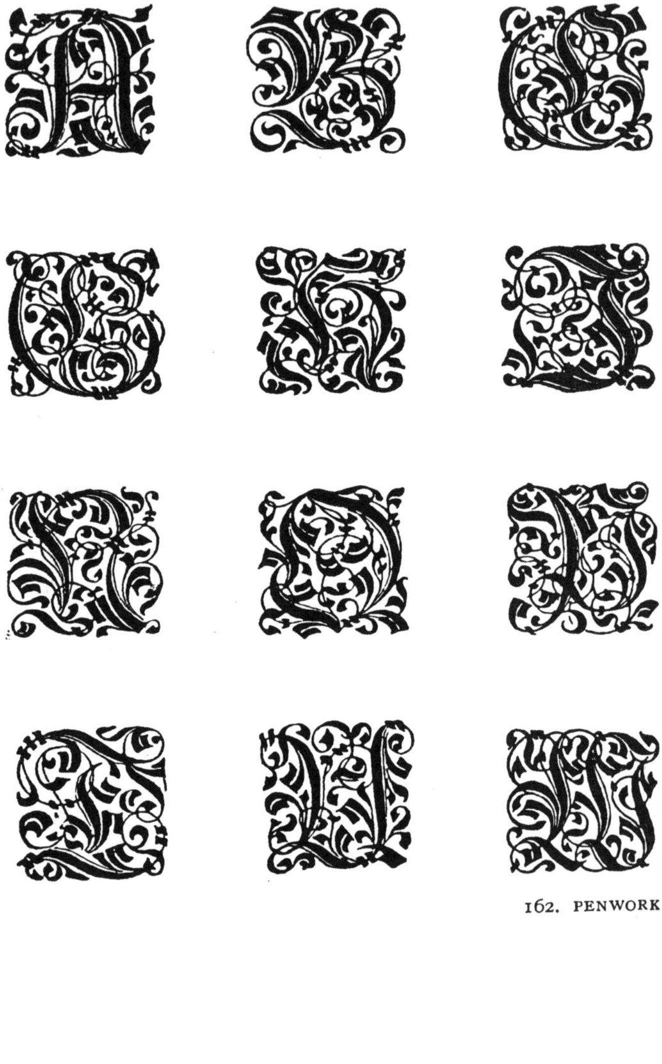

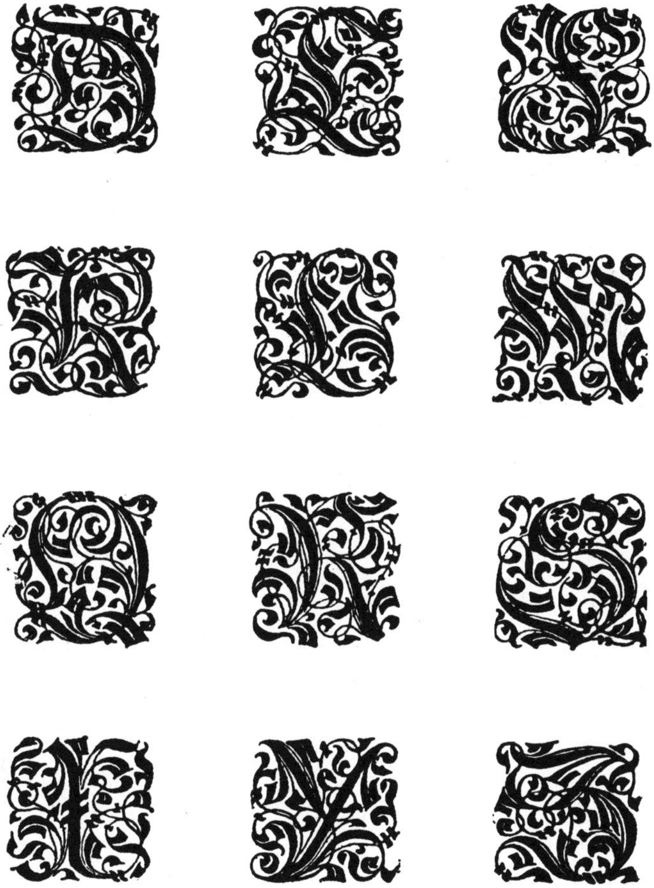

TTO HUPP.

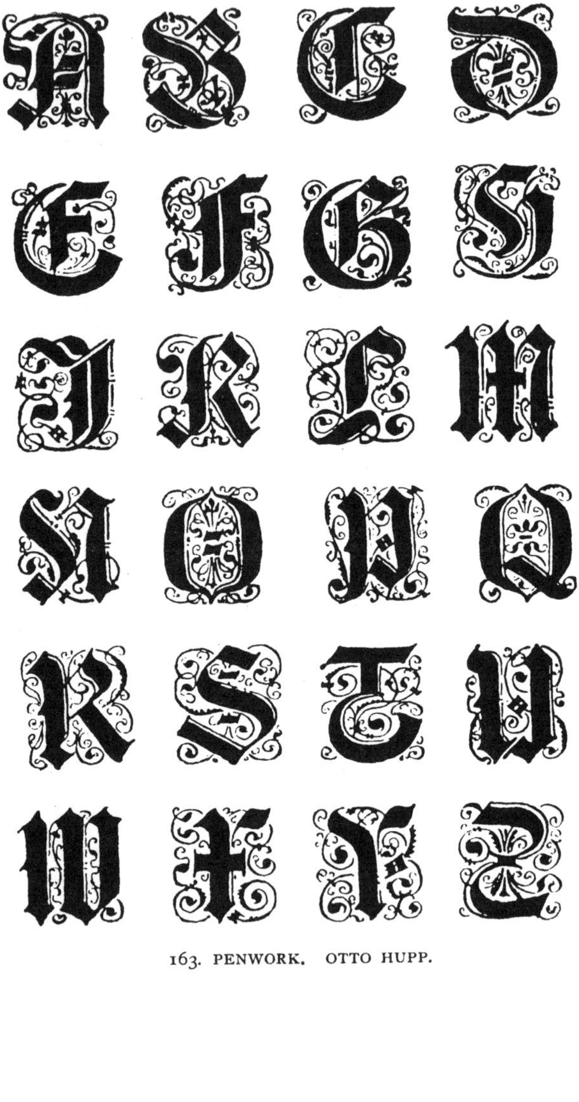

163. PENWORK. OTTO HUPP.

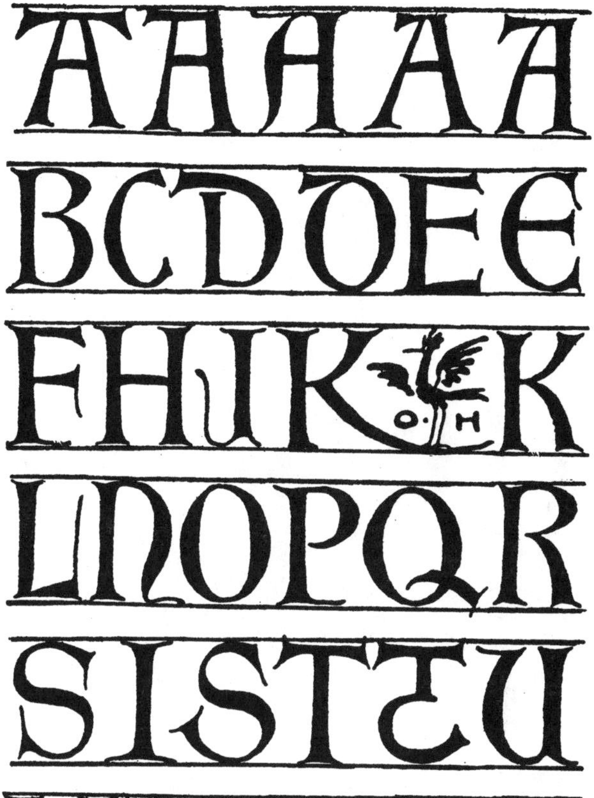

164. PENWORK. OTTO HUPP.

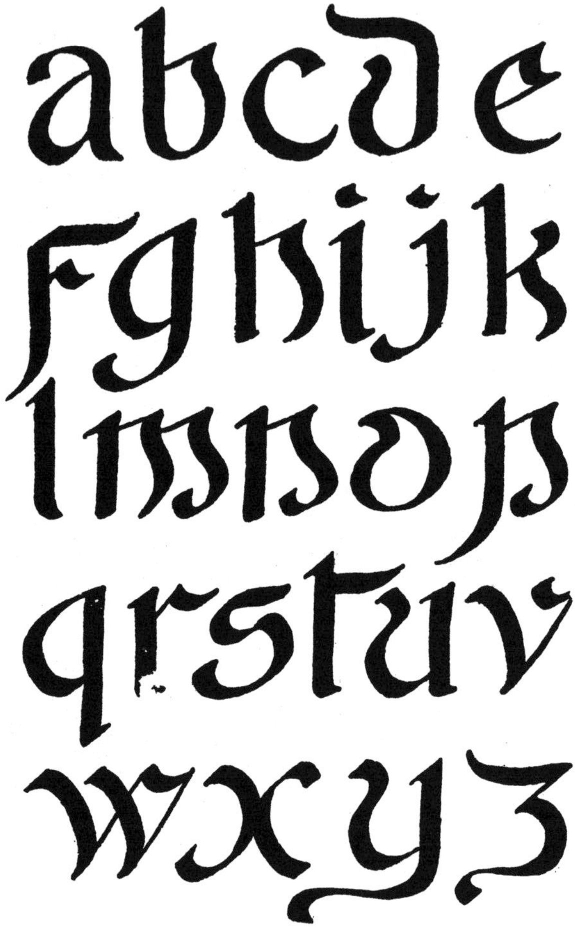

165. PEN WRITTEN. L.F.D.

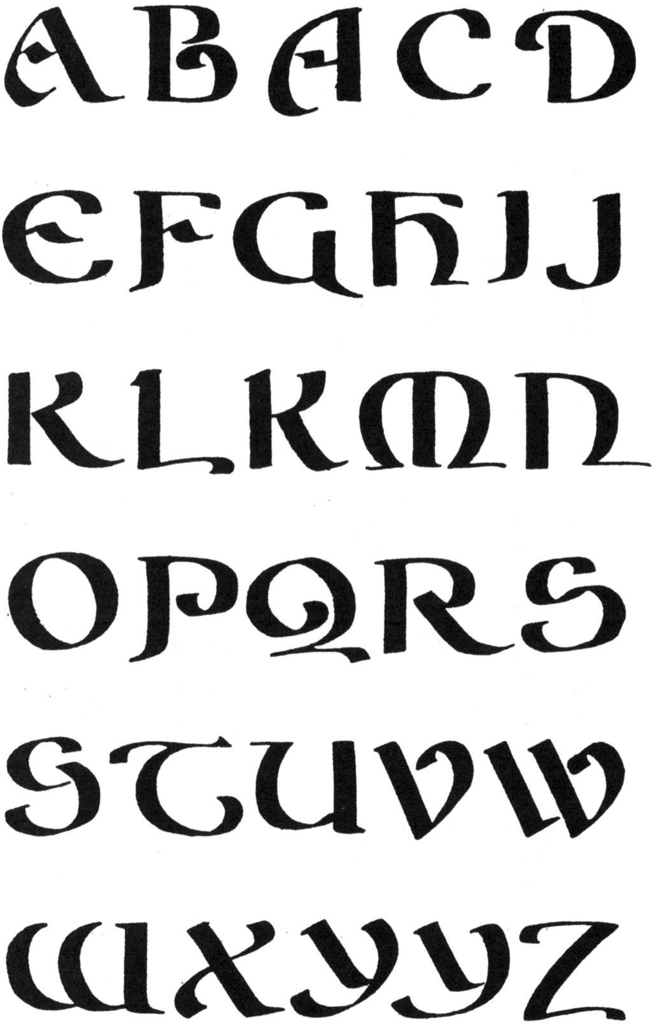

166. PEN WRITTEN. L.F.D.

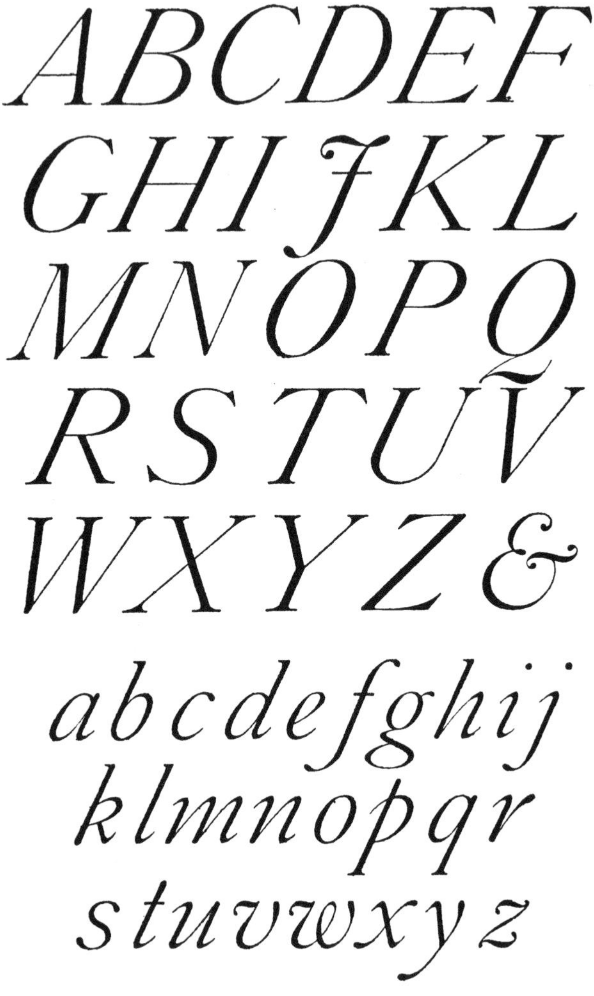

167. "OLD STYLE" ITALICS. J. VINYCOMB. PEN.

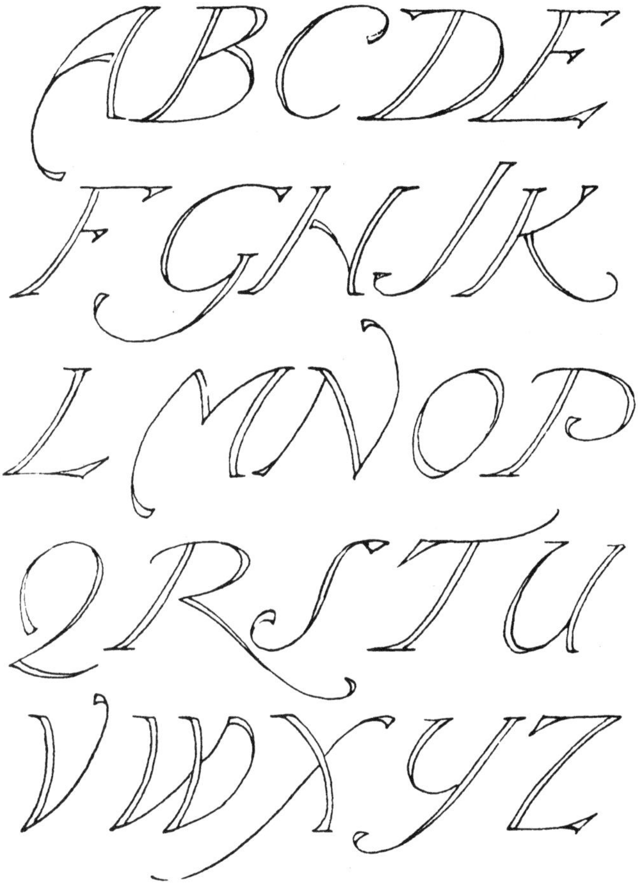

168. ITALICS. L.F.D.

ABCDEFG
HIJKLMMN
NOPQQRR
STVWXYZ
abcdefghijklmn
opqrstuvwxyz.
1234567890.

169. J. W. WEEKES.

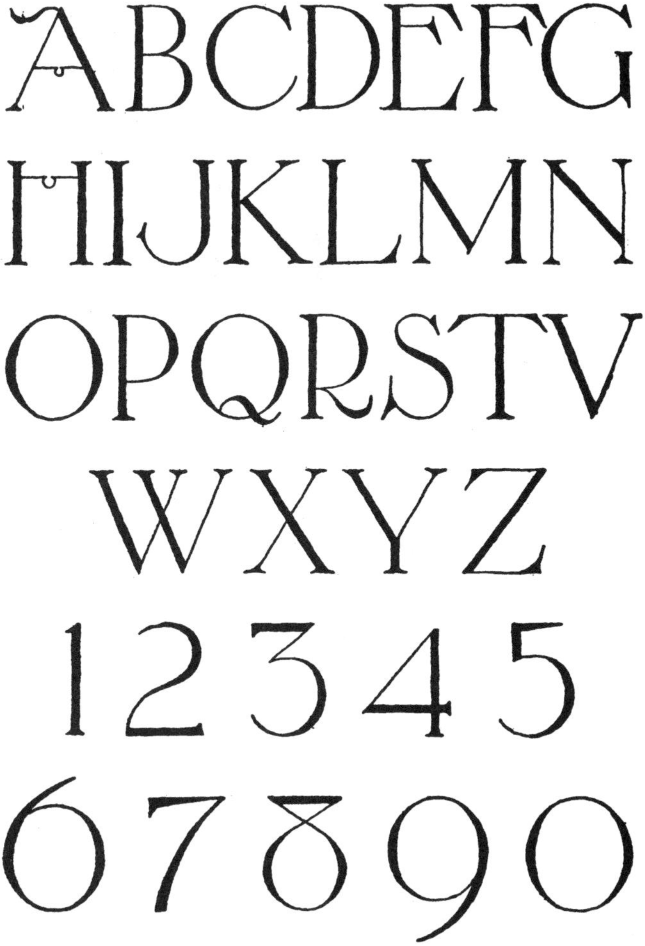

170. PENWORK. BAILEY SCOTT MURPHY, ARCHITECT.

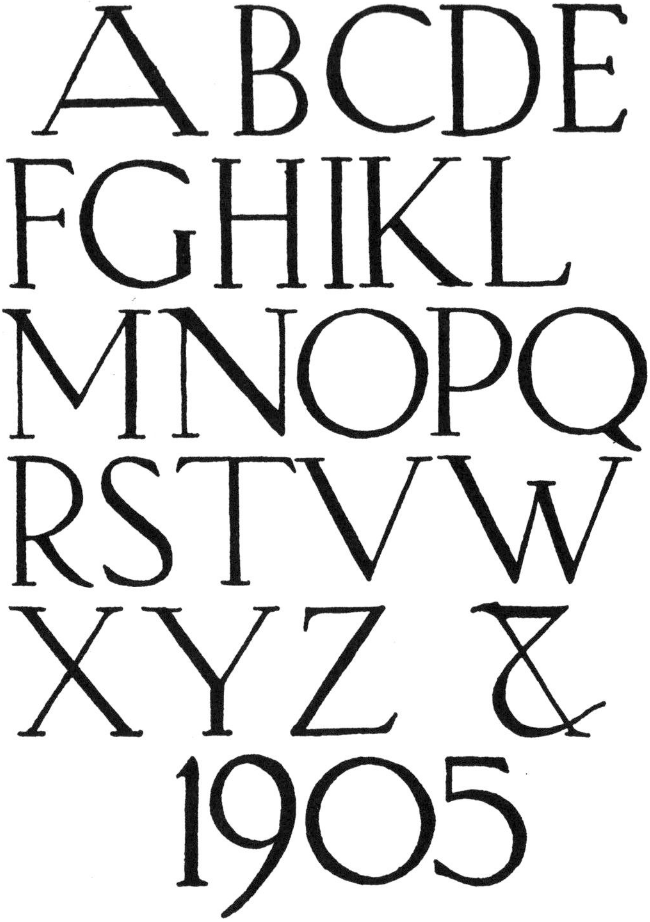

171 PENWORK. R. ANNING BELL.

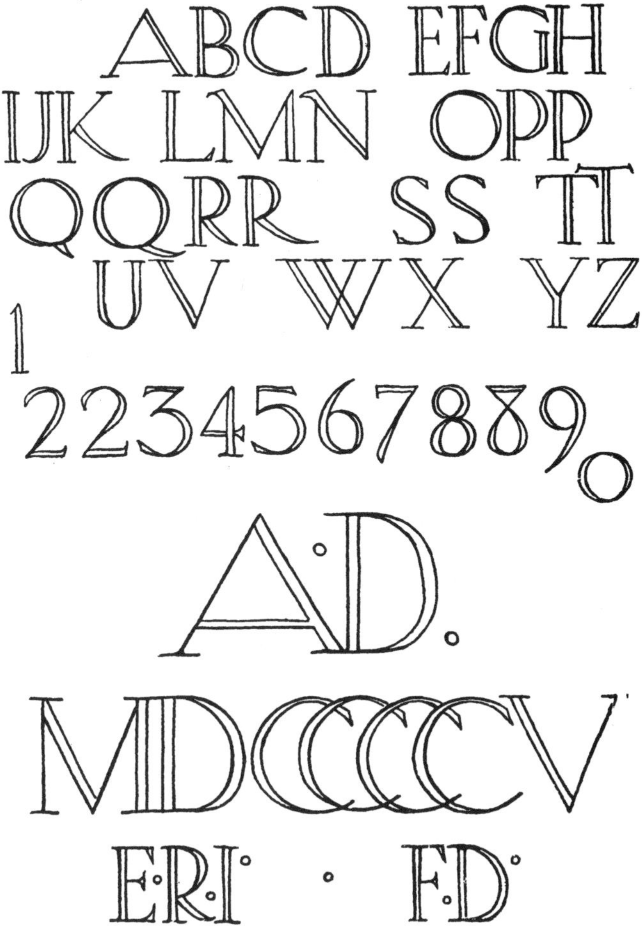

172. PENWORK. R. ANNING BELL.

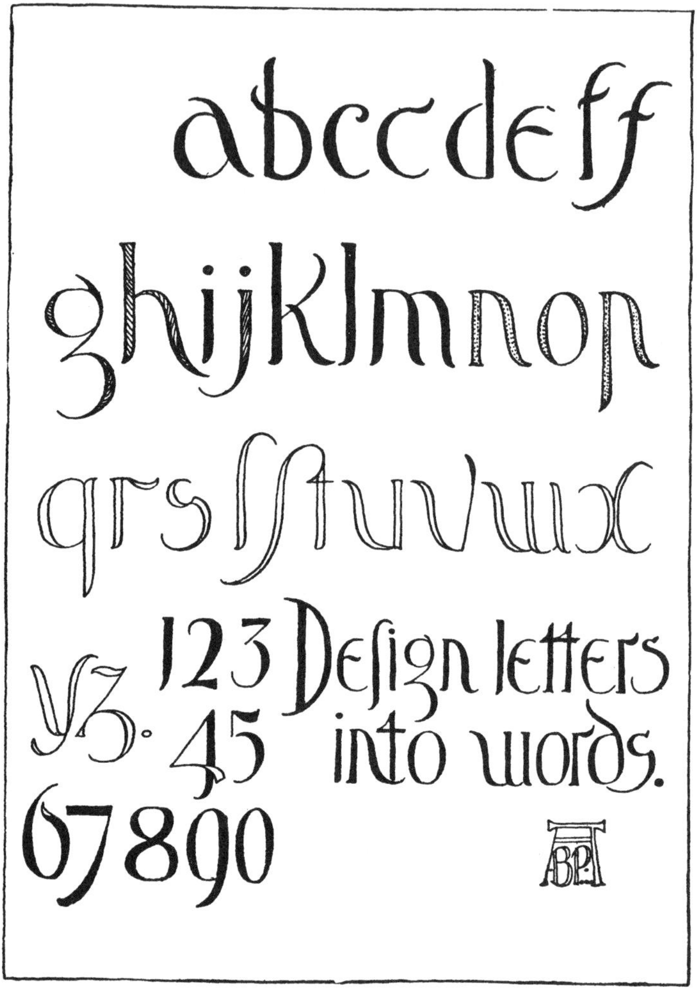

173. PENWORK. PROF. A. B. PITE, ARCHITECT.

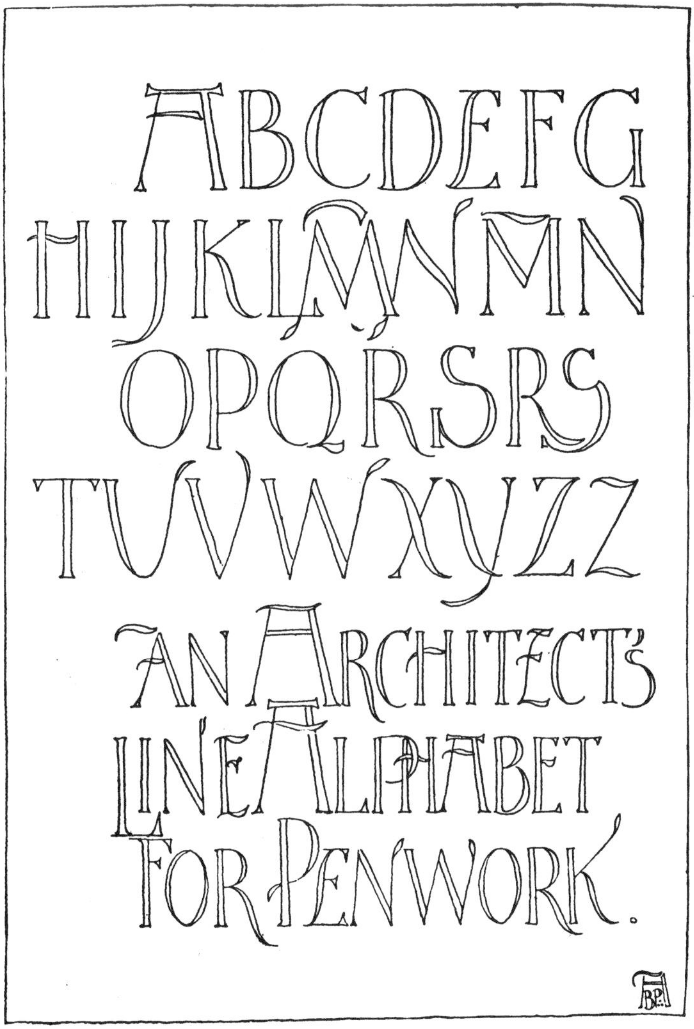

174. PENWORK. PROF. A. B. PITE, ARCHITECT.

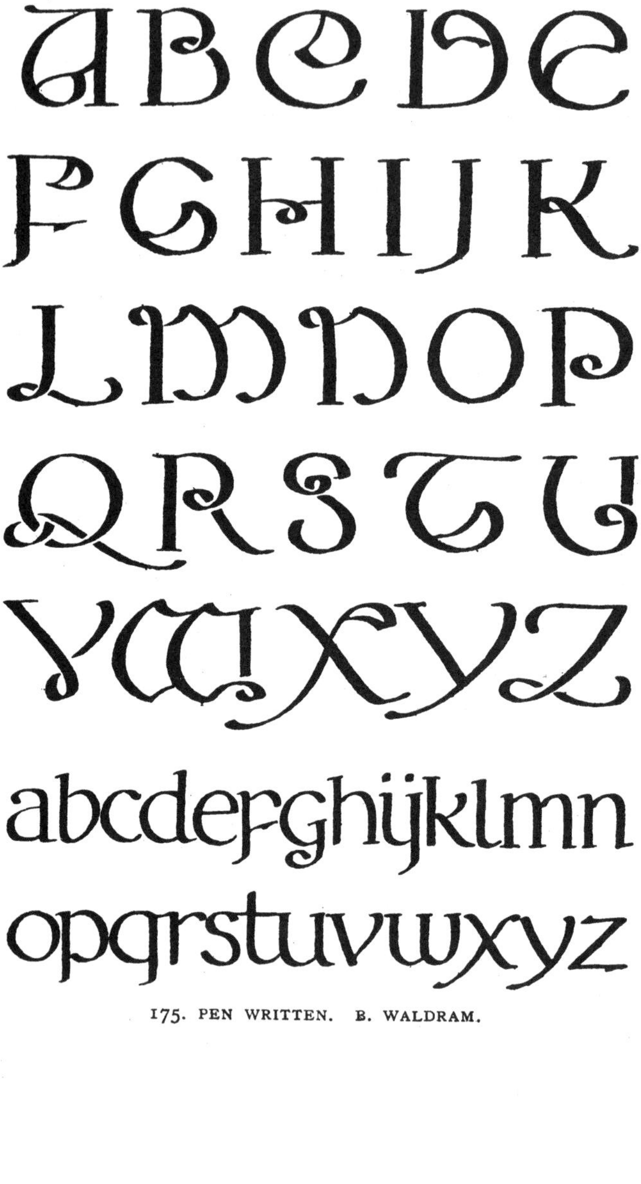

175. PEN WRITTEN. B. WALDRAM.

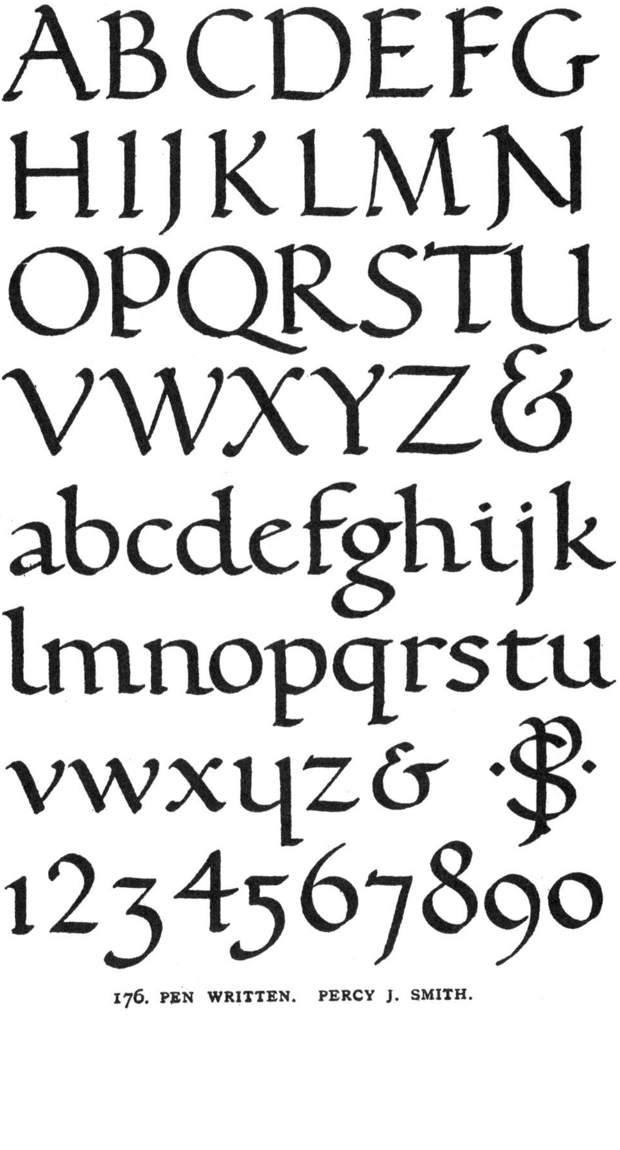

176. PEN WRITTEN. PERCY J. SMITH.

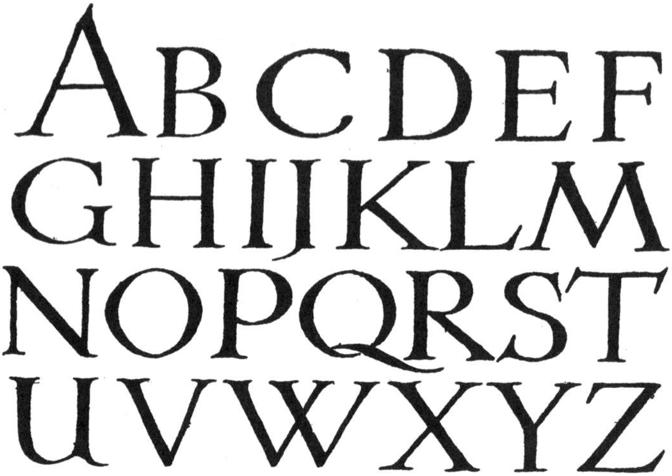

177. PEN-DRAWN "ROMAN" CAPITALS. B. WALDRAM.

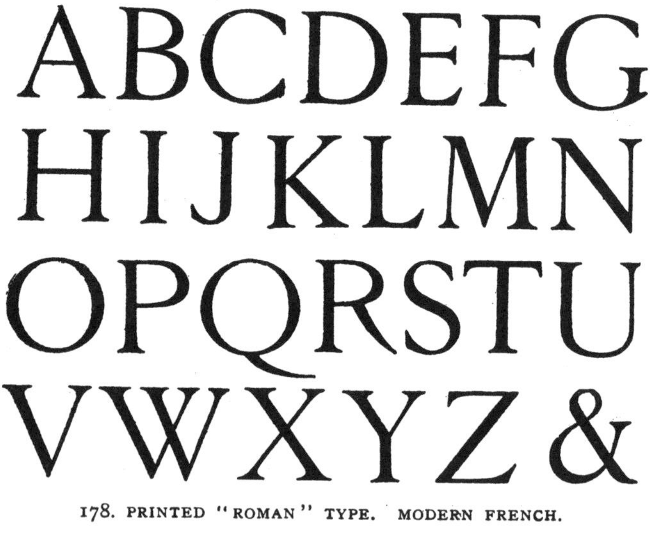

178. PRINTED "ROMAN" TYPE. MODERN FRENCH.

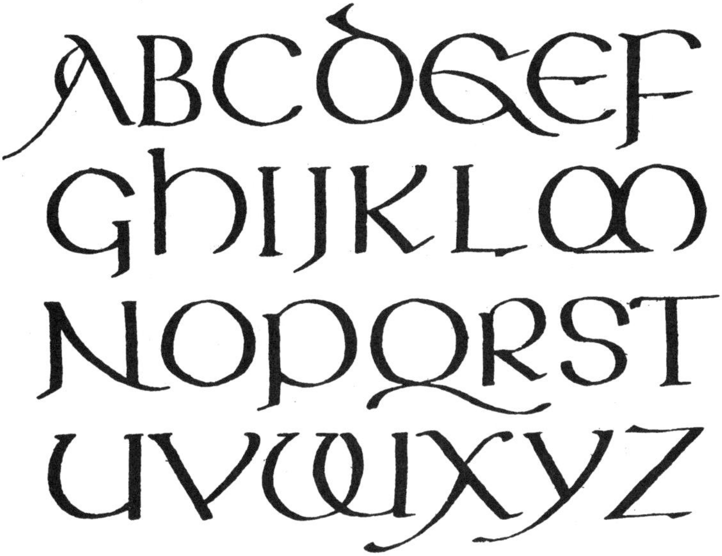

179. PEN-WRITTEN UNCIALS. B. WALDRAM.

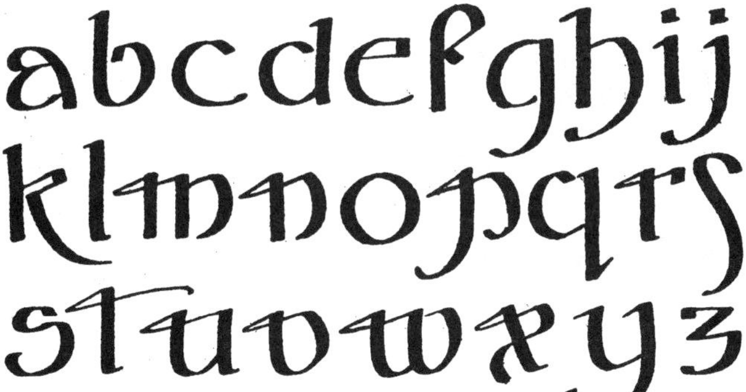

180. PEN WRITTEN. L.F.D.

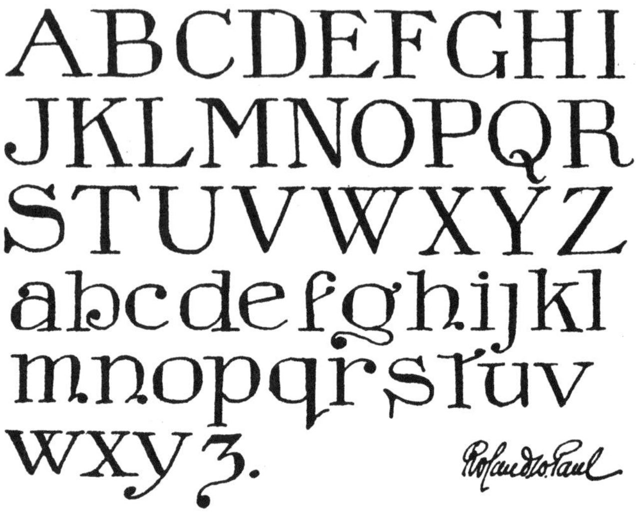

181. PENWORK. ROLAND W. PAUL, ARCHITECT.

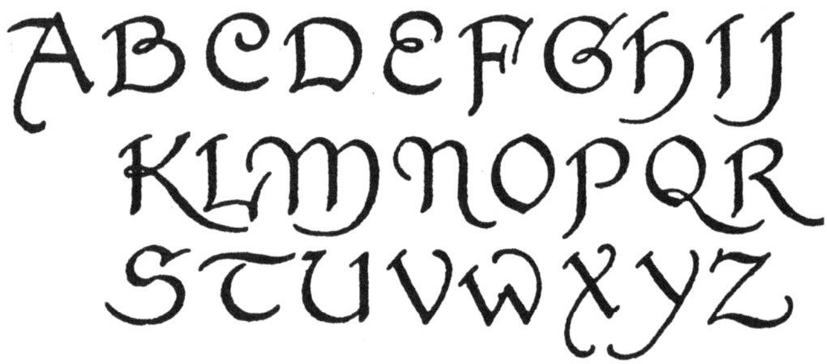

182. PENWORK. R. K. COWTAN.

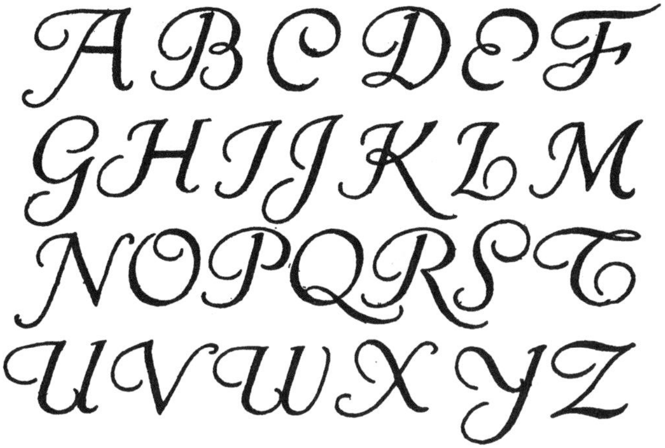

183. PENWORK. R. K. COWTAN.

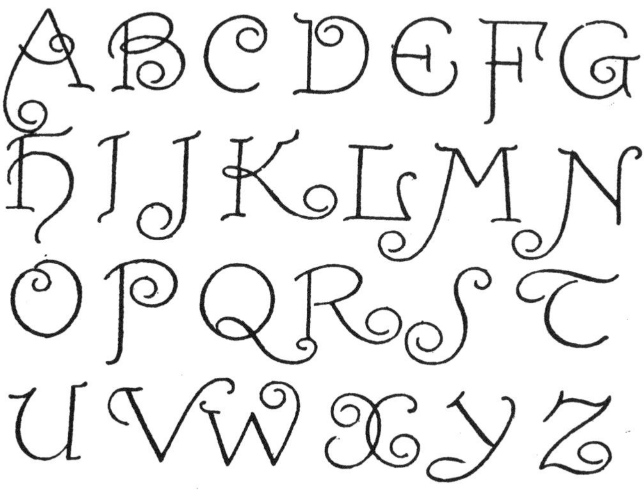

184. PENWORK. R. K. COWTAN.

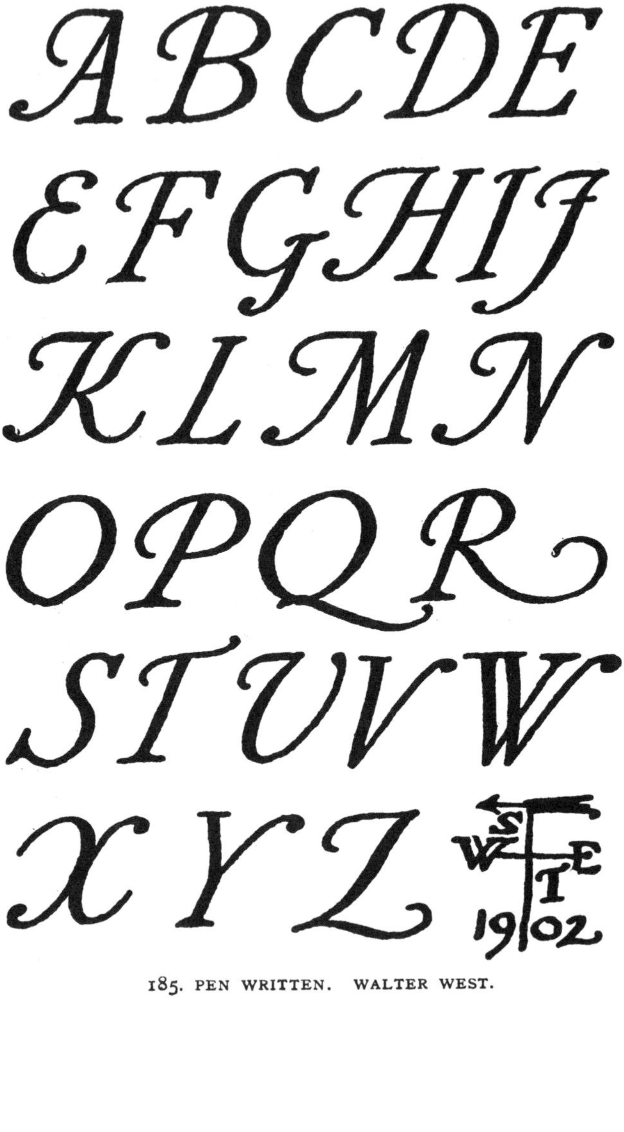

185. PEN WRITTEN. WALTER WEST.

abcdefghijklmn
opqrstuvwxyz

Of course the first question is that of materi:
al; and care must be taken to choose or de:
sign an alphabet, not only practicable in,
but suitable to, the medium in which it is
to be executed. One of the commonest errors
is that of taking a style of lettering excell:
ent when written on parchment or paper, with
a quill pen, and carving it, let us say for
example, on wood. Of course the result is
often, although by no means necessarily so,
incongruous in the extreme. Many letter-
forms are, indeed, interchangeable in this
way: but if it is desired to adapt the letter.
ing of one class of object to the purposes of

186. CURSIVE WRITING. SELWYN IMAGE.

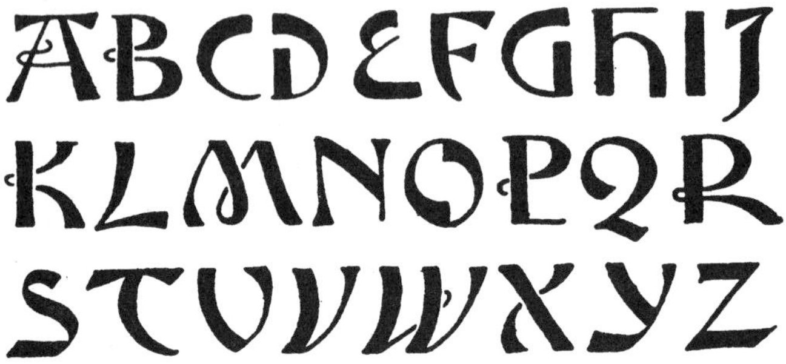

187. DESIGNED FOR ENGRAVING ON METAL; BUT NOT UNSUITED TO PENWORK. L.F.D.

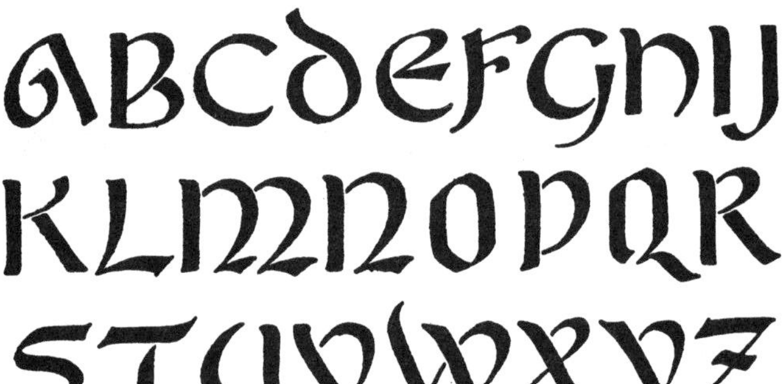

188. PEN WRITTEN. L.F.D.

ABCDEFG
HIJKLMN
OPQRSTU
VWXYZ &

abcdefghijkl
mnopqrstuv
wxyz

1234567890

189. FRENCH PRINTED TYPE. DESIGNED BY GRASSET (?).

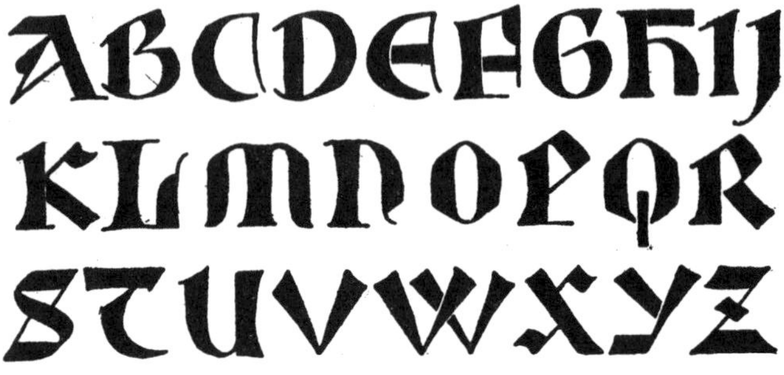

190. ENGRAVING. ADAPTED FROM MEDIÆVAL GOLDSMITH'S WORK.
L.F D.

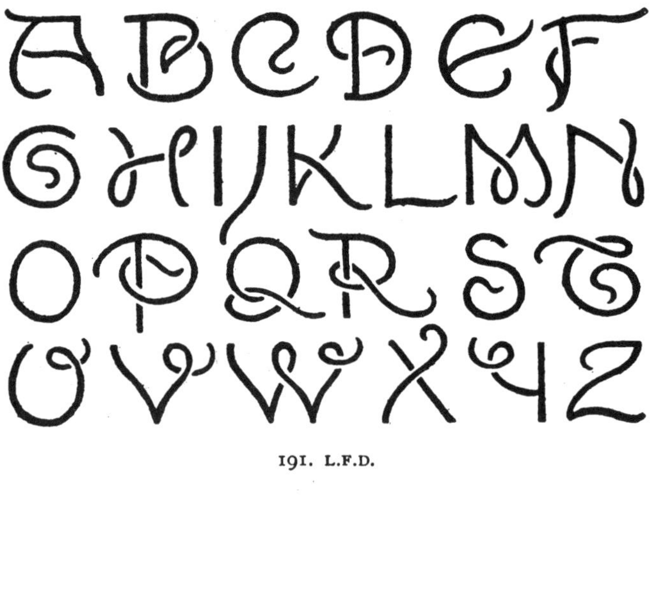

191. L.F.D.

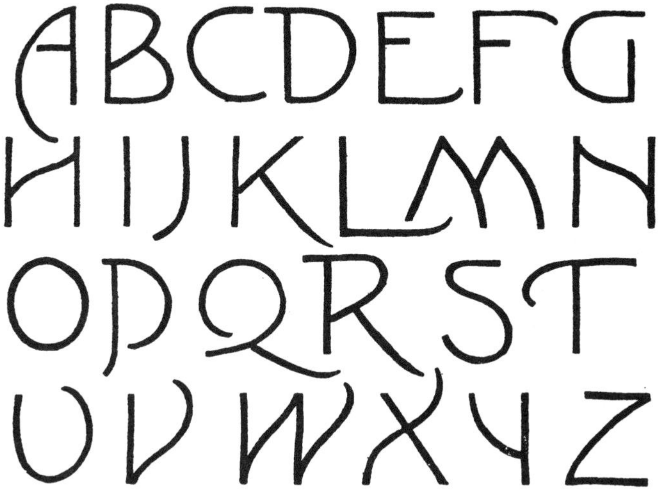

192. L.F.D.

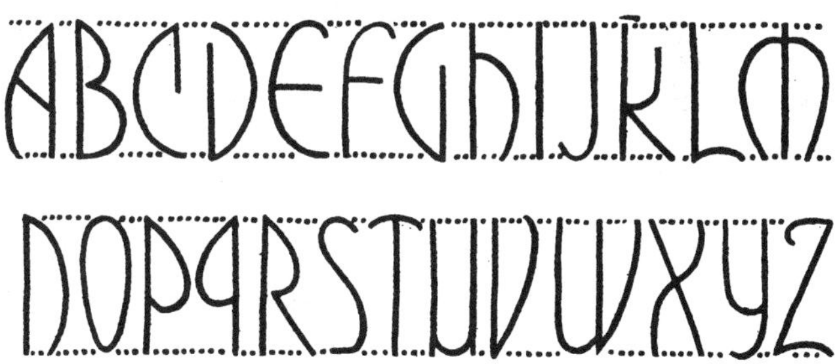

193. SCRATCHING. ADAPTED FROM OLD SPANISH. L.F.D.

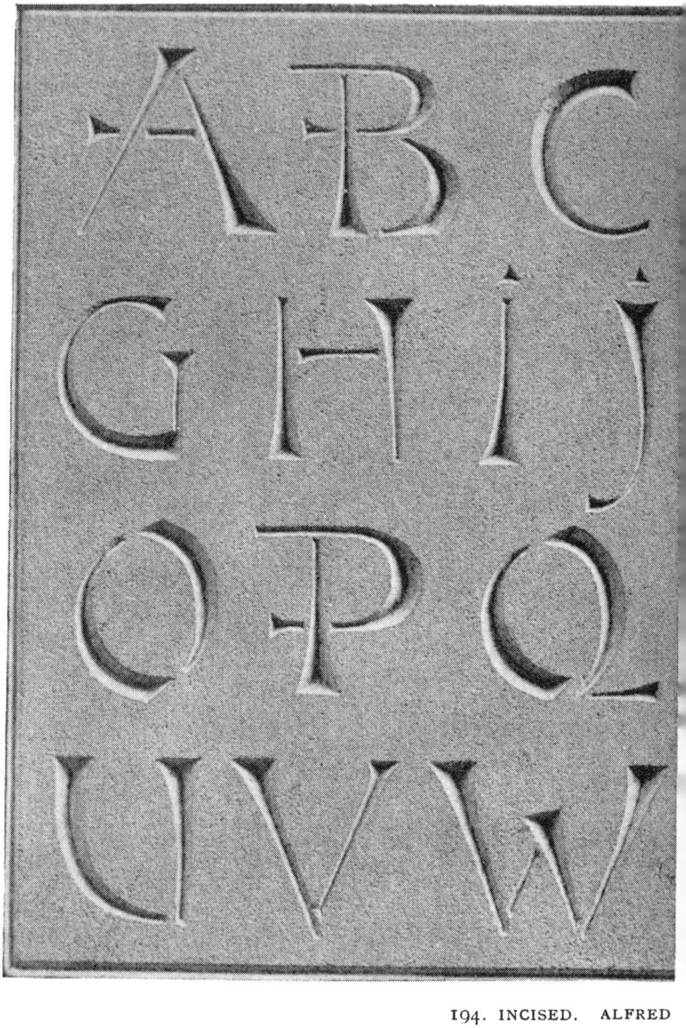

194. INCISED. ALFRED

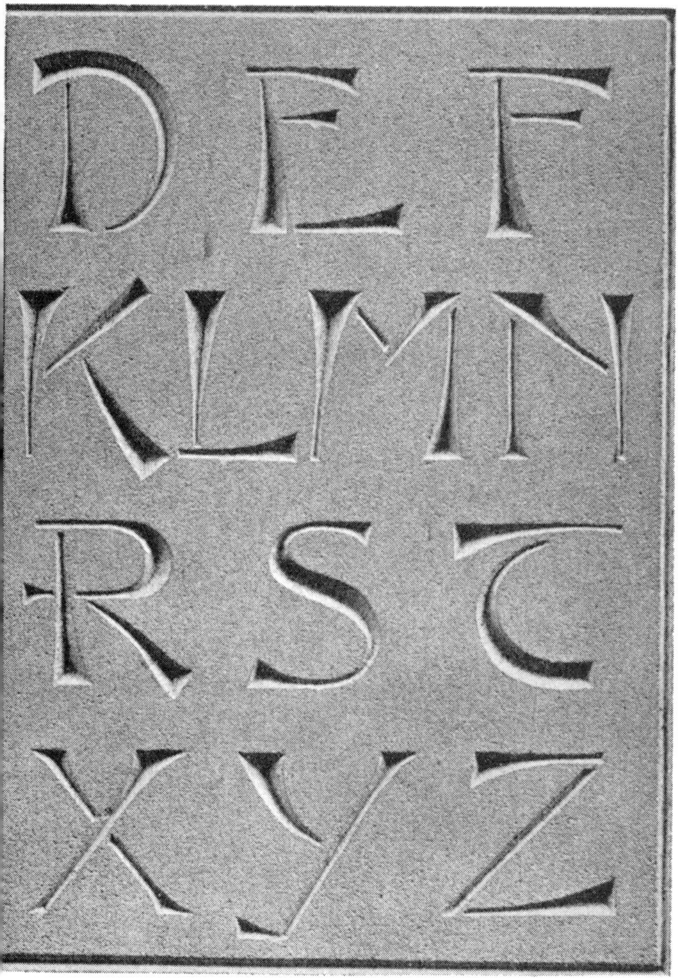

CARPENTER AND L.F.D.

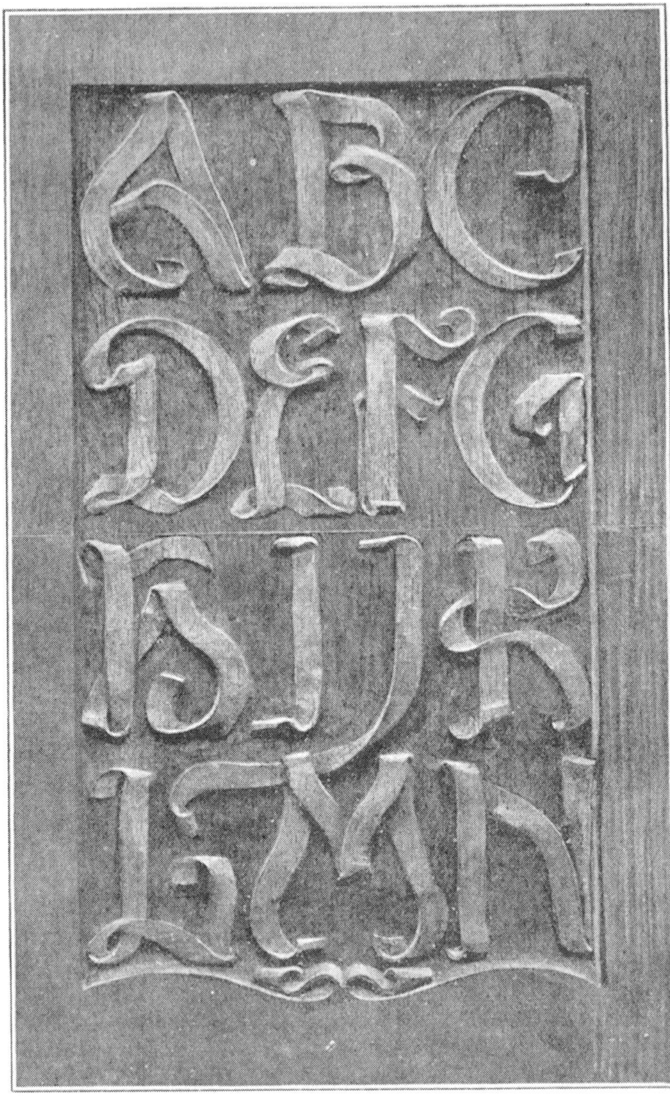

195. WOOD

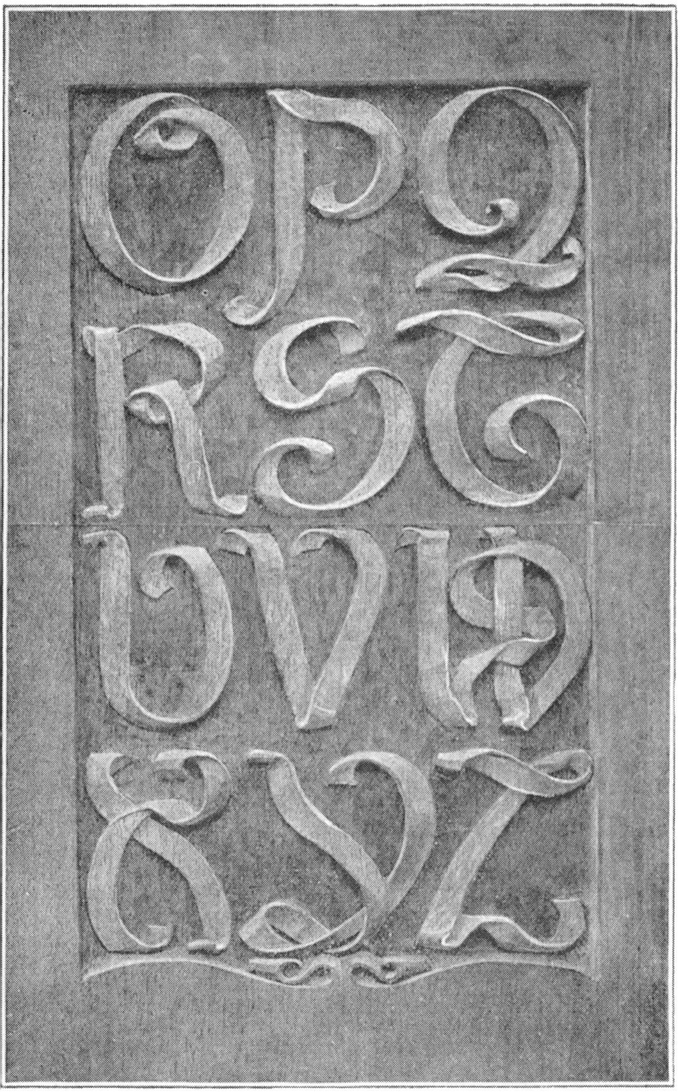

CARVING. L.F.D.

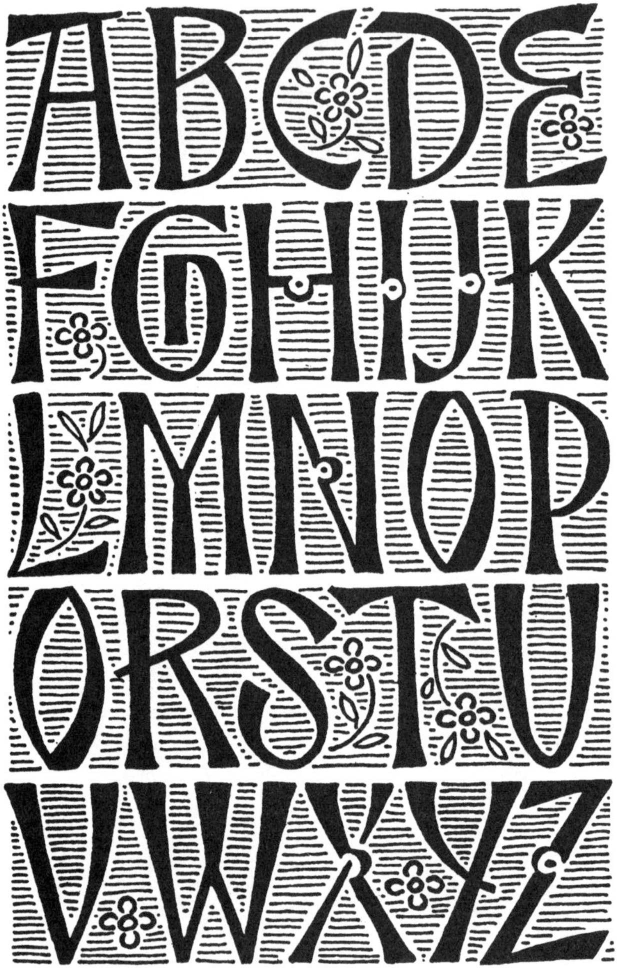

196. ENGRAVING ON SILVER. L.F.D.

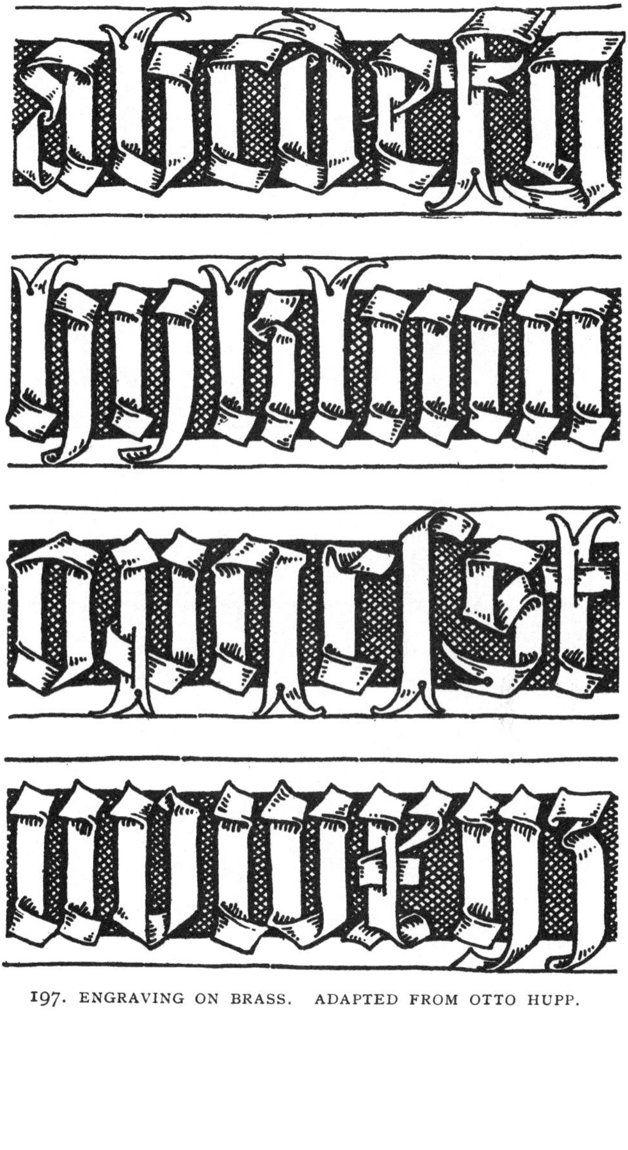

197. ENGRAVING ON BRASS. ADAPTED FROM OTTO HUPP.

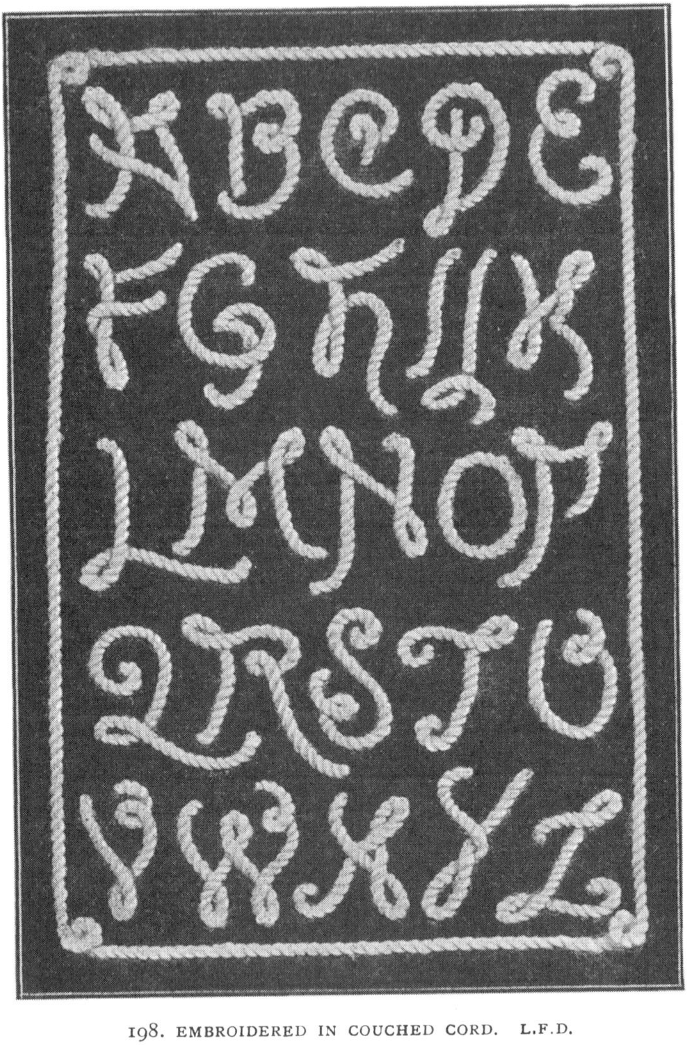

198. EMBROIDERED IN COUCHED CORD. L.F.D.

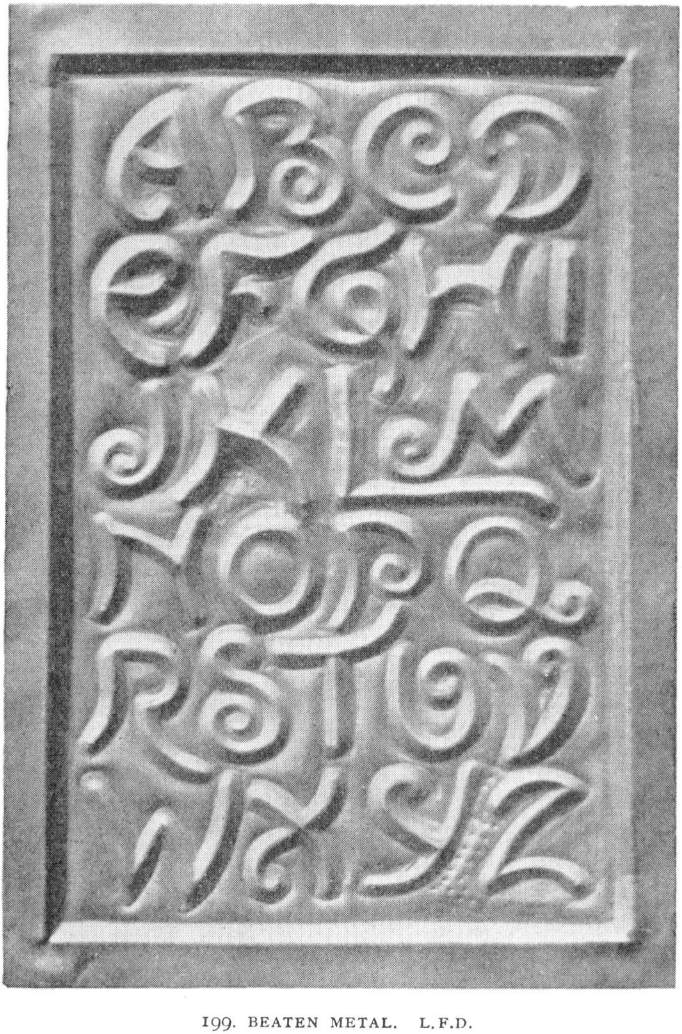

199. BEATEN METAL. L.F.D.

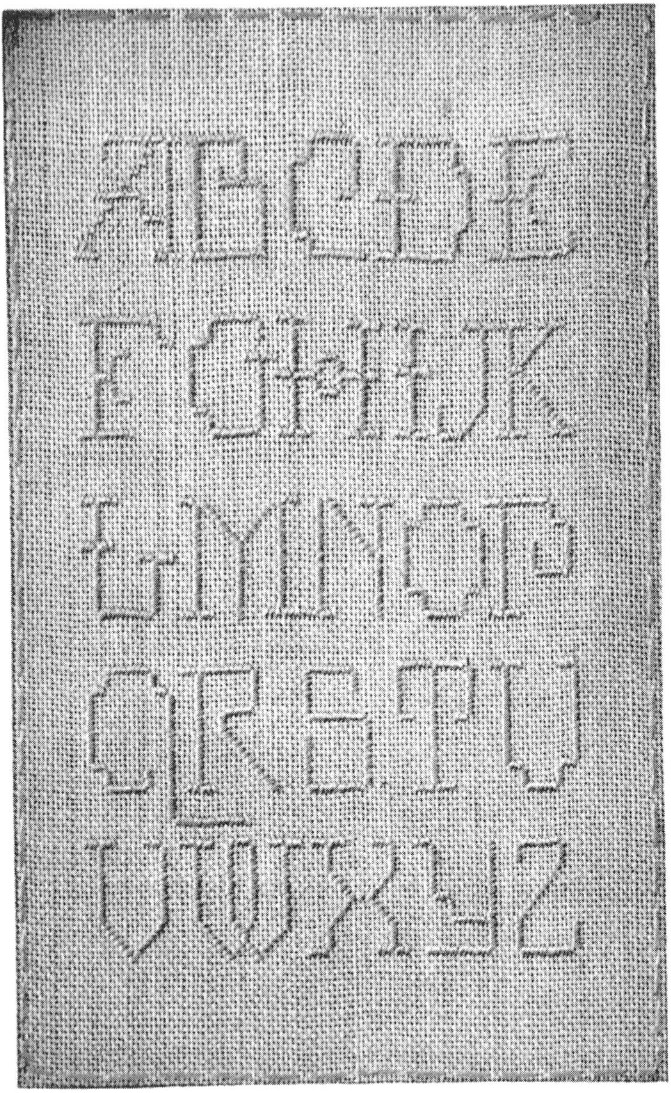

200. NEEDLEWORK. ADAPTED. L.F.D.

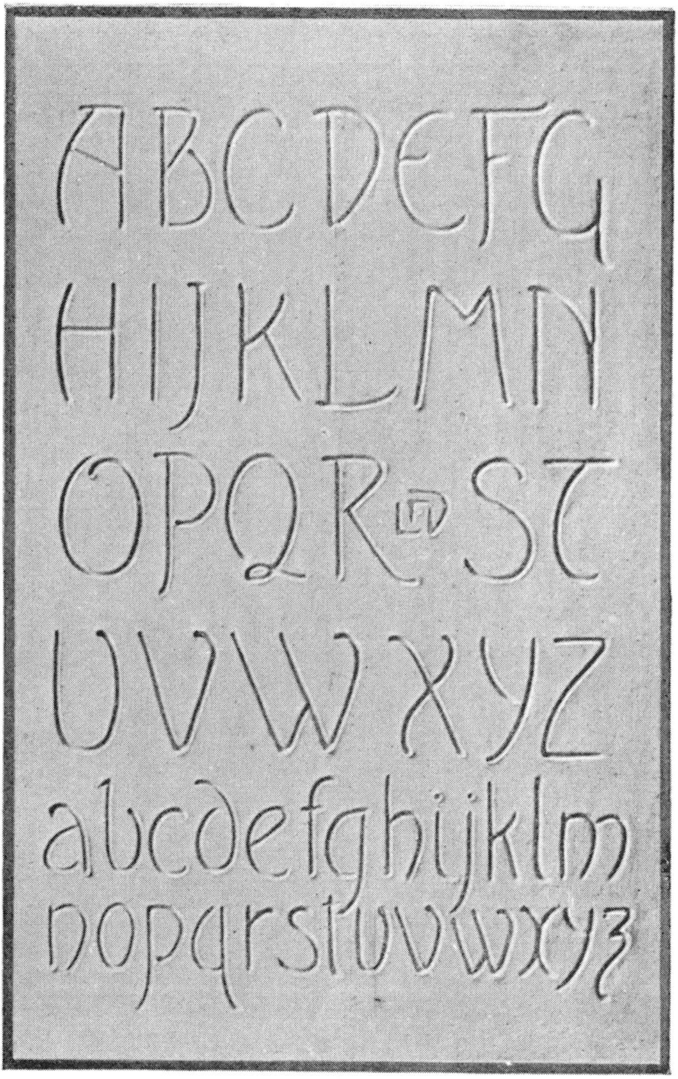

201. SGRAFFITTO. L.F.D.

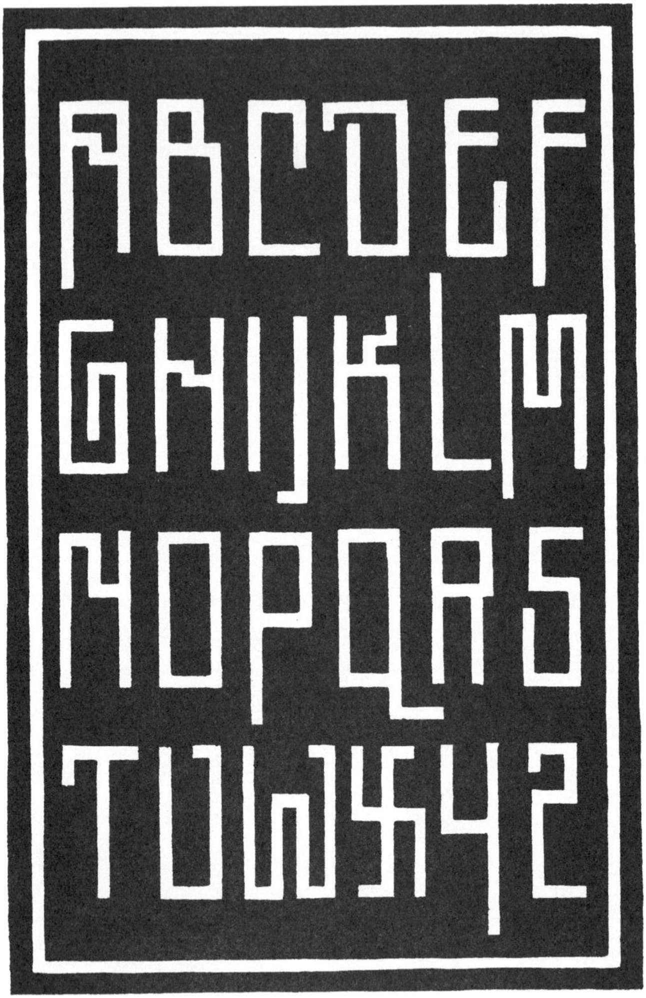

202. SQUARE-CUT. QUASI-CHINESE. L.F.D.

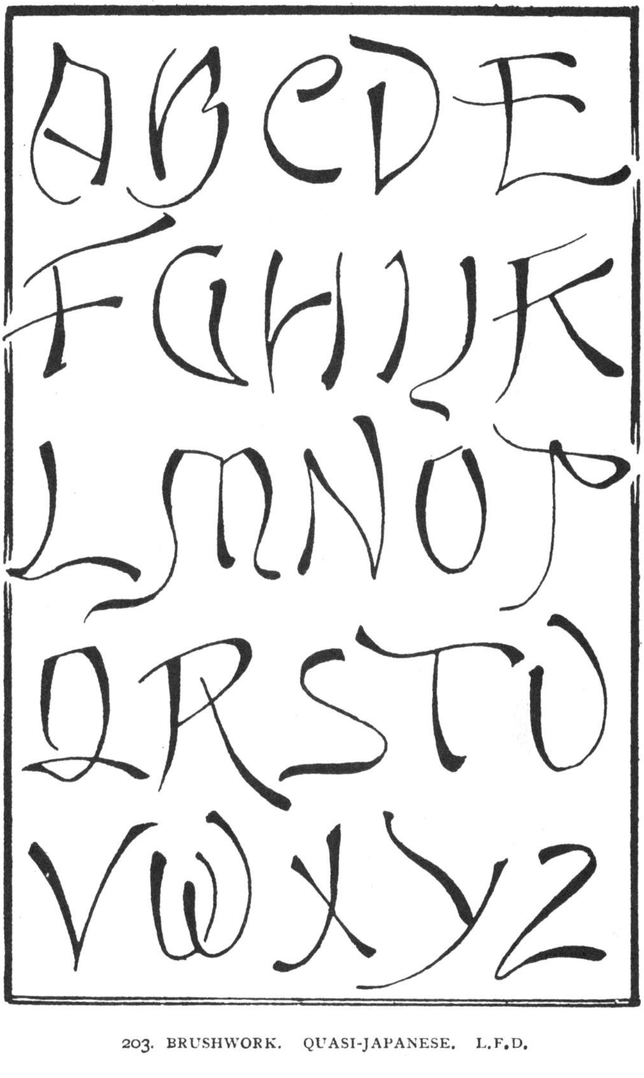

203. BRUSHWORK. QUASI-JAPANESE. L.F.D.

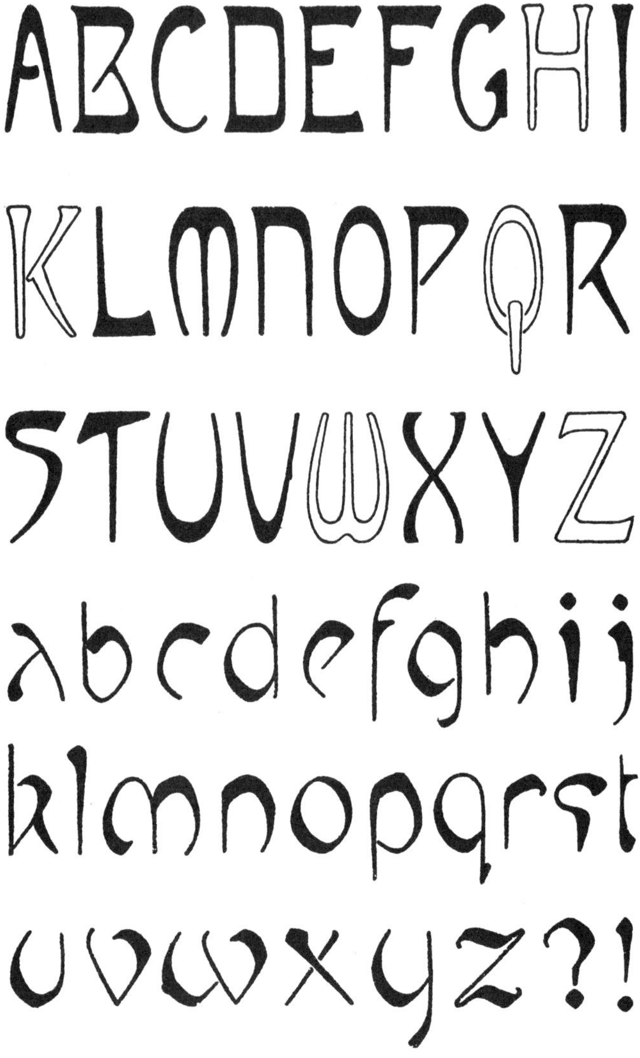

204. BRUSHWORK. MUCHA.

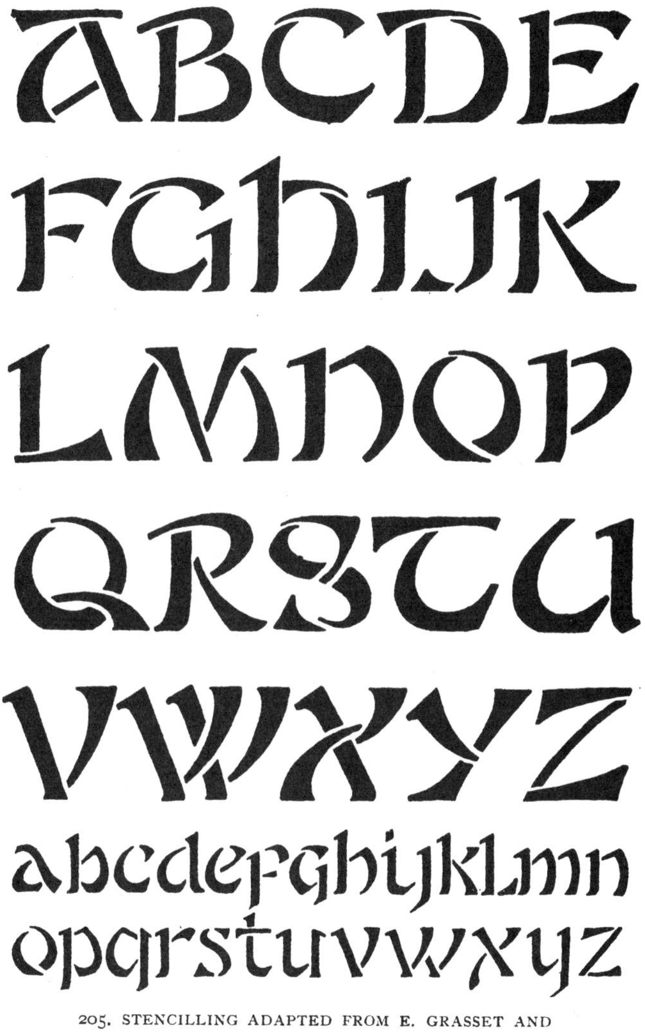

205. STENCILLING ADAPTED FROM E. GRASSET AND M. P. VERNEUIL.

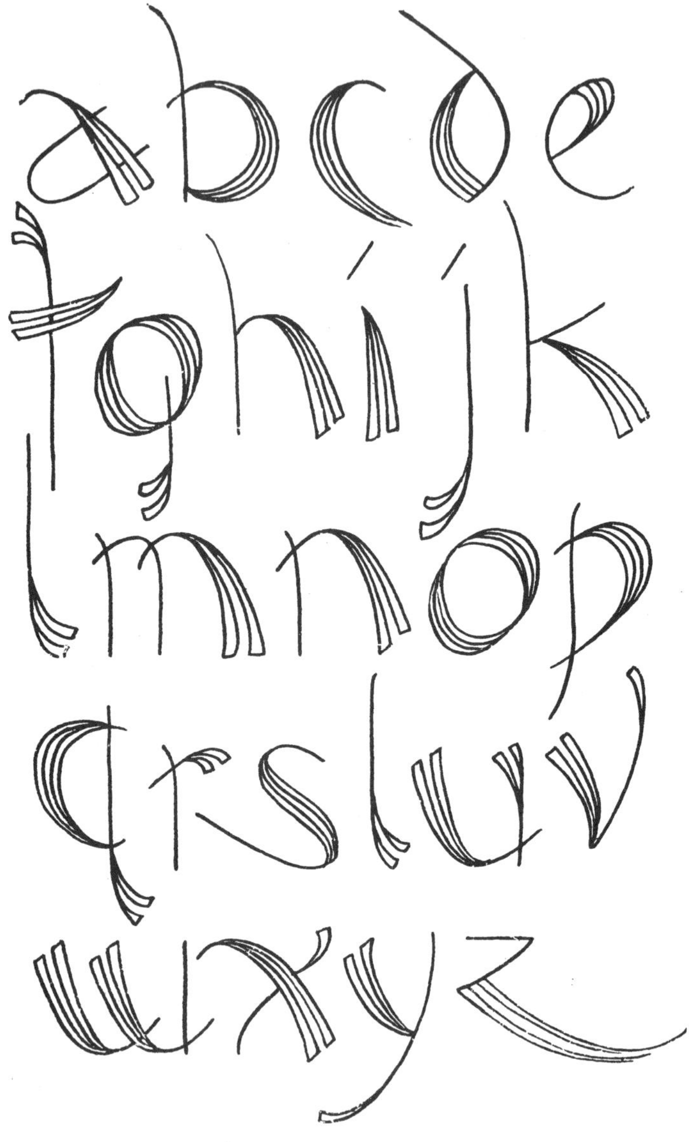

206. PENWORK. FRANZ STUCK.

MODERN ALPHABETS

IN WHICH THE INFLUENCE OF THE IMPLEMENT EMPLOYED IS NOT SO EVIDENT

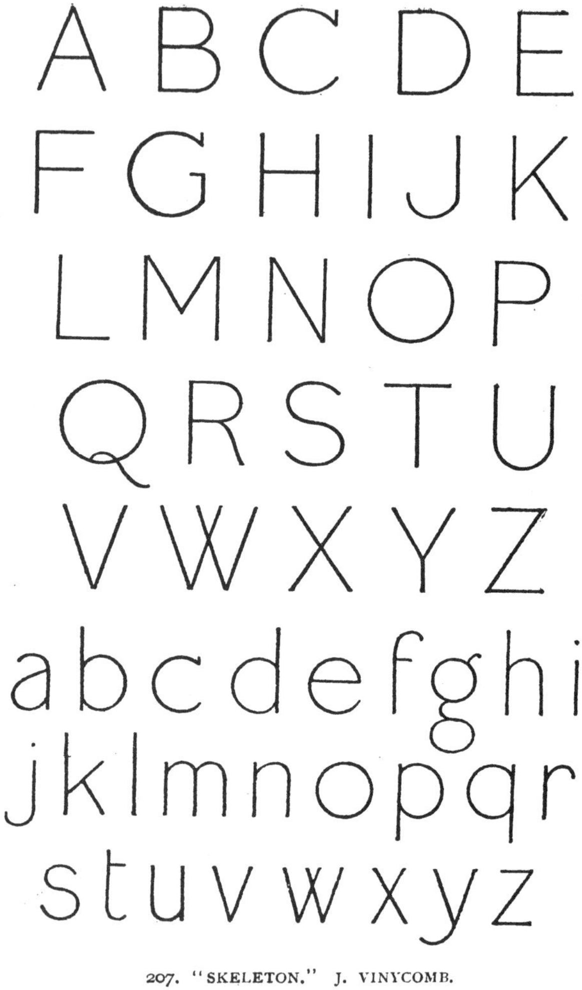

207. "SKELETON." J. VINYCOMB.

ABCDEF
GHIJKL
MNOPQR
STUVW
XYZ&&

abcdefghij
klmnopqr
stuvwxyz

208. "FRENCH." J. VINYCOMB.

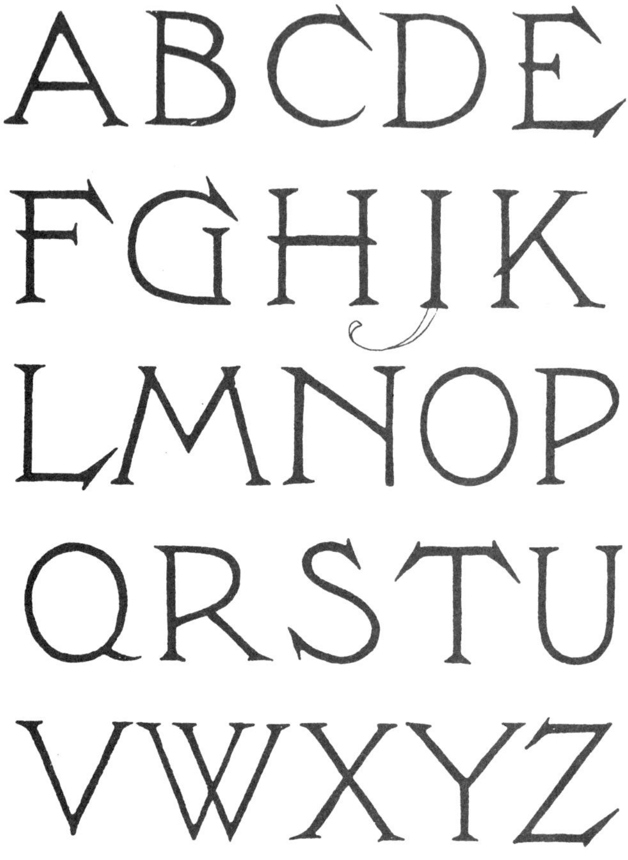

209. L.F.D.

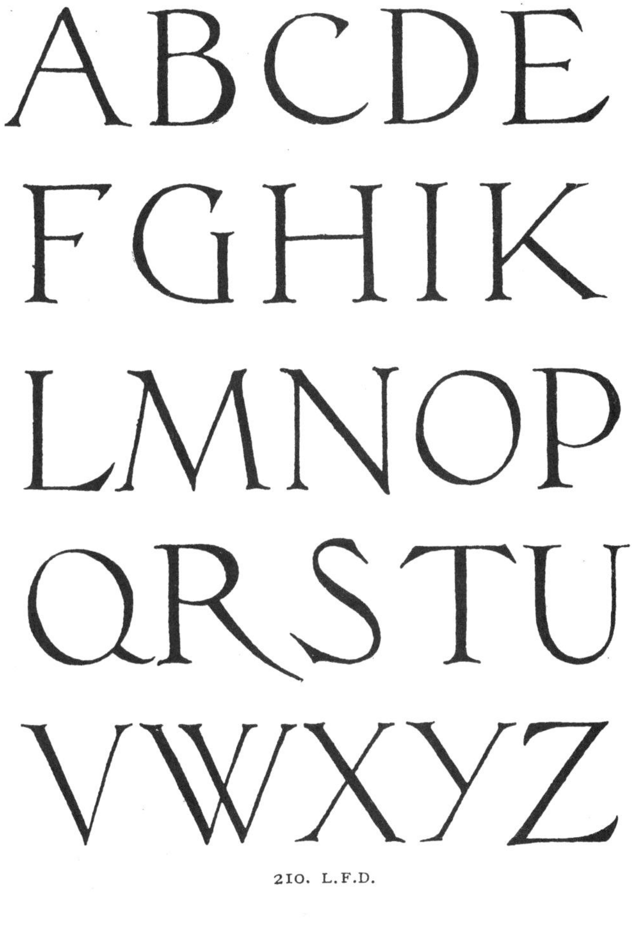

210. L.F.D.

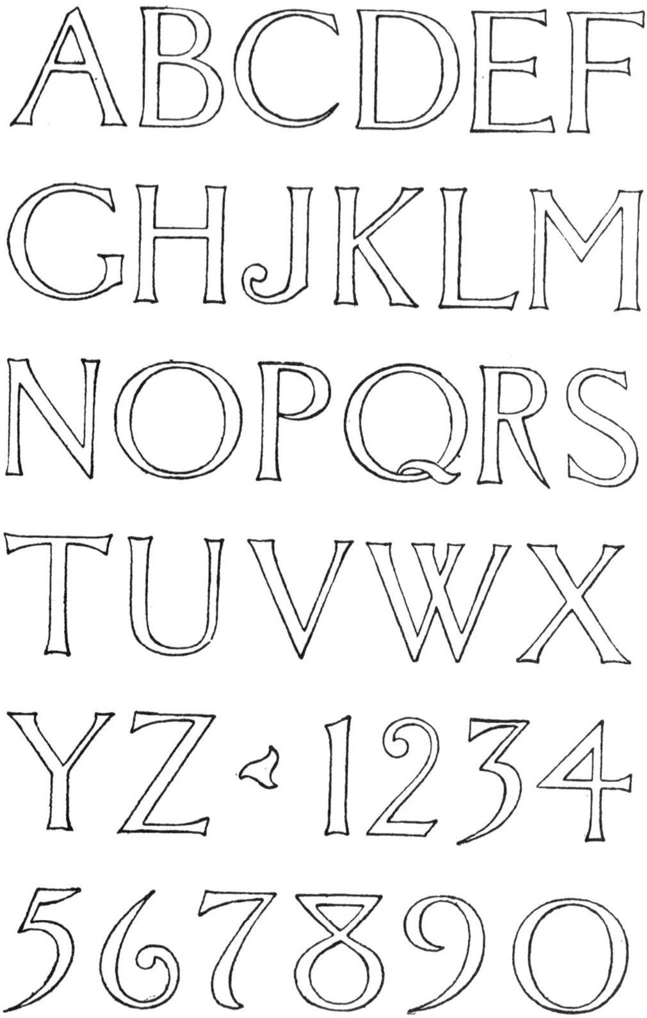

211. J. CROMAR WATT, ARCHITECT.

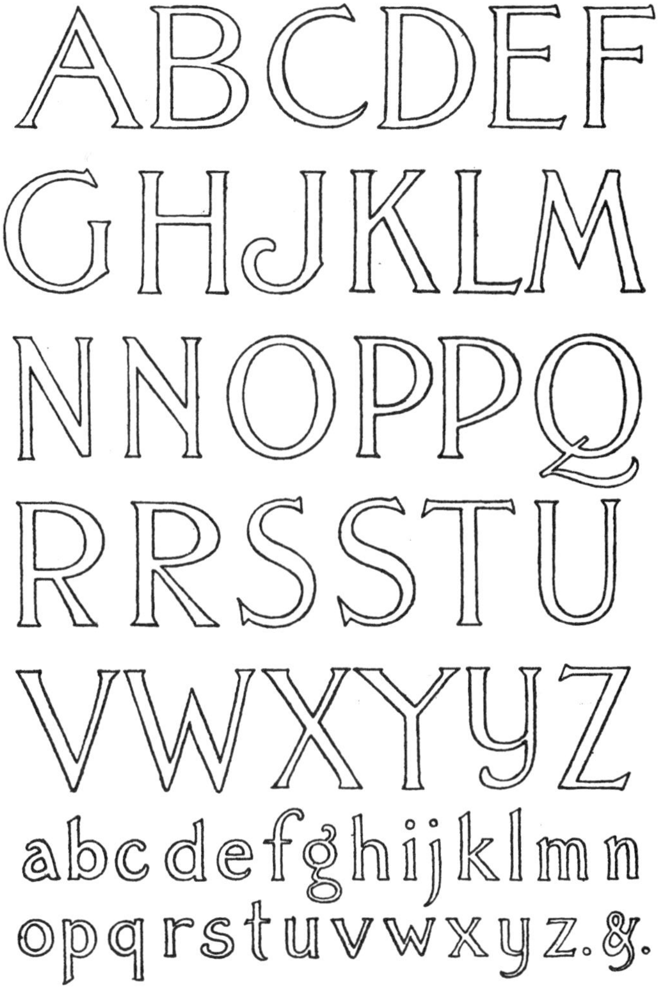

212. J. W. WEEKES.

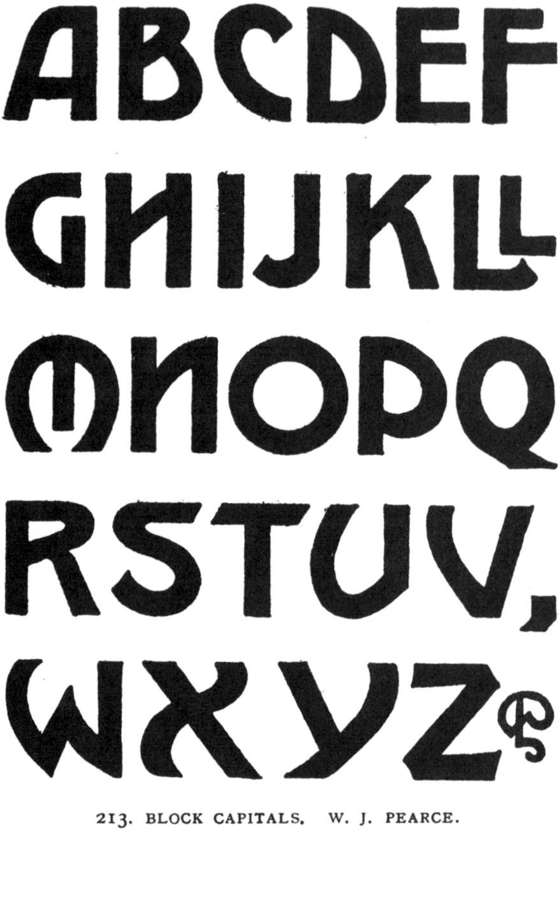

213. BLOCK CAPITALS. W. J. PEARCE.

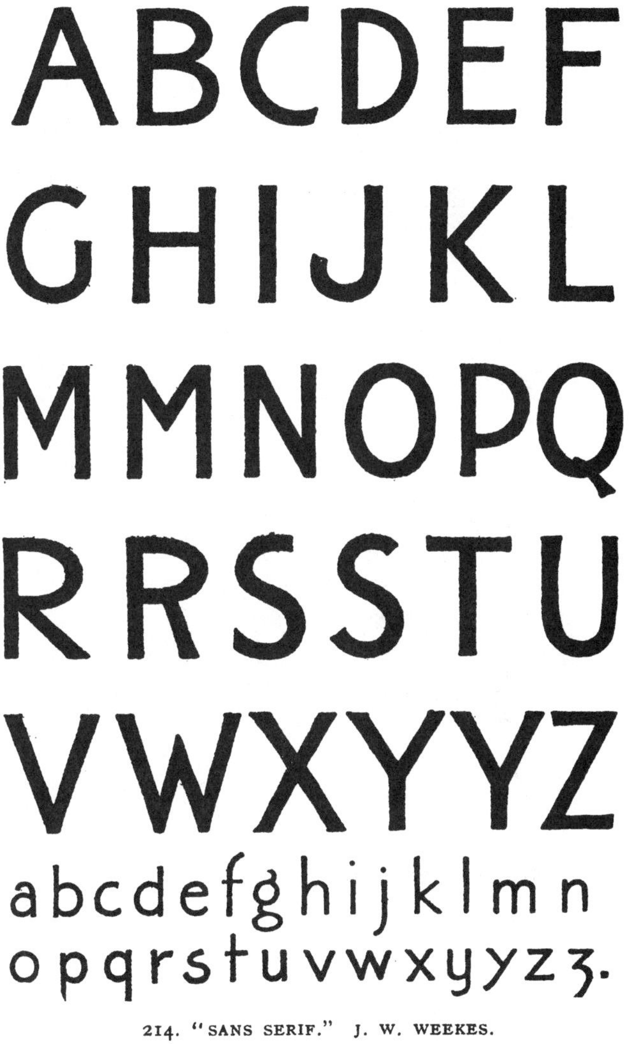

214. "SANS SERIF." J. W. WEEKES.

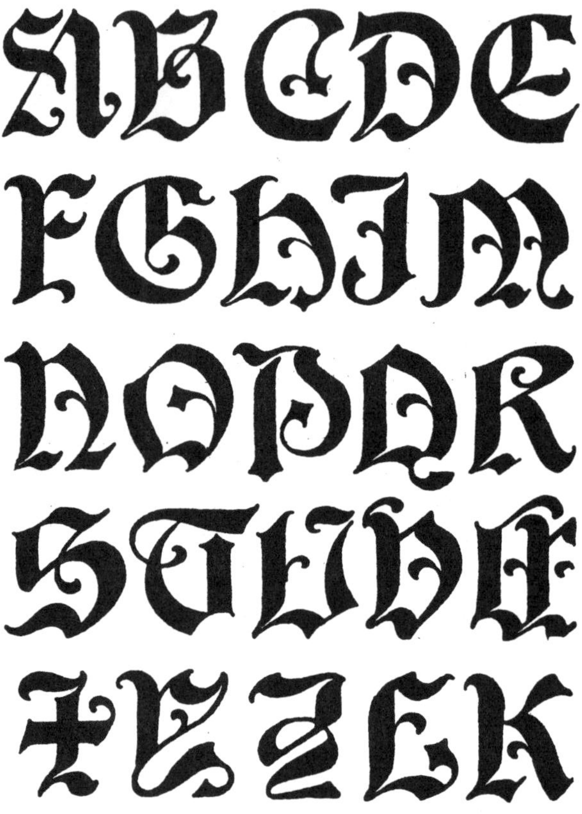

215. GOTHIC CAPITALS. W. J. PEARCE.

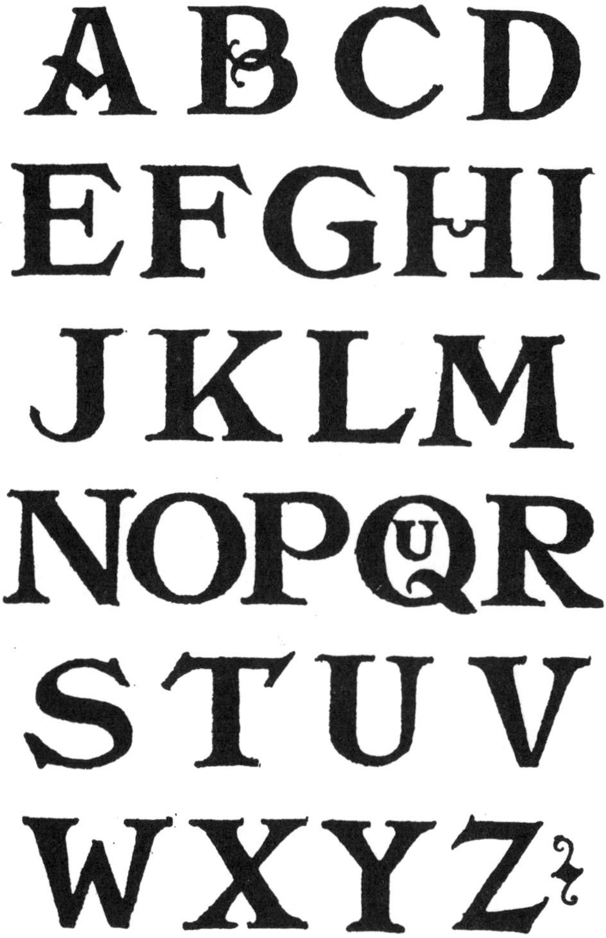

216. OTTO HUPP. "ALPHABETE UND ORNAMENTE."

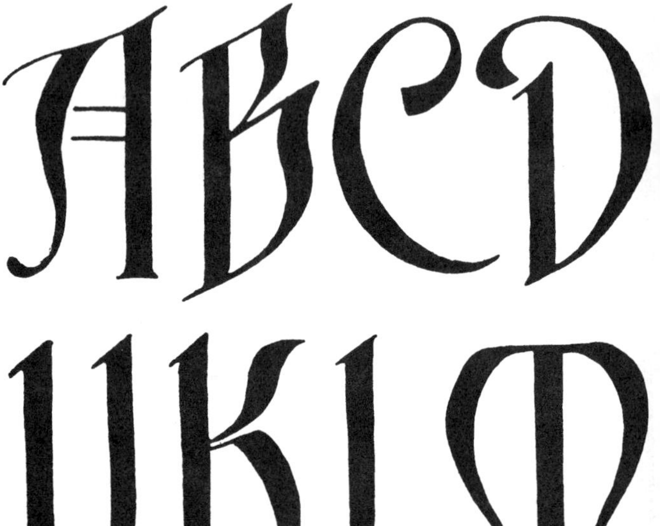
ABCD
IJKLM
RSTUV

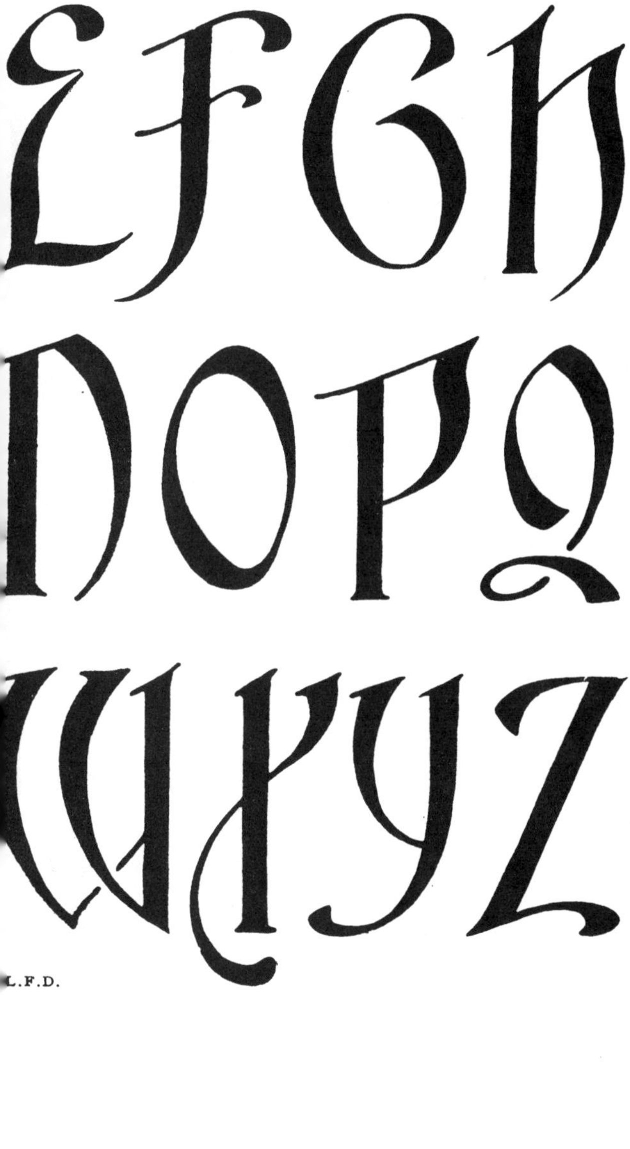

L.F.D.

A·B·C·D.

H·I·J·K·L

Q·R·S·T.

X·Y·Z.,;

EFGHIJKL

UVWXYZ. 12

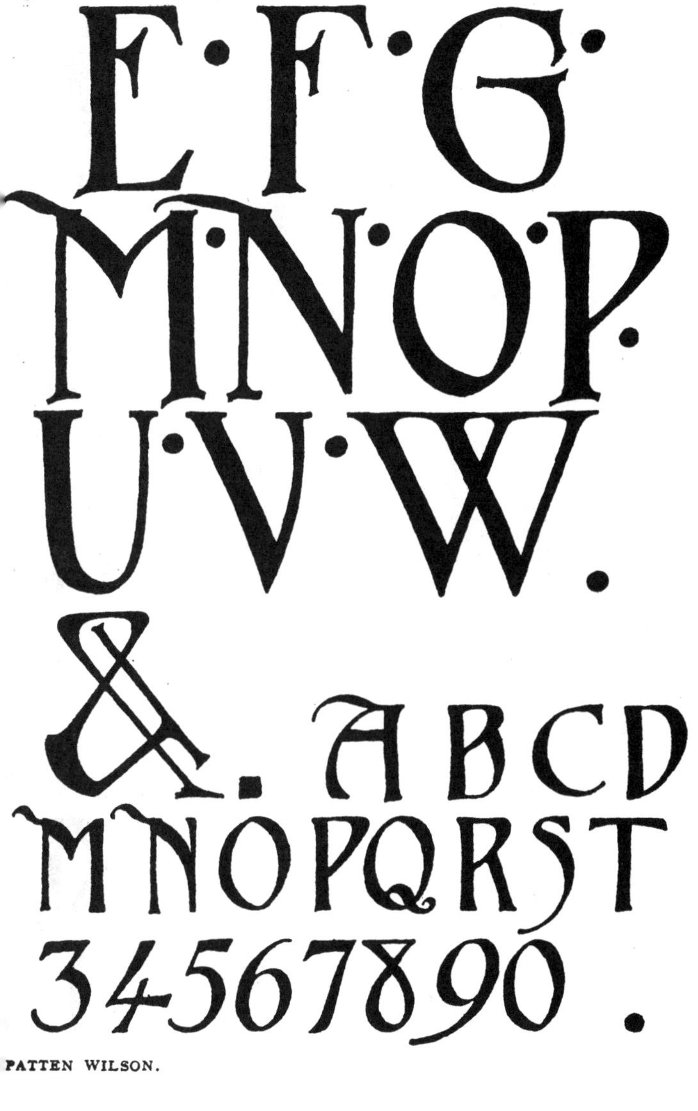

PATTEN WILSON.

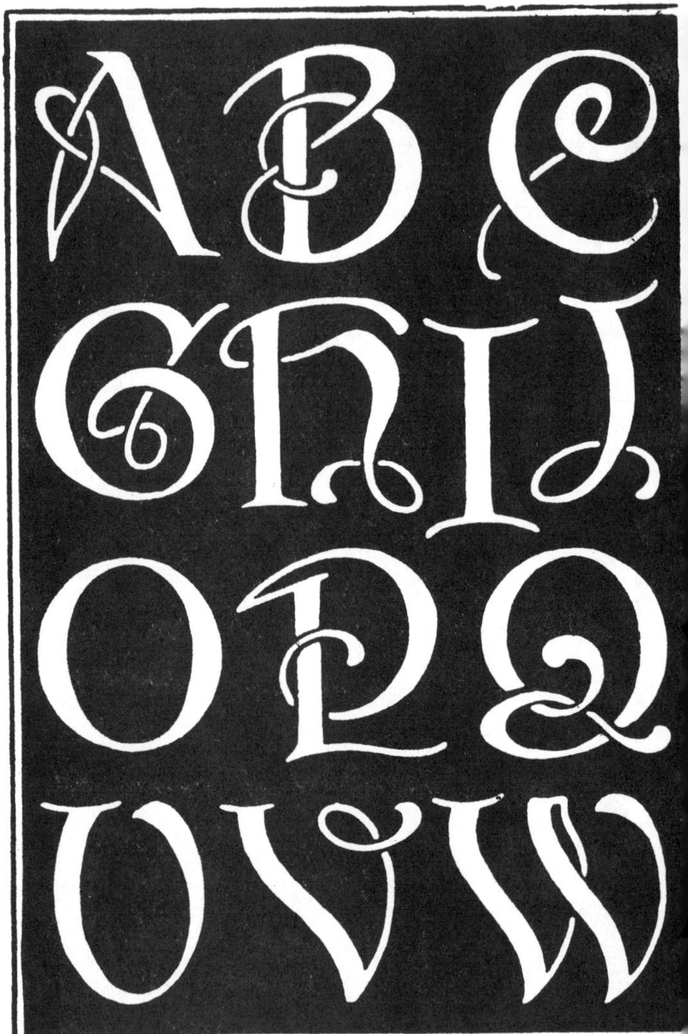

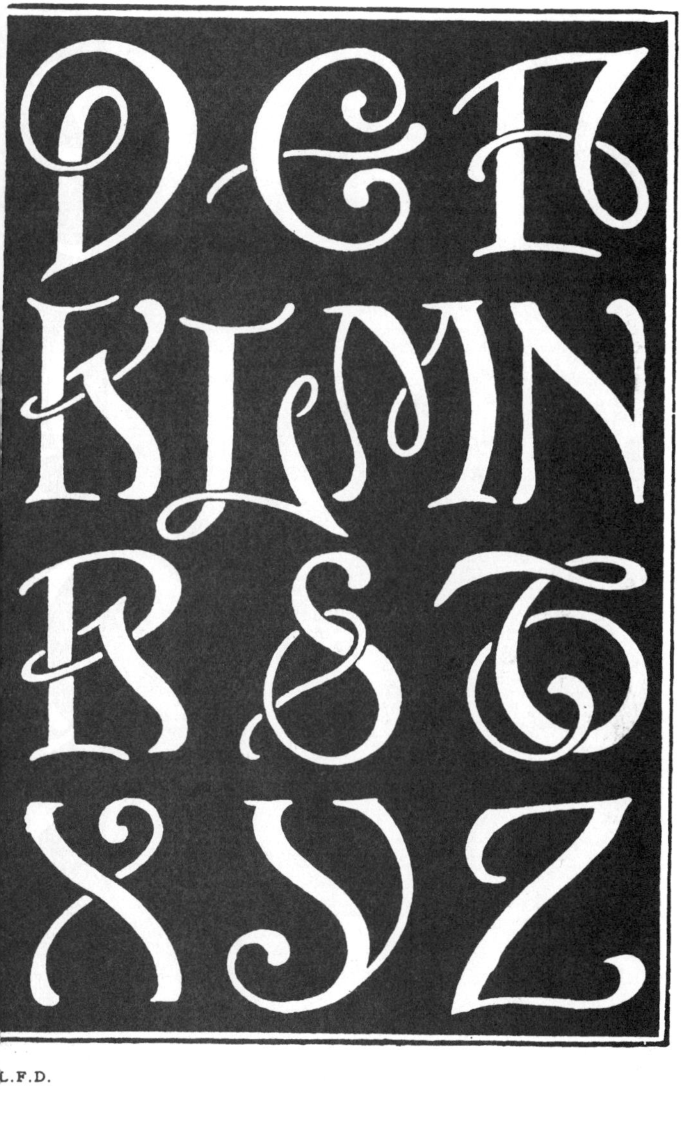

L.F.D.

ABCD
KLMN
STUV

220

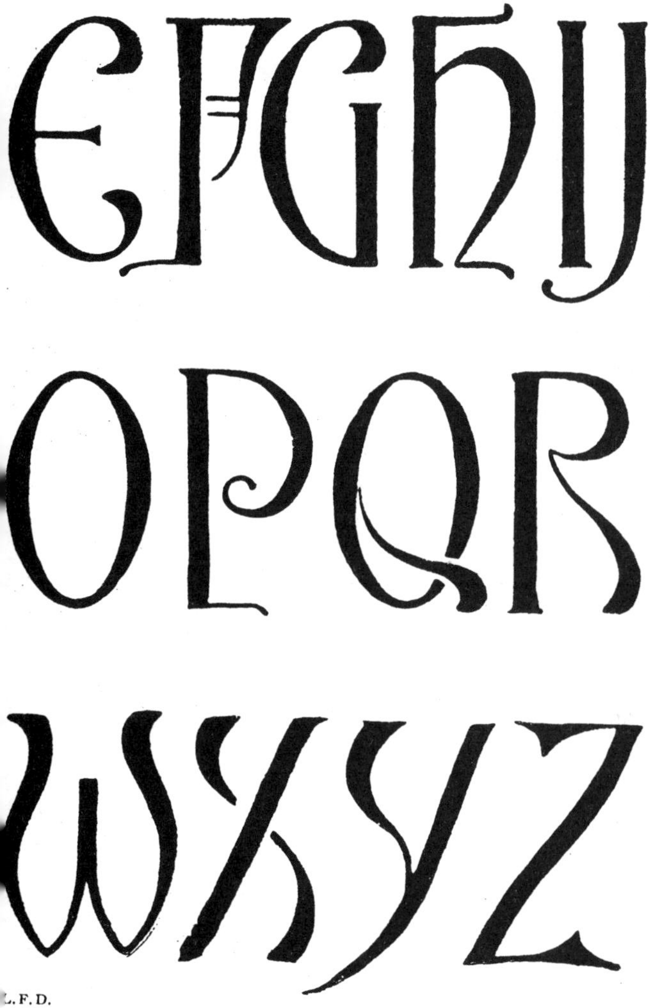

L. F. D.

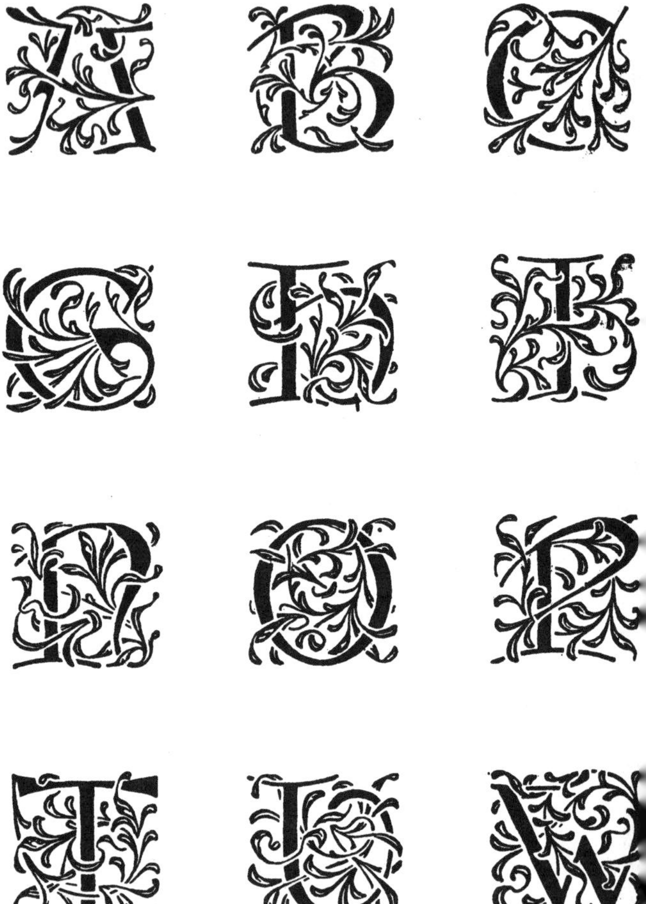

221.

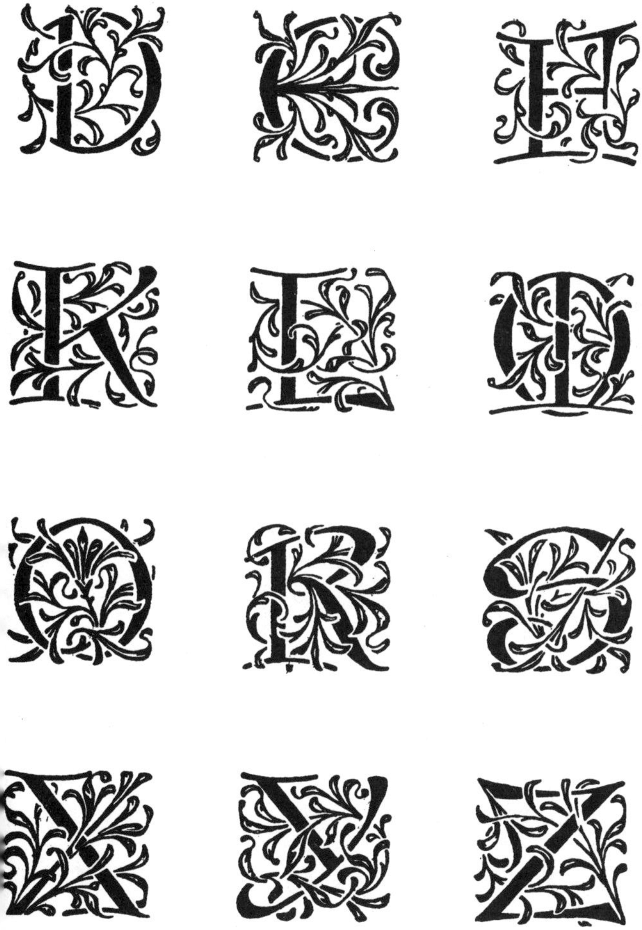

L. F. D.

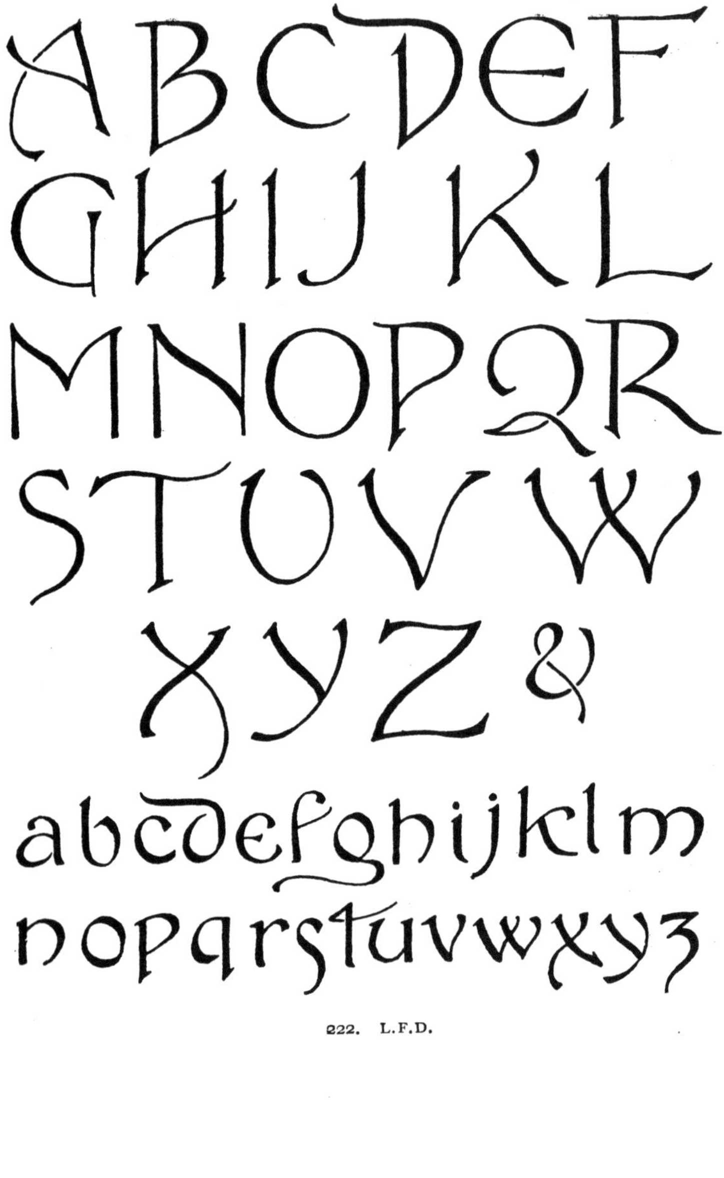
ABCDEF
GHIJKL
MNOPQR
STUVW
XYZ&
abcdefghijklm
nopqrstuvwxyz

222. L.F.D.

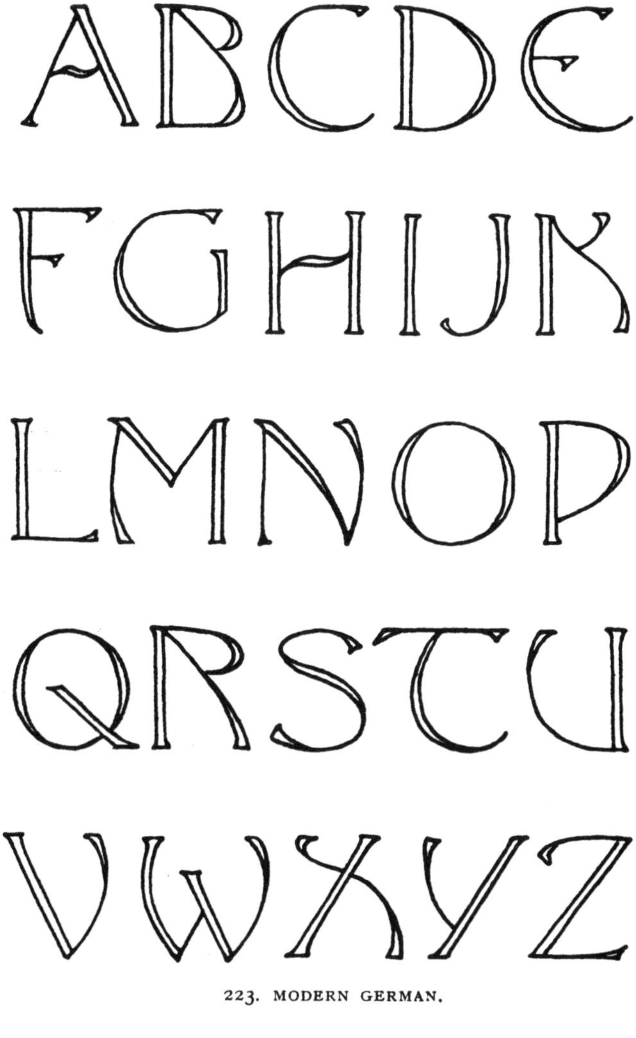

223. MODERN GERMAN.

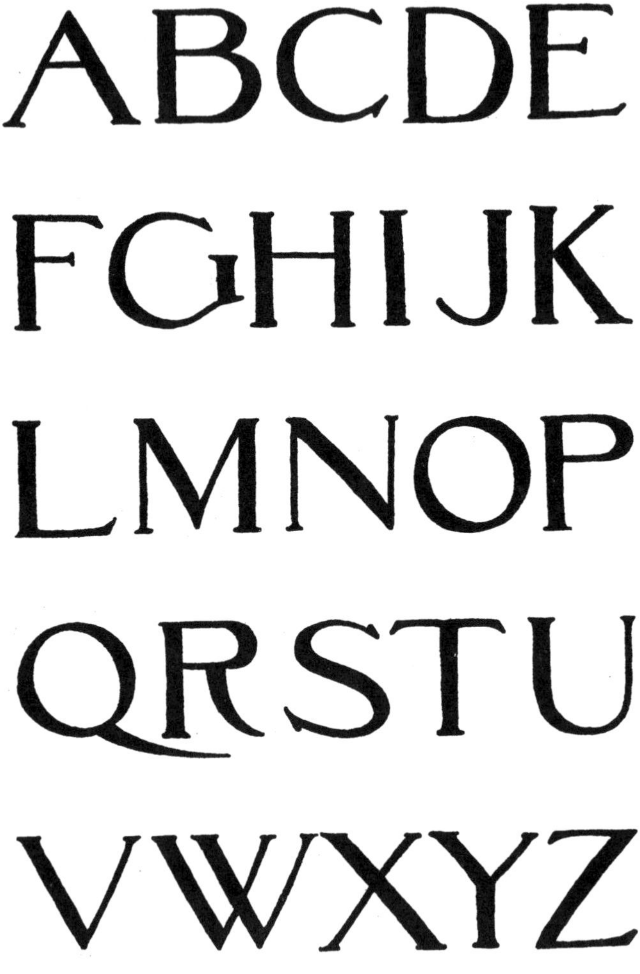

224. FRANZ STUCK.

AMPERZANDS AND NUMERALS

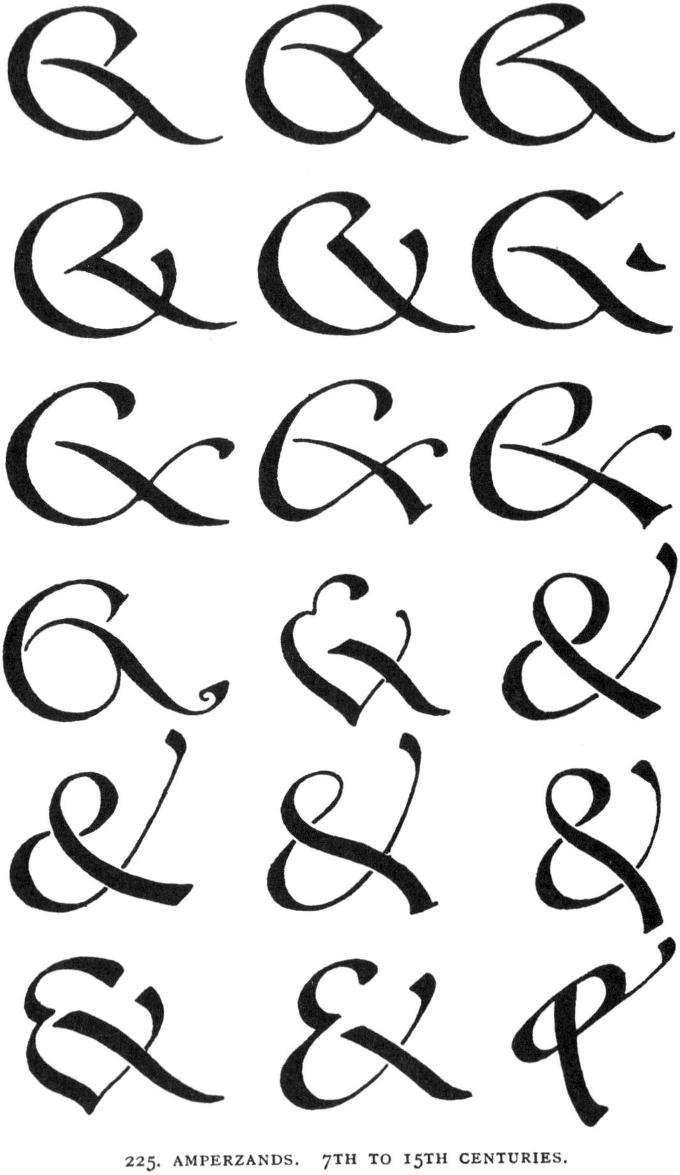

225. AMPERZANDS. 7TH TO 15TH CENTURIES.

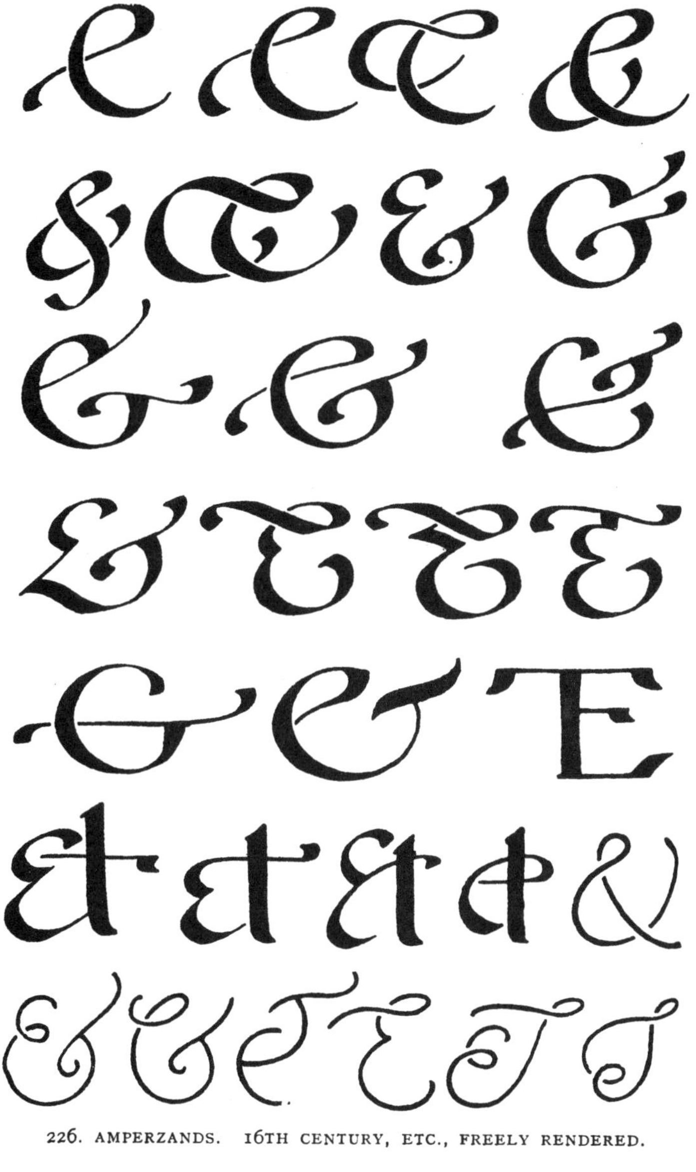

226. AMPERZANDS. 16TH CENTURY, ETC., FREELY RENDERED.

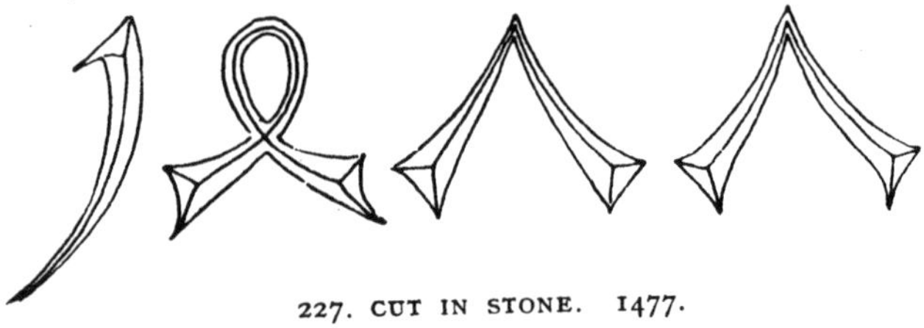

227. CUT IN STONE. 1477.

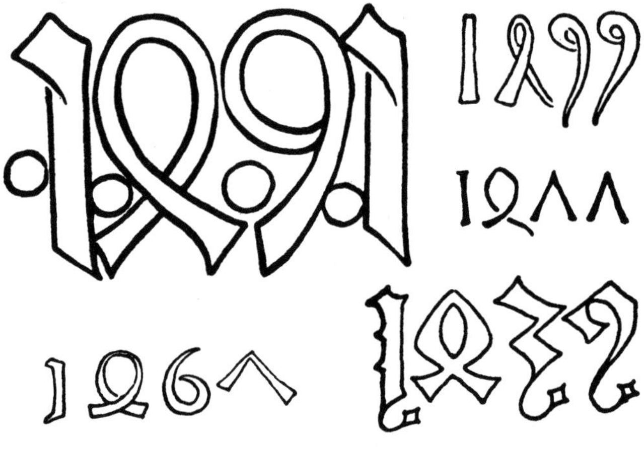

228. STONE AND BRASS. 1439-1491.

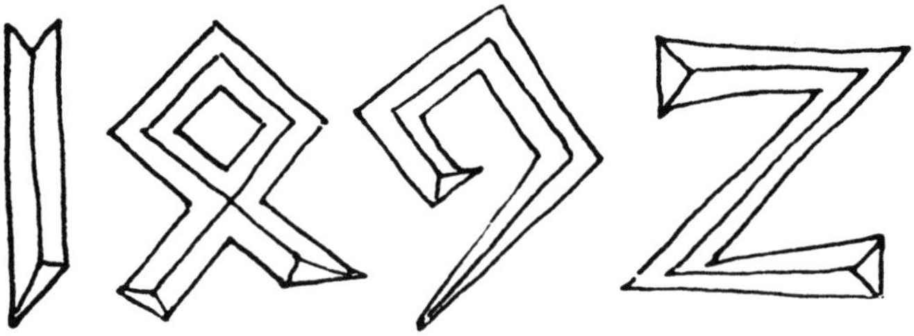

229. CUT IN STONE. 1492.

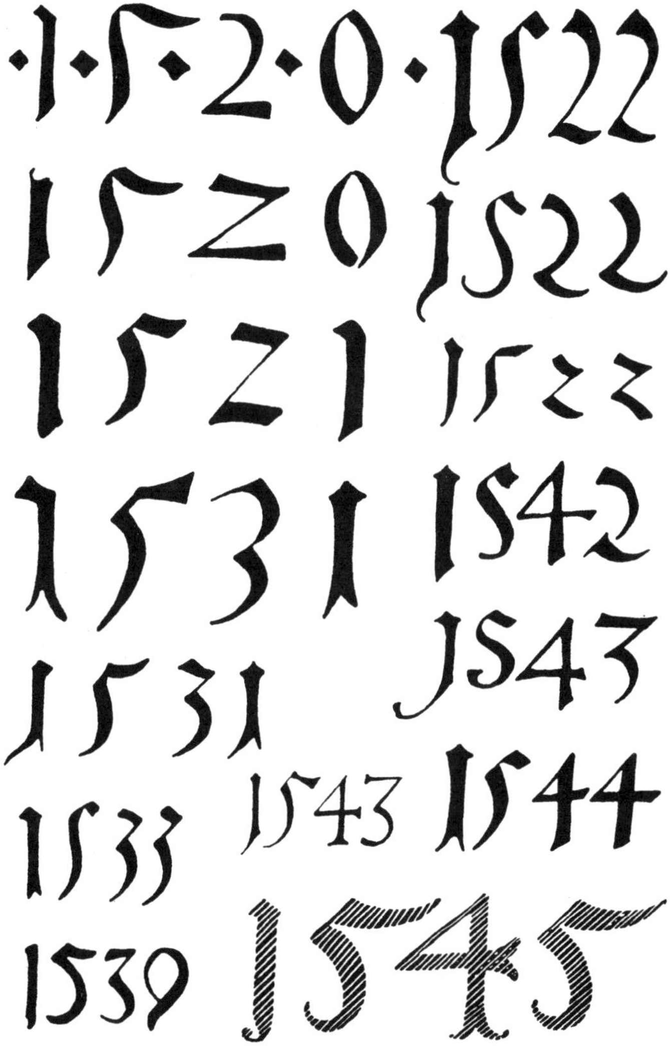

230. CHIEFLY BRASSES. 1520–1545.

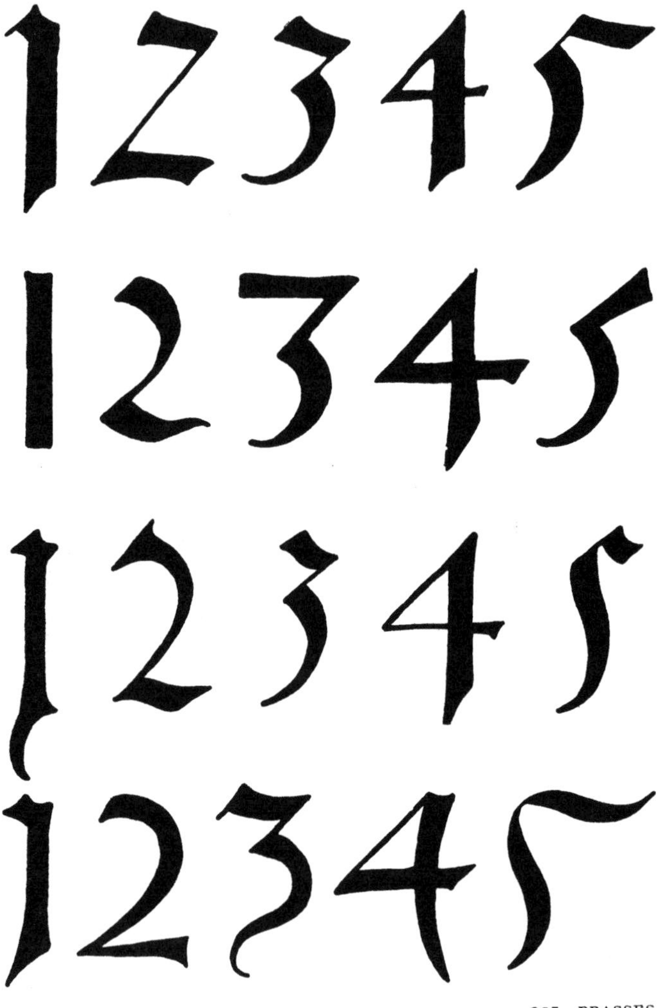

231. BRASSES.

67890

67890

67890

67890

1520–1598.

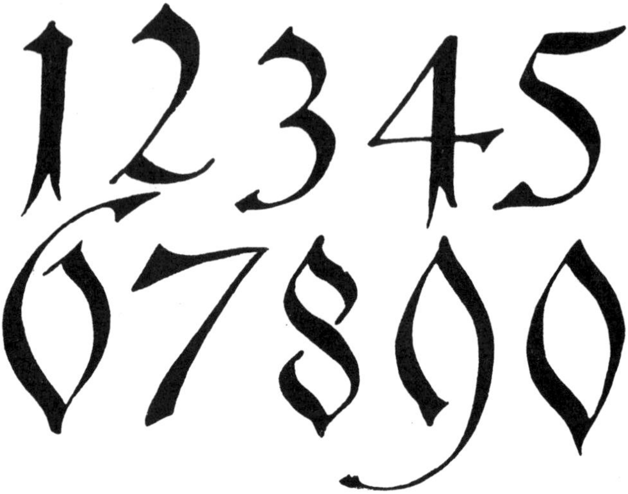

232. BRONZE. ABOUT 1550.

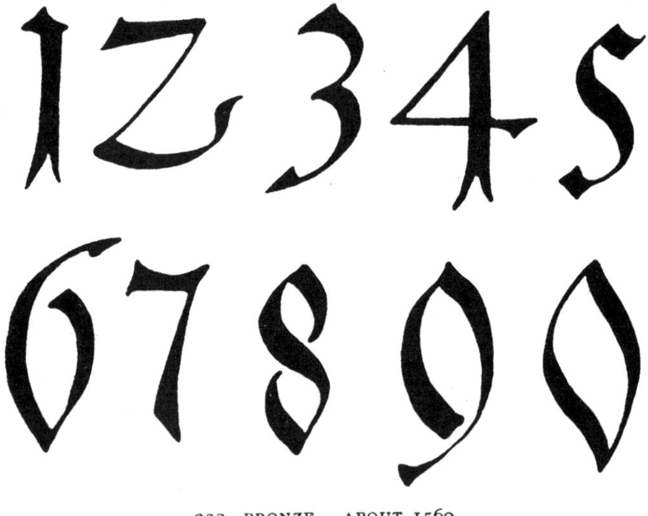

233. BRONZE. ABOUT 1560.

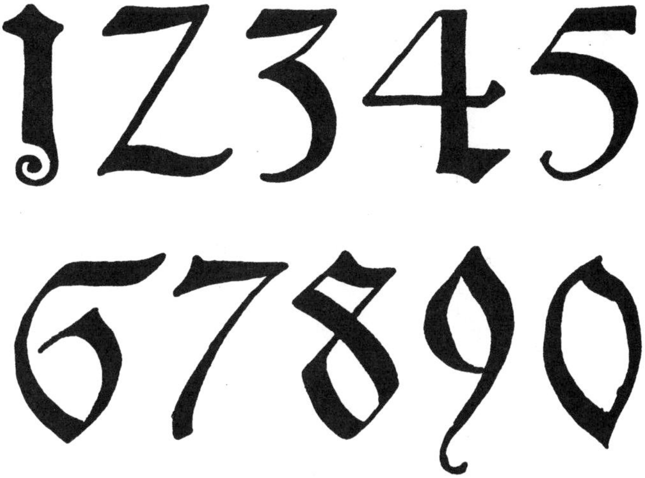

234. BRUSHWORK. FAIENCE. 16TH CENTURY.

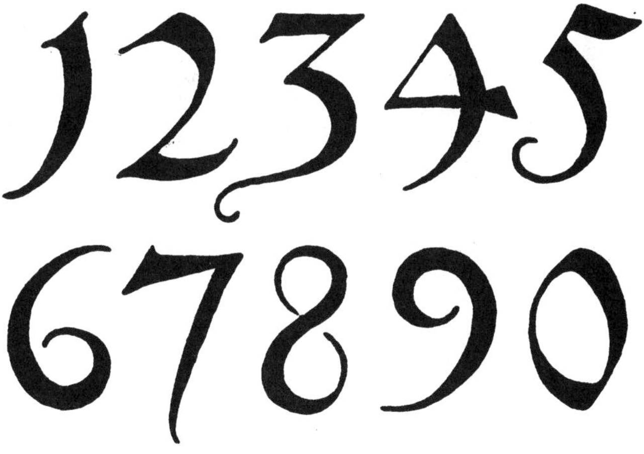

235. BRUSHWORK. 16TH OR 17TH CENTURY.

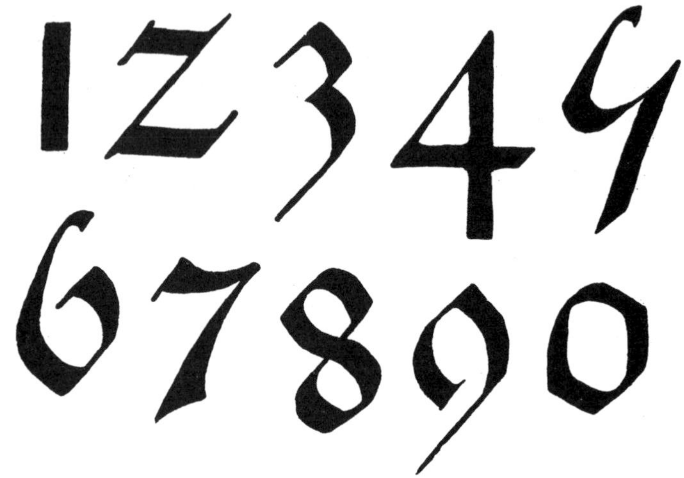

236. ITALIAN MS. 16TH CENTURY.

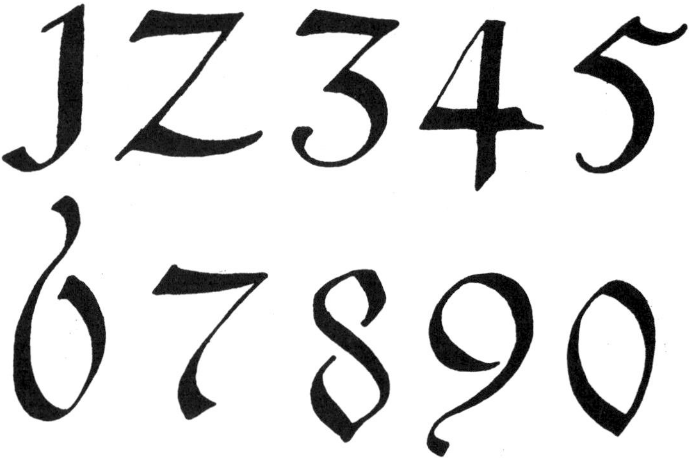

237. BRUSHWORK. GILT, ON BLACK. 1548?

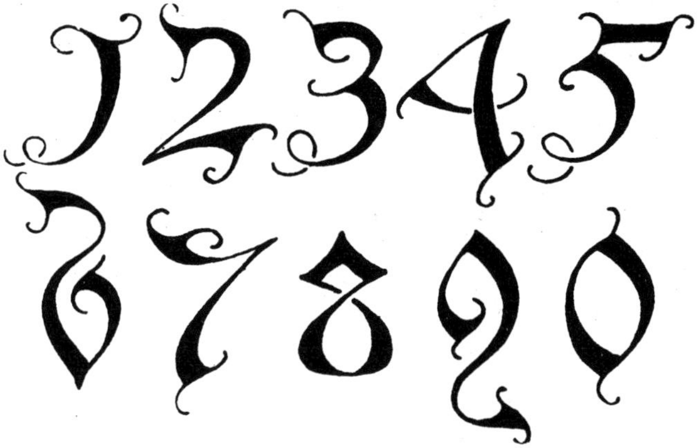

238. INCISED IN WOOD. GERMAN. 1588.

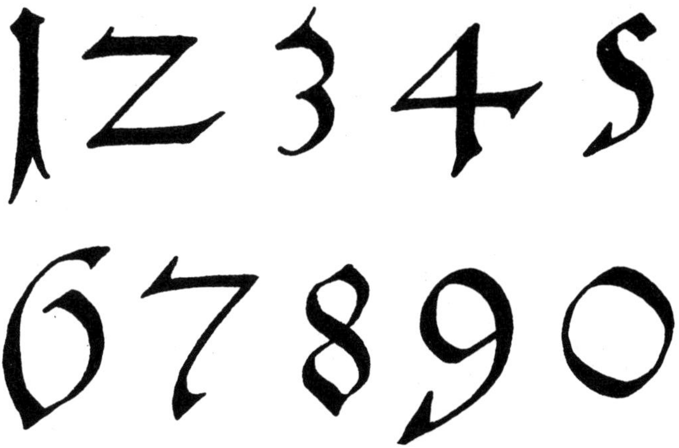

239. BRASS. 16TH CENTURY

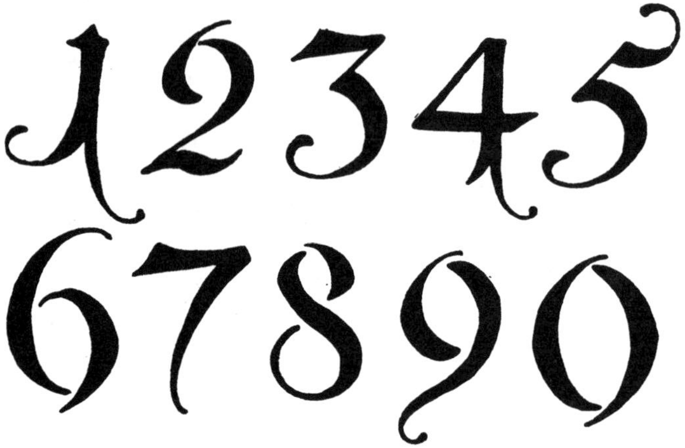

240. BRUSHWORK. 16TH CENTURY.

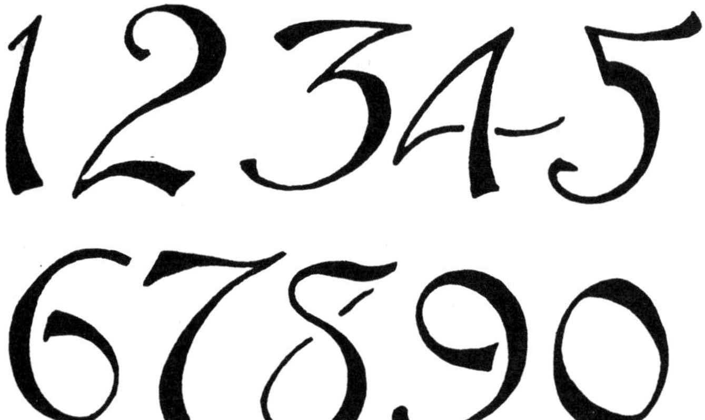

241. ABOUT 1700.

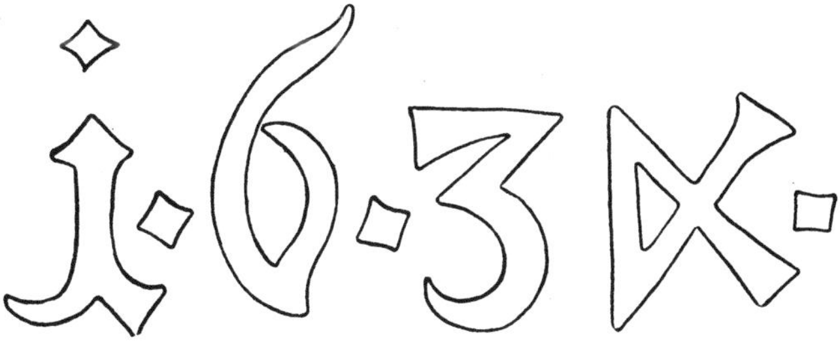

242. CUT IN STONE. 1634.

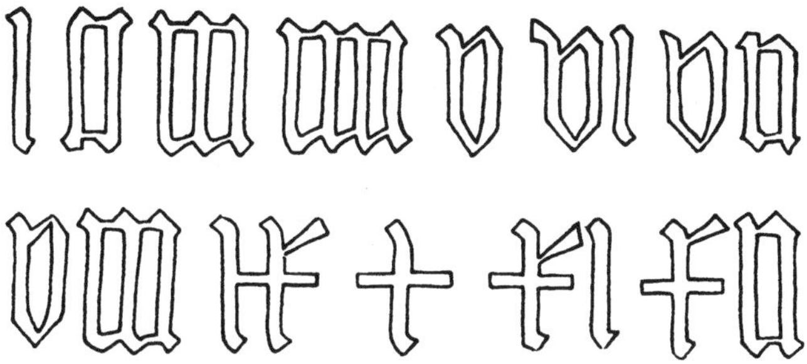

243. RELIEF IN BRASS OR BRONZE. 1647.

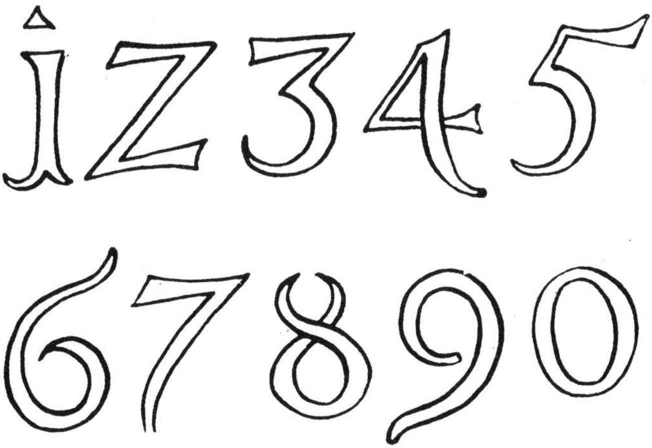

244. STONE. 1692.

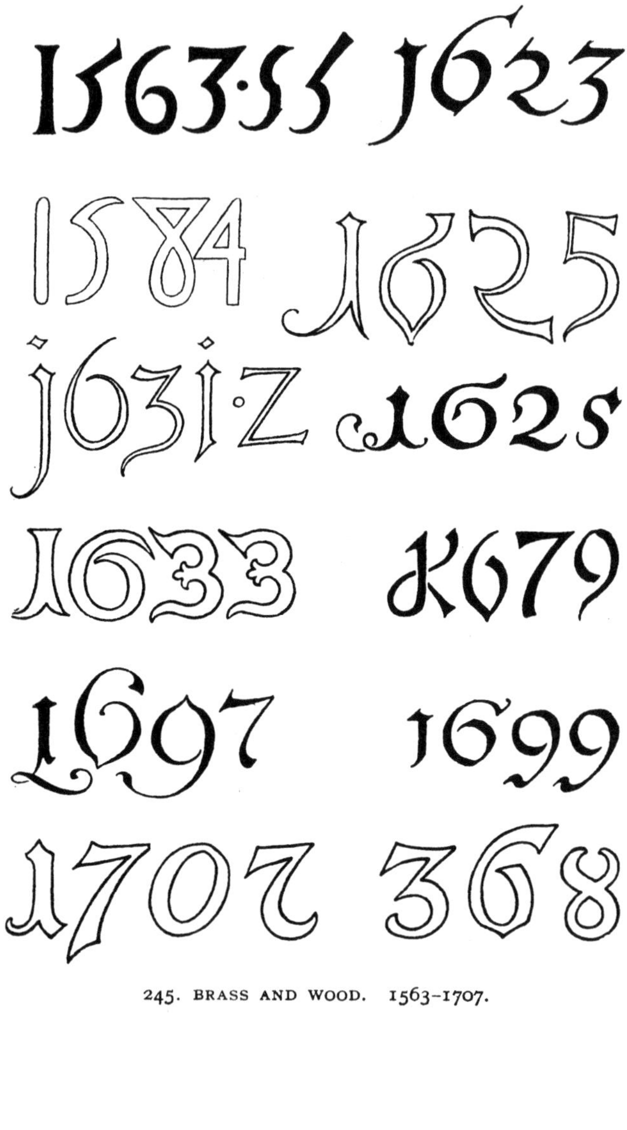

245. BRASS AND WOOD. 1563–1707.

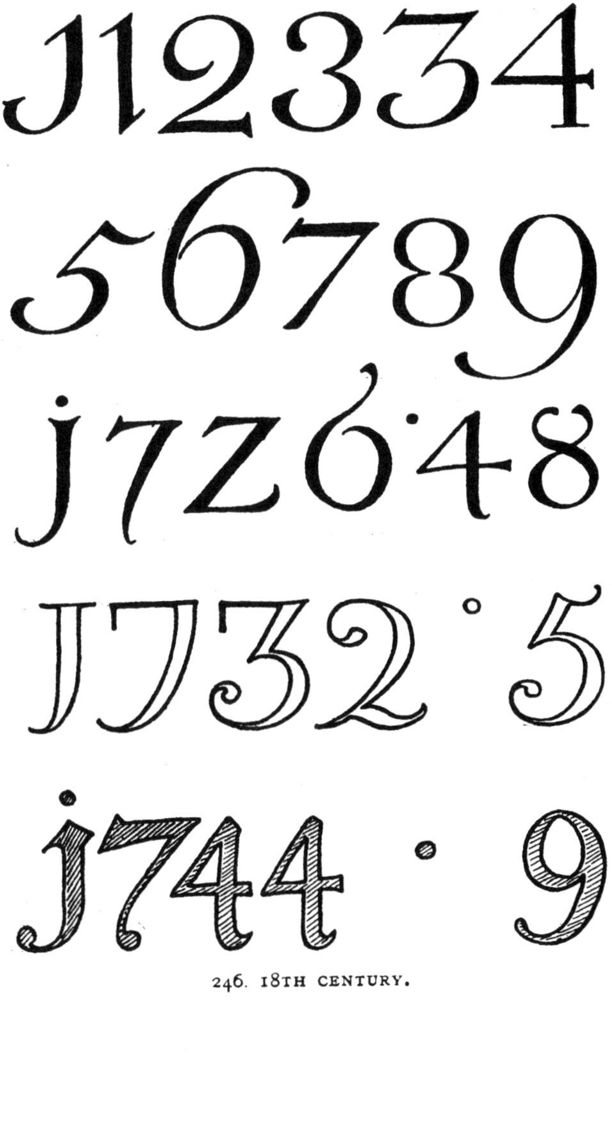

246. 18TH CENTURY.

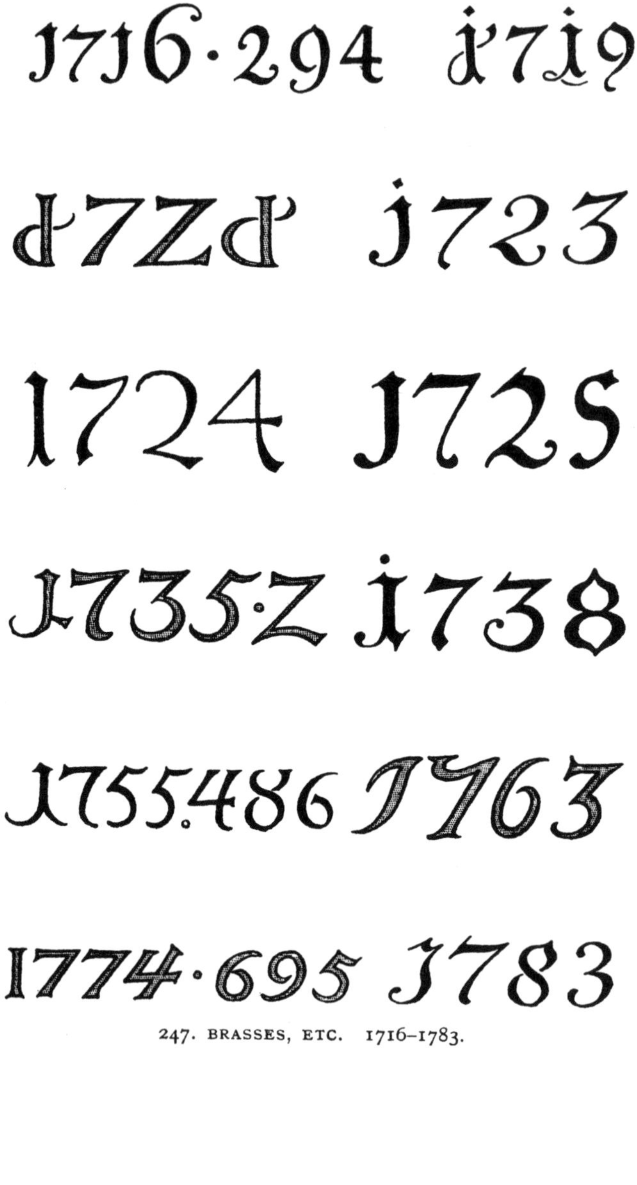

247. BRASSES, ETC. 1716–1783.

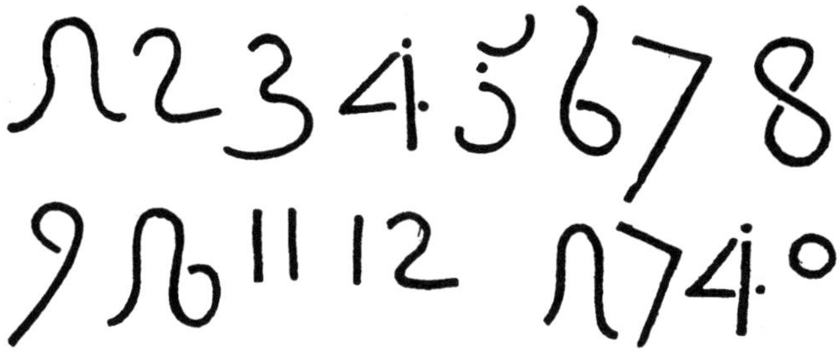

248. BRASS WIRE INLAY ON WOOD. 1740.

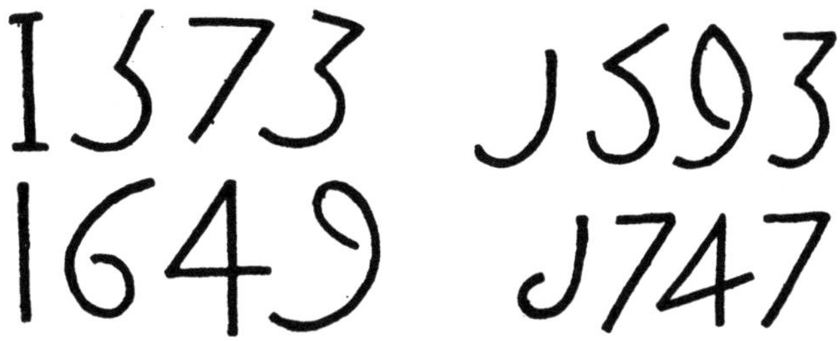

249. ENGRAVED ON STEEL, OR INLAID IN WIRE ON WOOD.
1573—1747.

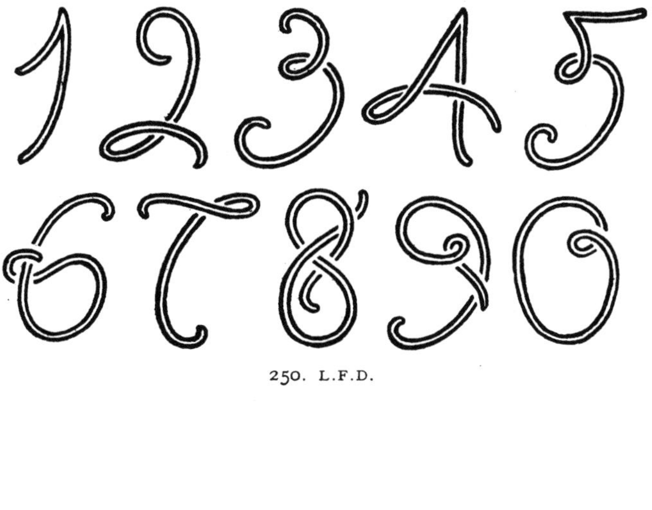

250. L.F.D.

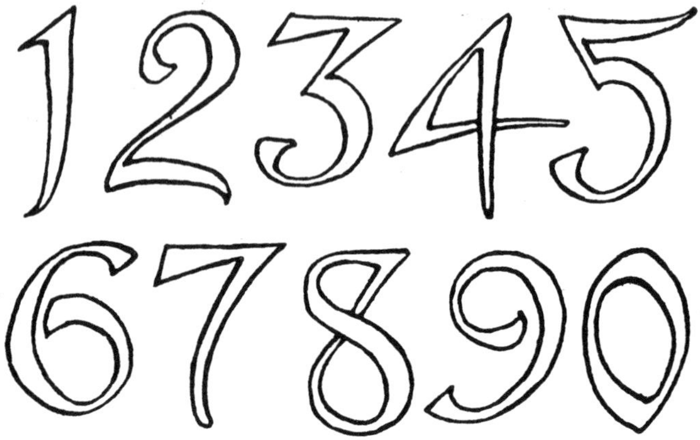

251. MODERN.

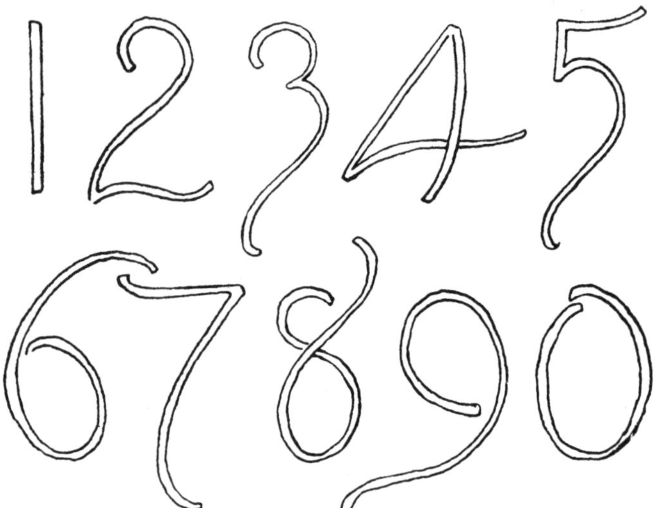

252. L.F.D.

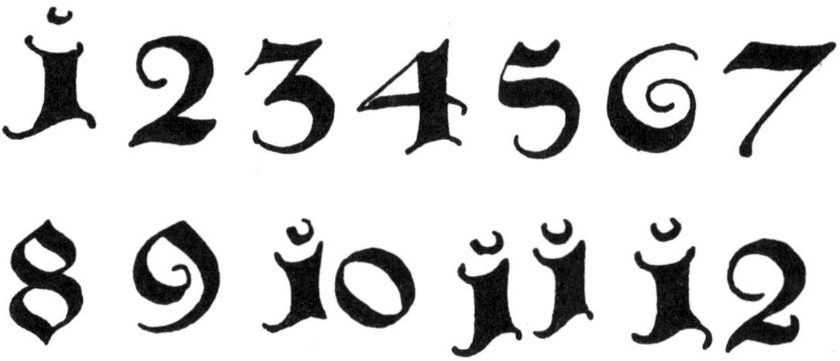

253. ALÖIS MÜLLER.

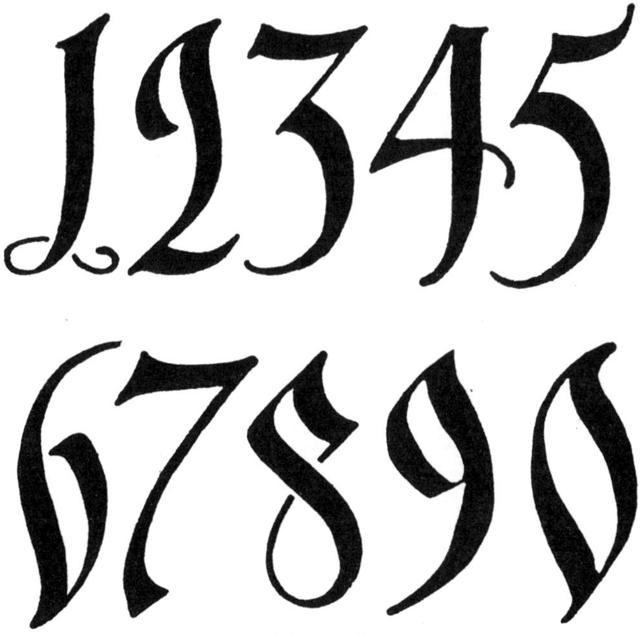

254. L.F.D.

INDEX OF ILLUSTRATIONS
ARRANGED UNDER ARTISTS, COUNTRIES, MATERIALS & PROCESSES, AND STYLES

NOTE.—*The reference numerals are to the figure numbers of the illustrations, and in no case to pages.*

BRADBURY, AGNEW, & CO. LD., PRINTERS, LONDON AND TONBRIDGE.